PENGUIN BOOKS

THE PENGUIN HISTORY OF THE CHURCH
Volume Five

Alec Vidler was born in 1899 at Rye in Sussex, and was educated at Sutton Valence School and Selwyn College, Cambridge. After serving as a curate in Newcastle and Birmingham he joined the staff of the Oratory House, Cambridge, in 1931. During the war he was Warden of St Deiniol's Library, Hawarden, founded by Gladstone. He was a Canon of St George's Chapel, Windsor, from 1948 to 1956 and prepared many middle-aged men for ordination during this period. From 1956 to 1966 he was Dean, and from 1956 to 1967 Fellow, of King's College, Cambridge, where he was also a university lecturer in Divinity from 1959 to 1967. He was a Litt.D. of Cambridge and an Hon. D.D. of the universities of Edinburgh and Toronto.

Dr Vidler edited the monthly *Theology* from 1939 until 1964. Among his many publications are *Secular Despair and Christian Faith* (1941), *The Orb and the Cross* (on Church and State, 1945), *Prophecy and Papacy* (on Lamennais, 1954), *Windsor Sermons* (1958), *A Century of Social Catholicism* (1964), *Twentieth Century Defenders of the Faith* (1965), *F. D. Maurice and Company* (1966), *A Variety of Catholic Modernists* (1970) and *Read, Mark, Learn* (1980). He edited *Soundings: Essays Concerning Christian Understanding* in 1962 and *Objections to Christian Belief* in 1963. His autobiography, *Scenes from a Clerical Life*, was published in 1977.

Dr. Vidler died in July 1991.

ALEC R. VIDLER

The Church in an Age of Revolution

1789 TO THE PRESENT DAY

PENGUIN BOOKS

PENGUIN BOOKS

Published by the Penguin Group
Penguin Books Ltd, 80 Strand, London WC2R 0RL, England
Penguin Putnam Inc., 375 Hudson Street, New York, New York 10014, USA
Penguin Books Australia Ltd, 250 Camberwell Road, Camberwell, Victoria 3124, Australia
Penguin Books Canada Ltd, 10 Alcorn Avenue, Toronto, Ontario, Canada M4V 3B2
Penguin Books India (P) Ltd, 11 Community Centre, Panchsheel Park, New Delhi – 110 017, India
Penguin Books (NZ) Ltd, Cnr Rosedale and Airborne Roads, Albany, Auckland, New Zealand
Penguin Books (South Africa) (Pty) Ltd, 24 Sturdee Avenue, Rosebank 2196, South Africa

Penguin Books Ltd, Registered Offices: 80 Strand, London WC2R 0RL, England

www.penguin.com

First published in Pelican Books 1961
Reprinted (with revisions and additional chapter) 1971
Reprinted with revisions 1974
Reprinted in Penguin Books 1990
10

The Penguin History of the Church
(formerly *The Pelican History of the Church*)

GENERAL EDITOR: OWEN CHADWICK

1. *The Early Church.* By Sir Henry Chadwick, Honorary Fellow and former Master of Peterhouse, Cambridge, and Regius Professor Emeritus of Divinity, Cambridge University.
2. *Western Society and the Church in the Middle Ages.* By Sir Richard Southern, formerly President of St John's College, Oxford.
3. *The Reformation.* By Owen Chadwick, Chancellor of the University of East Anglia and former Regius Professor of Modern History, Cambridge University.
4. *The Church and the Age of Reason, 1648–1789.* By Gerald R. Cragg, formerly Professor of Church History at Andover Newton Theological School, Boston, Mass.
5. *The Church in an Age of Revolution.* By Alec R. Vidler, formerly Fellow and Dean of King's College, Cambridge.
6. *A History of Christian Missions.* By Stephen Neill, formerly Professor of Philosophy and Religious Studies at the University of Nairobi and Assistant Bishop in the Diocese of Oxford.
7. *The Christian Church in the Cold War.* By Owen Chadwick, Chancellor of the University of East Anglia and former Regius Professor of Modern History, Cambridge University.

CONTENTS

Preface

THE period of history with which this book deals is fitly called 'an age of revolution'. It begins with the French Revolution which was more epoch-making than most events that are so described, and which itself had several further revolutions as its sequels. About the same time, Kant's copernican revolution in philosophy took place, and that has been no less prolific of upheavals in the world of thought. In the nineteenth century there were developments in the natural and mechanical sciences, in the structure of society, and in the study of history, not least of the history with which the Bible purports to be occupied, that were revolutionary in their consequences. It is unnecessary to specify the equally revolutionary changes that have been going on since the twentieth century began. The period has been an age of revolution in the broad sense that every area of human existence and every aspect of civilization have been subject to an unremitting dynamism, and what it has been it still is.

The Church, by which I mean the whole complex of Christian institutions, has inevitably been affected by what has happened in the world in which it is set. Although it has for the most part been conspicuous for its recalcitrance to change, and could plausibly be regarded as the chief rallying ground for all *laudatores temporis acti*, it has in fact been undergoing internal changes that add up to something like a revolution. I cannot attempt in this book to cover all the ground, or to provide a concise encyclopedia of church history since the French Revolution. What I have done is to select courses of events, phases of thought, crises and controversies, and movements here or there, which may serve to give a fair and representative impression of the most important things that have happened to the Church or in the Church during the period. Another author with the same purpose might have made a different and equally enlightening selection. I shall bear with equanimity any reproaches that are addressed to me about faults of omission. But I wish I had been able to say more about the ordinary life of Christian people in parishes and congregations which has gone on steadily from generation to generation and without which there would be no church history worth mentioning. It does not hit the headlines and it slips easily through the net in which historians try to catch what is unsteady and non-recurring and more readily open to public inspection.

Even within these limits, my selection of subjects for consideration has been deliberately restricted. This is a book about the history of the Church in Europe with an eye especially on Britain and with little more than a glance at Eastern Orthodoxy and American Christianity. Missionary expansion in other continents and the emergence of the 'Younger Churches', except as they form part of the history of the 'Older Churches', have been left out of account, because they are so various and so interesting as to require another book or series of books.

I am of course indebted to a large number of authors from whose historical studies and commentaries I have profited. If I have anywhere through inadvertence plagiarized their work without acknowledgement, I apologize. In two or three chapters, I have drawn some material from a book entitled *The Development of Modern Catholicism* (1933), in the writing of which I collaborated with the late Dr W. L. Knox. I wish to thank S.P.C.K., the holders of the copyright, for allowing me to do so.

A.R.V.

Preface to 1971 Edition

I HAVE amended the text in various places in order to bring it up to date, and have added a new chapter which seeks to take some account of what transpired during the 1960s. I am grateful to several correspondents who have sent me information and suggestions.

A.R.V.

1

The Gallican Church: The Revolution and Napoleon

'ANY considerate reader will admit', wrote F. D. Maurice in 1842, 'that as France has been the centre of the political, and Germany of the philosophical movements of the last hundred years, so England has been the centre of all religious movements.' This was, perhaps, to claim too much for England, but not for France or Germany. Certainly, the French Revolution was a great dividing-line in the political history of Europe, the sign of the downfall of the *ancien régime*, a sort of atomic bomb of which the fallout is still at work. It was a beginning as well as an end: the beginning of a still continuing series of attempts to build new structures to take the place of the system that had collapsed. The Church had been an integral, if not always a vital, element in the old system. Its establishment had been taken for granted. What would its fate be when the system in which it was established disintegrated?

This question arose wherever the forces that the Revolution released made their way, as they did everywhere sooner or later. But it was in France that the question was answered most strikingly, not so much in theory as by the swift pressure of events. Thus it is in France that the political impact of the age of revolution upon the Church can best be studied. Not that any stable solution was arrived at there, either in the years succeeding 1789 or at any subsequent time. Rather, it is the variety, the fluctuations, and the instability of the relations between Church, State, and society since 1789 that make French ecclesiastical history a paradigm both of the insecurity and of the survival of

Christianity in this age. What was writ large in France was written in lesser or derivative scripts elsewhere.

The position of the French Church on the eve of the Revolution was at first sight solid and even majestic. The clergy were a privileged class. The Catholic Church had no rivals, for since the revocation of the Edict of Nantes Catholics alone had the right of citizenship. The clergy had their own courts, and marriage was under ecclesiastical control. The Church possessed immense wealth and property, which was exempt from taxation. It had a monopoly of education and the care of the sick. But behind the imposing exterior there were grave abuses and sources of weakness.

In the first place, there was an absence of spiritual vitality, and without that a Church is ill-qualified to face an hour of crisis. Whereas in the seventeenth century Jansenism had had a bracing effect and there had been a flowering of mysticism, in the eighteenth century religion had become an uninspired moralism like Latitudinarianism in England, and in France there had been no counterpart to the evangelical revival. Monasteries and convents still abounded, but, in the case of the monks anyhow, their condition was deplorable. The number of novices was rapidly declining. Some large monasteries had only a handful of ageing monks left. The condition of the nunneries seems to have been better. But the spirit of the age had little use for the contemplative life. There was no convincing answer to the question: Why don't these indolent people do some useful work?

The secular clergy were much like their opposite numbers in England, though in France the higher appointments were more completely monopolized by the aristocracy. The bishops, accomplished and cultured men of the world, were more occupied with politics than with the spiritual care of their dioceses. It was said that they administered more provinces than sacraments! They lived in a state of magnificence, and often of absence. Saint-Sulpice, the principal seminary for the training of the clergy, was in a decadent state. The parish clergy were respectable and often given to good works, but were seldom remarkable for the ardour of their faith. Some of them were well-educated, though many rural priests knew more about agriculture than theology.

It was still the Age of Reason, of rational religion. There were no great theologians such as there had been in the seventeenth century. The clergy, like the laity, read and imbibed the rationalistic literature of the time: the science of the Encyclopedia; Voltaire's mockery of superstition; Rousseau's sentimental deism. The rights of man were more canvassed than the rights of God, and the clergy were naturally ambitious to secure *their* rights. They did not want to be slaves of the bishops any more than of the pope. There was even a current of presbyterianism, which prepared the way for the welcome that many of the clergy would give to the Civil Constitution to be promulgated by the Revolution.

The vast wealth of the Church was very unevenly distributed. Whereas most of the bishops and dignitaries could live in opulence and luxury, the inferior clergy, especially in the country, were generally poor and dependent on the precarious collection of tithes. This disparity in clerical remuneration and means of livelihood made for discontent and division in the Church and disposed the lower clergy to favour the idea of radical change.

As regards the laity, as a whole they remained attached to the Church, however much they might criticize its abuses. But among the intelligentsia, in Paris and the provincial centres of culture, there was much Voltairean scepticism and infidelity, so that in a crisis the Church would have its enemies as well as its friends. Opinions differ about how far hostility to the Church was focused in the masonic lodges. Many of the clergy belonged to them; they did not yet stand for the fierce anti-clericalism which subsequently became a mark of continental freemasonry.

All in all, it was a languid and a lukewarm, rather than a hopelessly corrupt Church that had to face the ordeal of the

Revolution. What was in the air in 1789 was not a violent tempest waiting to be unleashed in order to sweep the Church away, but a general desire for the removal of ancient abuses and the achievement of rational reforms. How then, when the Revolution came, did it bear upon the Church?

When in 1789, on account of the financial crisis, Louis XVI convened the States-General which had not met since 1614, the representatives of the nation were given an opportunity of ventilating their grievances and their aspirations. Petitions for the correction of abuses in the ordering of both Church and State flowed in from all over the country. But no one suggested or contemplated the demolition of either the monarchy or the Church, the twin pillars of the *ancien régime*. What was wanted and hoped for was a reform, not a revolution. A reform, it has been said, is a correction of abuses; a revolution is a transfer of power. But what starts as a reforming, often ends as a revolutionary, movement; and conditions were in fact ripe for a transfer of power from the old feudal aristocracy to the rising bourgeoisie.

When the States-General assembled, the nobles, who had expected to take charge, had quickly to surrender their privileged position, and the representatives of the bourgeoisie took the lead. They were liberal-minded and idealistic men, and they set about planning a general reform of institutions in the confident way that idealists do. They were really ill-qualified, or at least ill-prepared, to wield power and to control the vigorous process of change that had been set in motion. Consequently, the direction of affairs was destined to pass beyond them too into the hands of men who were at once harder-headed and harder-hearted, and within a year or two things were happening in France that no one had imagined or foreseen.

In its first phases the Revolution was not viewed with alarm by the rank and file of the Gallican Church. Quite the contrary. 'In a few days' time', wrote a priest at Orleans, 'I shall be ninety-eight years old. No day in my life has been as happy as that which I now see dawning. O Blessed

Sun beneath which so many virtues have sprung up!' When the States-General met, the action of the First Estate, that is the clergy, in throwing in their lot with the Third Estate, that is the financial, commercial, and professional classes, played a decisive part in breaking the power of the nobility, and indeed of the absolute monarchy, for there thus came into existence the National or Constituent Assembly, in which the bourgeoisie had the ruling voice.

The storming of the Bastille was a sign that forces had been released which could be controlled only if the Assembly quickly adopted large and drastic measures of reform. It was in an atmosphere of mingled panic and generous emotion that the clergy now renounced their privileges and, in particular, the tithes on which they depended for their subsistence. This and subsequent measures manifestly necessitated a reconstruction of the ecclesiastical system.

What form was the reconstruction to take, and who was to design it? The members of the Constituent Assembly were for the most part sincere Catholics: even the disciples of Voltaire or Rousseau still considered that religion was necessary for the people. All were interested in the reform of the Church. It is significant that it occurred to no one to turn to the pope for guidance or direction, so firm was the hold of the Gallican tradition. It was assumed that the king, who was now the executant of the will of the Assembly, was entirely qualified to authorize a new ecclesiastical settlement. So a committee of the Assembly, with a bishop as president, was appointed to work out a scheme of reform. It produced its report in April 1790. Its proposals were debated and amended and became law in July. The measure was known as the Civil Constitution of the Clergy; it provided for a reconstitution of the Church of France as part of the new French constitution.

The Civil Constitution of the Clergy rearranged the diocesan boundaries so that they became coterminous with the civil departments. Fifty-seven dioceses were suppressed. Archbishoprics were abolished, but there were still sees with metropolitan status. The Bishop of Rome ceased to have any authority over the Gallican Church, though this was said to be 'without prejudice to the unity of faith and the communion which will be maintained with the visible head of the universal Church'. In other words, the pope was accorded only a primacy of honour. Each bishop was to be *curé* of his own cathedral church. Cathedral chapters and other dignitaries were abolished, but the bishop was to have a staff or diocesan council without which he could not act in matters of jurisdiction. They were to be elected by the civil electorate of the department. Before the election the electors were to hear mass and to take an oath that they would consider only the interests of religion. The bishop-elect was to seek confirmation from the metropolitan or senior bishop, but not from the pope. He would simply inform the pope that he had been elected. *Curés* were to be elected in a similar manner.

The Civil Constitution should not be regarded as a reckless or revolutionary innovation. It implemented, in a somewhat extreme form, the pre-revolutionary Gallican principles. It corresponded on the whole to the kind of reforms that had been asked for in the petitions that had been prepared for the States-General. To the objection that it was being imposed by the civil power, the reply was made that it dealt only with ecclesiastical discipline and organization, which Gallicans held to be within the province of the civil power. It did not touch dogma. But ought it not to have been submitted to a national ecclesiastical synod or to the bishops for their approval? They unfortunately were nearly all drawn from the aristocracy, and could hardly have been expected to approve a constitution that would deprive them of many of their traditional privileges and powers, if not of their sees. Undoubtedly, the Civil Constitution would have had a much better prospect of success, if the Assembly had been resourceful enough to secure for it ecclesiastical as well as civil authorization, though it is not easy to suggest how in the circumstances this could have been done.

As it was, the pope delayed for eight months before giving his decision. In consequence, the king, who was a devout and scrupulously conscientious Catholic, had approved the Constitution before he knew that the pope condemned it. Moreover, there was great confusion and uncertainty among those Catholics who acknowledged the authority of the pope about what they ought to do. Towards the end of 1790 the king had reluctantly sanctioned a law according to which all bishops and *curés* then in office had to take an oath accepting the Civil Constitution, and they had to decide whether or not to obey, without being sure of the pope's will.

Exact figures cannot be given about how many clergy took the oath and how many refused, but the most reliable estimate seems to be that approximately fifty per cent swore and fifty per cent did not. Thus the effect of the Civil Constitution, whatever its merits, was to split the French Church in two, and for ten years it remained split. Nearly all the bishops were non-jurors and most of them emigrated; but there were just enough to supply episcopal consecration for the newly-elected bishops of the Constitutional Church. Talleyrand obliged, though he soon afterwards renounced his own orders.

These, however, were only the beginnings of troubles for the Church in France. At first, the non-jurors were allowed to carry on their ministry, but, when the conduct of the Revolution passed into more violent hands, they were pro-scribed as fanatics and counter-revolutionaries, and could say mass only in private at the risk of their lives. Many were driven into exile; others were massacred.

There followed the Reign of Terror and the campaigns of dechristianization, the cult of the goddess Reason and then of Robespierre's Supreme Being, and later the new religion of theophilanthropy. The Constitutional Church also now found itself under attack and some of its leaders apostatized, while others sought safety in contracting a marriage.

During these years there were several waves of assault on the clergy, but, when the worst was over, both the jurors and the non-jurors were able, spasmodically and gradually, to resume their ministry. It seemed that Catholicism, though disestablished, was still alive in the soul of the French people, despite all attempts to extirpate it. Nevertheless, when the Church began to lift up its head again, it was not only subject to the threat of further attacks; it remained fatally divided. The Constitutionals and the clergy loyal to Rome were bitterly set against one another, and in addition there were painful feuds among the pro-Roman clergy themselves which arose out of differences concerning the legitimacy of taking various oaths that the government continued to impose, and also between those who were republicans and those who were royalists. At the same time, the anti-clerical and anti-Christian forces remained strong both in the government and in the country, so that the future of Catholicism in France looked anything but bright.

It was the rise of Napoleon that transformed the scene. The genius of this extraordinary man showed itself in his achievements not only as a military commander but also as a statesman and administrator. He gave France the centralized, vigorous, and efficient government that was needed after the turmoil of the revolutionary years. He improved the finances of the country, promoted its economic prosperity, codified its laws, and constructed a system of public education which, like much else that he created, has endured to this day.

It was as a statesman too that he determined to bring to an end the schism in the French Church. To what extent, if any, he was himself a Catholic believer is a moot question, but he had a genuine sense of the part that religion can play in giving unity, cohesion, and contentment to a society. The social utility of religion was not, of course, an original idea of his: Voltaire, Rousseau, Chateaubriand, and many other guides of French thought, had in their various ways subscribed to it. But with Napoleon it was a maxim of policy. Here is one of several passages in which he expressed it. He is speaking of the 'mystery of religion'.

This mystery is not that of the Incarnation. I do not discuss that, any more than the other dogmas of the Church. But I see in religion the whole mystery of society. I hold ... that apart from the precepts and doctrines of the Gospel there is no society that can flourish, nor any real civilization. What is it that makes the poor man take it for granted that ten chimneys smoke in my palace while he dies of cold – that I have ten changes of raiment in my wardrobe while he is naked – that on my table at each meal there is enough to sustain a family for a week? It is religion which says to him that in another life I shall be his equal, indeed that he has a better chance of being happy there than I have.[1]

It was because he was convinced about the social utility of religion and of religious concord that Napoleon made up his mind to restore the unity and prosperity of the Church, despite the fact that many of his colleagues in the government were opposed to the project. It was a tough nut to crack, since, in order to succeed, he had to heal the schism between the Constitutional and the Non-juring Churches, and also to secure the cooperation and approval of the pope. The attempt to construct a church in France independently of the papacy had proved to be a failure: he would not repeat that mistake.

So he entered into negotiation with the Holy See for a new religious settlement, but it was he who laid down the lines on which it should be carried out. He insisted that the constitutionals and the non-jurors should be welded together, and to that end that all the bishops of both churches should hand in their resignations or, failing that, have their sees declared vacant by the pope. A new hierarchy would then be nominated – by himself as First Consul – and the former constitutional bishops were to have a fair share of the new appointments. This was a specially bitter pill for the papacy to swallow in view of all that it – and the non-jurors – had said about the Constitutional Church. However, a heavy price was worth paying for the restoration of the Church in

1. Paul Droulers s.j. *Action pastorale et problèmes sociaux sous la Monarchie de Juillet.* 1954, p. 117.

France and all that might follow from it. So Napoleon got his way in this as in most other matters. The papal negotiators were able to secure only a few modifications of his plans. Eventually a concordat was concluded in July 1801: it was to govern the relations of France with the Holy See for over a century.

The confiscation of church property that had taken place during the Revolution was accepted by the pope, and instead the bishops and other clergy were to be paid stipends by the State. This made them much more dependent on the civil government than they had been before the Revolution, and in the long run they would be inclined to turn more and more for support to the papacy against the domination of the State. In this respect, Napoleon unintentionally gave a fillip to ultramontanism. Still more ultramontane in its implications was his recognition that the pope had authority to demand the resignation of French bishops, which would never have been allowed by the royal government before the Revolution.

Napoleon was more papal than the papacy itself was disposed to be at this point, because he saw no other way of healing the schism, but in reality he was set upon retaining the liberties and privileges which the Gallicans had always claimed. He demonstrated this at once, for, as soon as the concordat had been agreed and published, he promulgated on his own authority a set of 'Organic Articles' which laid down restrictions on the exercise of papal authority in France and which were extremely obnoxious to the papacy.

While he wanted to appear, and at the time did appear to the majority of French Catholics, to be the saviour and restorer of the Church, we can now see that his intention in the whole proceeding was to use and exploit the Church for his own purposes. He had hoped to find in Pope Pius VII, upon whom he was able to exercise a strange fascination, a compliant instrument for his designs. In that, however, he proved at last to have misjudged his man, for although at times the pope made surprising concessions – as when he came to Paris for the imperial coronation – he refused to be wax in the emperor's hands, even when he was driven out of the papal states and imprisoned in France.

The resistance of Pius VII was indeed one of the factors that led to the downfall of Napoleon. Nevertheless, as a result of the concordat the Church of France had been given a new lease of life. Although it had been dreadfully weakened during the Revolution, and had laboured under many inhibitions during the Empire, it had an opportunity of regaining its place in the life of the French people.

In 1814 it was impossible to say whether the Church would take the opportunity. Its external fabric had been substantially restored, but there had been no equal revival of spiritual life or of theological thought. There had been little scope under the Empire for training a body of priests with a sense of mission to a society whose traditional loyalties had been dissolved. Nor had conditions been favourable to a renovation of Christian thought. No Catholic writers had arisen who were capable of counteracting the influence of the heirs of Voltaire and Rousseau or of meeting the challenges to faith that the Age of Reason had bequeathed. Chateaubriand's apology for Christianity in *Le Génie du Christianisme* (1802) had been little more than sentimental. So far as Christian philosophy and theology were concerned, events in France had revealed the bankruptcy of the old order without provoking the germination of anything radically new.

2

Theological Reconstruction in Germany

ON 16 July 1804 Schiller, the German poet and dramatist, wrote to a friend: 'In the dark time of superstition Berlin first kindled the torch of rational religious liberty. . . . Now in this age of unbelief there is another kind of renown that might be won. . . . Let Berlin now add warmth to light, and thus ennoble the Protestantism of which this city is destined some day to be the capital.' His hope for the future of Germany, and of Berlin in particular, was to be largely fulfilled. For it was there that new religious ideas were to be generated that would arouse both enthusiasm and alarm, far and wide. Mark Pattison, surveying the state of theology in 1857, could say: 'Extinct in Italy, and all but so in France, it is now in Germany alone that the vital questions of Religion are discussed with the full and free application of all the resources of learning and criticism which our age has at its command.' It is still broadly true to say that the Germans set the pace in the development of theology.

F. D. E. Schleiermacher (1763–1834), who is commonly described as 'the father of modern theology', certainly brought warmth as well as light into Protestantism. His earliest book, *Religion: Speeches to its Cultured Despisers* (1799), was a bold attempt to recover for religion the position it had lost in the intellectual world. Religion was not a sop for the uncultured or a consolation for the aged, but the noblest ingredient in the intellectual life of mankind. Schleiermacher became the most eminent and influential theological professor of his time, and he worked out a radically new system of dogmatics. Any theologian today who reads for the first time his principal work, *The Christian Faith* (1821–2), will be astonished to find how many theological ideas, which he had supposed to be of much more recent origin, are adumbrated there.

This remarkable man was at the confluence of all the currents of thought and social movement that agitated the world at the beginning of the nineteenth century. The evangelical piety of the Moravians among whom he was brought up, the rationalism of the *Aufklärung* (the Enlightenment), the critical idealism of Kant, the romanticism of Frederick Schlegel with whom he lived and collaborated in Berlin, the patriotic cause of resistance to Napoleon and of the regeneration of Prussia – all these left their mark upon him, as would also the reunion of the Lutheran and Reformed Churches in Prussia which was prompted by the third centenary of the Reformation.

The eighteenth century had been the Age of Reason. Weary of the wars of religion and of barren disputes about insoluble questions, men had embraced with relief the notion that all the religion and morality that were necessary could be quite simply ascertained. Reason was a light that was universally diffused among mankind. It was given to all by nature, and it sufficed. Ancient beliefs and institutions should be submitted to it and judged by it. What survived the test was 'natural religion', a simple, ideal abstract, in contrast to the positive religions that had their origin either in ignorance of natural causes or in the ambition of priests and kings.

Immanuel Kant (1724–1804), 'the German Socrates', whom Schleiermacher had met as well as studied, stirred up the mud at the bottom of this stream of common sense. What is reason? he asked. What are its powers and its limitations? His answers were by no means plain: in fact, they have provided matter for philosophical discussion ever since. But roughly speaking, so far as theology was concerned, his teaching had two sides. On its negative side, Kant insisted that human knowledge is knowledge only of phenomena or appearances, not of *noumena* or things-in-themselves. He therefore denied that it was possible to have a rational metaphysics or a rational theology, since they purported to get at things-in-themselves, or the ultimate realities. The traditional arguments for the existence of God, being meta-physical, thus went by the board.

But what Kant took away with one hand he seemed to give back with the other. Although in theory or along the line of pure reason there is no escape from agnosticism as regards ultimate reality, yet in practice there is in man's consciousness a sense of unconditional moral obligation that makes sense only if belief in God, freedom, and immortality is postulated. The categorical imperative – which says 'thou shalt do this' or 'thou shalt not do that' whatever the consequences – requires (1) a *God* who is entitled to say 'thou shalt'; (2) that 'thou shalt' can be said only where 'thou canst' can also be said, hence *freedom* also must be postulated; and (3) that, since the moral perfection which man feels himself obliged to seek cannot be realized within the bounds of this life, *immortality* must also be postulated. Thus Kant vindicates religious belief by analysing the moral consciousness. Religion is the recognition of all our duties as divine commands. It is 'the faith which puts the essential of all worship in the moral nature of man'. Schleiermacher went on from where Kant left off: from the moral conscious-ness to the religious consciousness.

Schleiermacher was also a child of romanticism. He was sensible of the fact that man is a being possessed of emotion and feeling as well as of thought and will. Romanticism, in contrast to rationalism, places content above form, the aesthetic above the moral, the concrete above the abstract. It views the universe not as a machine but as a work of art, and man as a mirror of the universe. The romantic spirit chimed in with the warm piety and deep devotion to the person of Jesus which Schleiermacher had learned from the Moravians, and which had been only temporarily sub-merged when he found that he must break with the naïve traditional orthodoxy of his parents.

A great theologian, however, is always more than a

sounding-board, and Schleiermacher was more than a product of his antecedents. His greatness consists in the fact that he propounded a new and comprehensive interpretation of Christianity. He repudiated the traditional idea that religion is a compendium of fixed doctrines that must be accepted on faith. He looked for himself at the springs of religion in human experience, as at a living reality that existed in its own right whatever philosophy might have to say about it. Instead of trying to argue others into agreeing with him, he sought to awaken in them an experience akin to his own.

He found the starting-point of religion in man's feeling of absolute dependence. 'God is given to us in feeling in an original way; and if we speak of an original revelation of God to man or in man, the meaning will always be just this, that, along with the absolute dependence which characterizes not only man but all temporal existence, there is given to man also the immediate self-consciousness of it, which becomes a consciousness of God.' By 'feeling' Schleiermacher meant not only sensation or emotion, but an intuitive contact with reality. In the feeling of absolute dependence God is grasped directly as the 'Whence' of all things.

This feeling lies at the bottom of all religions and in all of them there is a measure of revelation. What distinguishes Christianity is the idea of redemption by Christ. The essential thing about Christ was not his teaching, or the miracles, or the fulfilment of prophecy, but his perfect God-consciousness, 'which was a veritable existence of God in him'. He is the one perfect revelation of God in the human race. His work as redeemer consists in imparting to others the strength of his consciousness of God.

Sin is the antithesis or incompleteness of the consciousness of God in man, the result of a strife between the lower and higher impulses. Redemption means being brought out of the condition in which the consciousness of God is dimmed or enfeebled into a condition in which it is vivid and strong and capable of growth. Sin is social as well as individual: its operation in one individual produces evil in others. Likewise redemption is a corporate process. Through the fellowship that Jesus founded, the Church, fellowship with God is communicated and sustained. Schleiermacher teaches that the Church is the body of Christ, an organism animated by the Holy Spirit, but that it is also human and mutable. Unlike many German theologians, he attached importance to the Church's autonomy and freedom from control by the State. The perfection of the Church cannot be realized in this world: the final consummation lies beyond. The traditional doctrine of the last things (death, judgement, heaven, and hell) contains prophetical articles that cannot be clearly understood. Schleiermacher was not sure whether there was a definite warrant for believing in personal immortality.

A paragraph or two can only hint at the fertility and freshness with which he reinterpreted the entire scheme of Christian theology on the basis of the Church's continuing experience of the work of Christ. He offered an emancipation from the forensic and external presentation of doctrine that was to be found in the conventional text-books of Protestant scholasticism, and his appeal to experience and the common life of believers enabled him to discard those features of traditional orthodoxy which the natural science or the historical and literary criticism of the time were showing to be untenable.

In some of these matters his teaching naturally became outmoded; for example, he accepted the Fourth Gospel as a primary source for the life of Jesus. But his work as a whole came to bear the same relation to subsequent Liberal Protestant theology as the *Summa* of St Thomas does to Thomism or as Calvin's *Institutes* do to Reformed theology. It is a Roman Catholic writer[1] who has said that 'the influence of Schleiermacher's ideas has been immense. It can be said without exaggeration that his name altogether

1. L. Cristiani in *Dict. théol. cath.* XIV, 1505.

dominates the Protestant theology of the nineteenth century
and that the twentieth century remains subject to the same
impress.'

Dr Karl Barth, who has done much to obliterate that
impress, still recognizes that it was a great virtue in Schleiermacher that he sought to relate theology to all that was best
in the non-theological world. 'He did not do this retro-
spectively, trotting behind the times, as theologians so often
do, but in advance of the time, as a born man of the age,
and further as one dedicated to the achievement of a
better future'.[1] But Barth also suggests that Schleiermacher
transformed *faith*, as it is understood in the New Testament,
into a *gnosis*. He recalls that Schleiermacher on his death-
bed celebrated Holy Communion with his family, using
water instead of wine which the doctor had forbidden him
to drink. Was this a parable of his theology? 'But there can
be no doubt of the fact that Schleiermacher wanted to celebrate the Holy Communion. He wanted in his Christology,
whose content might perhaps be compared with the water,
to proclaim Christ.'[2] Barth here poses a question that has
not yet been finally answered.

*

The reconstruction of theology undertaken by G. W. F.
Hegel (1770–1831) was based on quite a different plan and
informed by quite a different spirit, but in the nineteenth
century its influence was scarcely less pervasive. Like
Schleiermacher, Hegel was a professor at Berlin, but they
had little in common. Hegel treated Schleiermacher's
teaching with contempt. He said that if religion is founded
only on the feeling of absolute dependence, then the best
Christian would be the dog whose sense of dependence on his
master is absolute. Whereas Schleiermacher was a preacher
and participated in the social life and movements of his
time, Hegel was by comparison an academic, a philosopher

1. K. Barth. *From Rousseau to Ritschl.* 1959, p. 315.
2. ibid., p. 313.

pure and simple. Though he had a life-long interest in religion and as a young man contemplated a clerical career, he was without the warm personal piety and devotion to Christ as a historic and living person which Schleiermacher had learned from the Moravians. Nor does Hegel ever seem to have gone through a period of intense spiritual conflict. A. M. Fairbairn drew an apt and picturesque contrast between the two men:

> Hegel now massive, majestic like a swollen river running between bank and bank and bearing down whatever stood in its course, and now strung, tense, like a charged catapult shooting out a criticism in a metaphor or argument that went straight and strong through any defensive armour; Schleiermacher nimble, subtle, graceful, like the streamlet that leaps as it runs making beauty for the eye and music for the ear.[1]

At first sight, it is strange that, when Kant had just barred the way to the construction of metaphysical systems, Hegel should proceed to construct one in which he claimed that the substance of all previous philosophies was contained. As W. T. Stace has said:

> No sooner had Kant ... cried 'Halt!' to philosophy than philosophy, forming its adherents into a sort of triumphant procession, proceeding, so to speak, with bands playing and flags waving, marched victoriously onward to the final assault, confident of its power to attain omniscience at a stroke, to occupy the very citadel of reality itself. And strangest of all, this was done with the very weapons which Kant had forged.[2]

Hegel, like Kant, was an idealist, that is they both took their stand upon consciousness and its contents. But Hegel rejected Kant's assertion that only phenomena can be known by pure reason. The conception of unknowable *noumena* is self-contradictory, since, if things-in-themselves are unknowable, we have no means of knowing that they

1. A. M. Fairbairn. *The Place of Christ in Modern Theology.* 1849, pp. 282f.
2. W. T. Stace. *The Philosophy of Hegel.* 1924, p. 43.

are unknowable. For philosophy everything must be knowable. The Absolute itself lies open to the human mind. So Hegel declared: 'The nature of the universe, hidden and shut up in itself as it is at first, has no power which can permanently resist the courageous efforts of the intelligence: it must at last open itself; it must reveal all its depth and riches to the spirit, and surrender them to be enjoyed by it.'

According to Hegel, the world was to be explained as the working out of a rational principle, namely spirit or the Absolute Idea, which is 'the idea of a self-consciousness which manifests itself in the difference of self and not-self, that through this difference and by overcoming it, it may attain to the highest unity with itself'. Nature and history are an evolving process, through which spirit is realizing itself. It becomes self-conscious only in man. The process is dialectical. That is to say, the rational principle, in order to develop, differentiates itself in forms that inevitably conflict with each other, but are ultimately reconciled. This movement from thesis through antithesis to synthesis is everywhere at work and can be detected at all levels. Here is Karl Barth's description of the Hegelian dialectic:

> Where the triple beat of thesis, antithesis, and synthesis rings out and it rings out everywhere, the Hegelian wisdom resembles one of those old villages of weavers where once, day after day, the sound of the same machines could be heard from every house: where this rhythm sounds there is the whole and centre of this philosophy. ... What makes for Hegel's genius ... [is] the fact that he dared to want to invent such a method, a key to open every lock, a lever to set every wheel working at once, an observation tower from which not only all lands of the earth, but the third and seventh heavens, too, can be surveyed at a glance.[1]

But for Hegel the truth as pure thought or as a conceptual theory could be understood only by philosophers. The masses of mankind were not capable of this, and so the truth had to be translated to them in the pictorial or figurative forms of religion. All religions served this purpose to some extent.

1. op. cit. pp. 289f.

Christianity was the one absolutely true religion because the inner meaning of its figurative expressions was identical with the principles of true (that is Hegelian) philosophy.

So, for instance, he explains the Trinitarian dogma: 'As pure abstract idea, God is Father; as going forth into finite being, the element of change and variety, God is Son; as once more sublating or cancelling this distinction, and turning again home enriched by this outgoing in so-called manifestation or incarnation, God is Holy Spirit.' This is a typical piece of Hegelian theologizing, and in this way he interpreted the whole scheme of Christian doctrine as a figurative expression of his philosophical system. His intention was to enable Christianity to understand itself, but it is a question whether he did not change it into something else. In his system God is subordinated to the Absolute, Christ is a logical construction and not a living person, evil is raw material on the way to becoming good or spirit, redemption is not an event in time but an eternal truth, the resurrection and ascension of Christ mean that the universal which became particular returns into itself.

This transformation of theology into philosophy is not generally viewed nowadays with a kindly eye by either theologians or philosophers, but Hegel's system had a grandeur, even if it was a grandeur that could not last. Even those who regard his whole system as perverse may allow that in some respects he had a valuable positive influence on subsequent thought. As C. C. J. Webb said:

Hegel helped to turn the current of men's thoughts into two at least of the channels in which they have since been running. By giving *history* a standing, so to speak, in philosophy . . . he gave a new dignity to historical study, much as Bacon in his day had given a new dignity to the study of nature; and he also made the notion of *development* central.[1]

Hegel enjoyed immense prestige during his lifetime, but soon after his death his followers began to disintegrate and

1. C. C. J. Webb. *A Century of Anglican Theology*. 1923, pp. 29f.

to separate into opposing parties. There was a right wing
that treated him as the champion of orthodox Christianity.
On the other hand, the left wing, notably in Feuerbach,
divested the Hegelian system of religious and ethical meaning and turned it into a thoroughgoing atheism. Between
the right and left wings there were various mediating schools.
On any showing, Hegel gave a new impetus to philosophical
theology. In one way or another, by attraction or repulsion,
Hegelianism fascinated the nineteenth century, and we shall
come across a good many traces of its influence.

*

After the aridity of the Age of Reason there was as much
need for a reconstruction of Catholic as of Protestant theology. At the beginning of the nineteenth century Herder said
that the Church of Rome was like an ancient ruin into which
no new life could enter, and it looked like that. Catholic
theological teaching was based on a dry and decadent
Cartesianism. The romantic school of writers and artists
brought fresh air into this stuffy atmosphere. For example,
Frederick Schlegel (1772–1829) said that poetry, in order
to be able to give expression to the infinite mysteries of life,
needed a mythology like that of the ancient Greeks or
early Christians. At first he proposed to create a new religion that would absorb the French Revolution as Christianity
had absorbed the Roman Empire. 'I am thinking of founding a new religion,' he wrote to Novalis, 'or at least of help-
ing to preach it. Perhaps you are better qualified to make a
new Christ – if so, he will find in me his St Paul.' If Catholicism could be presented to such men as a living faith, it
would evidently fall on receptive soil, and in the event a
number of them did become converts.

Stimulated by romanticism, a revival of Catholic theology
took place at various centres in Germany, notably at
Tübingen. Tübingen is one of the German universities where
Catholic and Protestant faculties of theology exist side by
side. The Catholic faculty dates from 1817: it had an able

and enterprising group of theologians, which included John Sebastian Drey (1777–1853) and John Adam Möhler (1796–1838). They sought to do for Catholicism what Schleiermacher was doing for Protestantism.

They were determined to show that their faith had nothing to fear from historical criticism or philosophical discussion. The ideas of organism, in contrast to mechanism, and of development, in contrast to a fixed and closed system, were fundamental for them. Their theology was dynamic. Dogmas should be regarded not as abstract and isolated propositions, but in relation to the living whole of which they formed a part. They are the fruit of the perpetual effort of the Church to translate into intellectual terms the life of faith. All religion is revelation: Christianity is the revelation that completes and synthesizes all partial revelations, preserving whatever is true and durable in them. Tradition is not a fixed set of fossilized statements, but the Word of God living in the faithful. It is constantly developing and has constantly to be rethought in the light of the total movement of human culture.

They maintained that Catholicism is the complex whole of which Protestantism is a one-sided distortion, and they contrasted the universality of the Catholic Church with the nationalism and territorialism with which Protestantism was compounded. They were criticized as innovators by conservative Catholics, and as time went on they modified some of their more daring proposals for doctrinal restatement and ecclesiastical reform, for, to begin with, they had called in question such long-standing customs as clerical celibacy, private masses, communion in one kind, and a Latin liturgy. It cannot be said that they were viewed with official favour in the Roman Church, but they had staked out a claim for the ideas that reason and revelation, nature and supernature, liberty and authority, are not opposed to one another but are complementary, and that Catholicism is capable of meeting not only Protestantism but historical criticism, science, and philosophy in an open encounter.

3

Christianity in England, 1790–1830

THE principal effect of the French Revolution on the English was to stiffen their conservatism and so to postpone the pressure for reform in Church and State which everywhere made itself felt sooner or later in the nineteenth century. The Revolution and the Napoleonic wars also deepened the insularity of the English. In particular, the English intelligence was insulated from the new philosophical and theological movements that were centred in Germany. So far as the Church in England was concerned, there were no political or intellectual upheavals in the first quarter of the century. What we have to do in this chapter is to take stock of a comparatively settled state of affairs which must be understood if the peculiar character of the subsequent transmutation of Christian institutions and Christian thought in England is to be intelligible.

It is true that the first phase of the French Revolution was welcomed and applauded by many observers in England. It was the downfall of a feudal despotism, and it was considered to be overdue. That the French should seek to establish the constitutional liberties upon which the English prided themselves was highly commendable. Some went further and experienced the intoxicating sense of being in at the opening of a new era in human history, in which ancient abuses and corruptions were going to be for ever swept away, and liberty, fraternity, and equality to be realized at last. 'Bliss was it in that dawn to be alive.'

The alarm about the real meaning of the Revolution in France was sounded by Burke in his famous *Reflections* (1790). He had been provoked into writing by Dr Price, a leading dissenter, who had congratulated the French on

carrying further the principles of the English Revolution of
1688. Burke's thesis was that the English understanding of
politics was the precise opposite of the French. The English
were traditionalist, gradualist, empirical, whereas the French
were dangerously doctrinaire idealists. His warnings seemed
to be prophetic and fully justified as the Revolution turned
into the Terror. Most of those in England who had at first
welcomed it changed their minds when they heard of the
massacres, the execution of the king, and the Jacobin
excesses. Naturally the sense of horror was intensified when
England found itself at war with France.

Dread of the terrible things that were happening across
the Channel was enhanced by the threat to all established
institutions at home voiced by Tom Paine's *The Rights of
Man*, which was published in 1791 and sold by tens of
thousands. Tom Paine was a declared republican and was
regarded as a notorious infidel. Burke had extolled the
Church of England as the source and sanction of social
stability, and so it was. What was going on made churchmen
more averse than ever to change. Bishops rivalled one
another in denouncing subversive teaching, the spirit of
democracy, and the blasphemous character of the revolutionary movement. The effect of the French Revolution in
England was therefore to strengthen the forces of conservatism, and to set the clock back. Had it not been for this
reaction, parliament might have been reformed, the dissenters, Catholic and Protestant, freed from their disabilities,
and the slave trade abolished a generation earlier than they
were.

Let us look first at the Church of England, then at the
other Christian communities. J. A. Froude hit off the temper
of the Establishment, as it was then appropriately called.

The French Revolution had frightened all classes out of advanced ways of thinking, and society in town and country was Tory in
politics, and determined to allow no innovations upon the inherited
faith. It was orthodox without being theological. Doctrinal problems were little thought of. Religion, as taught in the Church of

England, meant moral obedience to the will of God. The speculative part of it was accepted because it was assumed to be true.
The creeds were reverentially repeated; but the essential thing was
practice. People went to church on Sunday to learn to be good,
to hear the commandments repeated to them for the thousandth
time, and to see them written in gilt letters over the communion-
table. About the powers of the keys, the real presence, or the
metaphysics of doctrine, no one was anxious, for no one thought
about them. It was not worth while to waste time over questions
which had no bearing on conduct, and could be satisfactorily
disposed of only by sensible indifference.[1]

Pluralism, absenteeism, sinecures, extremes of clerical
poverty and wealth went unchallenged. The bishops on the
whole were good, conscientious, and respectable men. It
would not be fair to say that they regarded themselves only
as officers of State. Some of them, at any rate, showed by
their utterances that they had a high sense of the divine
character of the Church. Van Mildert, who became Bishop
of Durham, in his Bampton Lectures (1814) included among
'the *essential* doctrines of the Church' 'the ordinances of the
Christian Sacraments and Priesthood', and added: 'We
are speaking now . . . of what in ecclesiastical history is
emphatically called THE CHURCH; that which has from age
to age borne rule upon the ground of its pretensions to
Apostolical Succession.' You might think you were reading
the Oxford Tracts of the 1830s. But no: although these
things were sometimes said, they made no real impression
on the public mind. Those who at this time were known as
'High Churchmen' were so in the sense that they were
jealously concerned to preserve the property and privileges
of the Church as a national institution. They were politically,
rather than theologically, High Church. Froude's father
who was Archdeacon of Totnes, was a High Churchman of
the old school. 'The Church itself he regarded as part of
the constitution; and the Prayer Book as an Act of Parliament which only folly or disloyalty could quarrel with.'

1. J. A. Froude. *Short Studies on Great Subjects.* 1886, IV, pp. 239f.

He 'upheld the Bishop and all established institutions, believing that the way to heaven was to turn to the right and go straight on'.

There were of course variations within the general picture, and there were certain groups or tendencies with marks that distinguished them from the ordinary ecclesiastical conventions: the Evangelicals, a more theologically-minded run of High Churchmen, and a miscellaneous group that may be conveniently designated 'Liberal'.

Among the heirs of the eighteenth-century evangelical revival[1] who now formed a party within the Church of England, the foremost name in this period is that of Charles Simeon (1759–1836), who exercised a profound influence both in Cambridge and far beyond. Macaulay said of him (in 1844): 'As to Simeon, if you knew what his authority and influence were, and how they extended from Cambridge to the most remote corners of England, you would allow that his real sway was far greater than that of any primate.' Bishop Charles Wordsworth reckoned that 'Simeon had a much larger following of young men than Newman, and for a much longer time'. That may have been so, but Newman's influence at Oxford was more concentrated and dramatic: as a writer Simeon was not to be compared with him, and whereas Newman was a fascinating personality, Simeon, despite his being a Fellow of King's, seems to have been something of a bore. He was very definitely a *church* Evangelical. While like all Evangelicals he attached primary importance to conversion and faith in the atoning death of Christ, he was also a sacramentalist with a concern for church order and church ordinances.[2]

There were two other notable manifestations of Evangelicalism in this period: the Clapham Sect and the Religious Societies. Sydney Smith, the clerical wit of the age, has been credited (apparently without foundation) with having given

1. Cf. G. R. Cragg. *The Church and the Age of Reason*. Penguin Books, 1960, pp. 141ff.
2. See Charles Smyth. *Simeon and Church Order*. 1940.

the Clapham Sect its name or nickname. It was a group of distinguished Evangelicals who lived at Clapham – then a village, three miles across the fields from London. Actually, they were more like a large and united family than a sect. There was the Rector, J. Venn (1759–1813), son of an earlier Evangelical divine; Henry Thornton (1760–1815), a leading banker, also son of an eminent Evangelical father; William Wilberforce (1759–1833), perhaps the greatest orator of the age (Thornton and Wilberforce were Members of Parliament); Zachary Macaulay (1768–1838), who had been a Colonial Governor, father of Lord Macaulay; and James Stephen (1758–1832), a distinguished lawyer, who married Wilberforce's sister and was also father of famous descendants.

These rich and prosperous men lived in comfort, but they also practised an almost monastic austerity, rising early and giving much time to prayer and Bible reading and self-examination. They consecrated themselves to good works and noble causes, above all to the abolition of the slave trade. King George III, even when he was in his right mind, and the official classes generally, looked upon the Evangelical leaders at Clapham as dangerous revolutionaries, but they were nothing of the sort. They were indeed full of benevolence and philanthropy towards the poor – 'the lower orders' – but they believed that they should be kept in their place. The Clapham Sect has been somewhat unjustly accused of being concerned about the miseries of black slaves in the West Indies while ignoring the sufferings of the poor in England. But they interested themselves a great deal in the social as well as in the moral and religious needs of the industrial poor, for example in the provision of hospitals and education. They denounced the barbarity of the criminal law and the state of prisons, and they were ahead of their time in being willing to allow State interference in order to improve factory conditions. Still, it would be true to say that they worked *for* rather than *with* the poor. All their activities derived from their deep sense of accountability to God for the use of their gifts, their time, and their opportunities.

First and foremost among the religious societies, for which the Evangelicals were responsible, was the Church Missionary Society, in the foundation of which Charles Simeon played a principal part. After a precarious beginning it did splendid pioneering work in carrying the Gospel to the heathen. Henry Martyn (1781–1812), one of Simeon's most gifted and brilliant disciples, was the brightest star in the early galaxy of missionaries.[1] Then the church Evangelicals from the first supported the Religious Tract Society, which had been founded by Dissenters. Out of it arose a much larger undertaking, the British and Foreign Bible Society, which was also interdenominational. High Churchmen were hostile to it or held aloof, because it seemed to depreciate the importance of the Church, but it had an immense success in disseminating translations of the Bible throughout the world.

Other societies which the Evangelicals founded were the London Society for Promoting Christianity among the Jews, the Colonial and Continental Church Society, and at a later date the Church Pastoral Aid Society for the provision of more clergy. These religious societies proved to be a powerful bond between evangelicals and welded the party together, but also led to their displaying some of the less admirable – 'holier than thou' – characteristics which all organized religious parties are prone to develop.

As regards the theologically-minded High Churchmen, they also produced a group of friends, united by family ties, which has been called the Clapton Sect or the Hackney Phalanx, from the circumstance that a number of them lived in that area. The central figure was Joshua Watson (1771–1855), a prosperous wine merchant who retired from business in 1814 and devoted the remaining forty years of his life to voluntary work for the Church.[2] They were High

1. See Constance E. Padwick. *Henry Martyn.* 1925.
2. See A. B. Webster. *Joshua Watson.* 1954.

Churchmen in that they prized and cultivated the Laudian tradition. They saw the incarnation rather than the atoning death of Jesus Christ as the central Christian dogma, and they exalted the place of the Church in the scheme of man's salvation. They were generous in supporting humane and philanthropic causes.

They saw the need for the Church to rouse itself so that it could minister to the rapidly increasing population of England. Their contact with ecclesiastical and political leaders enabled them to stir the government as well as the bishops to take action, both in the provision of new churches and in the promotion of education. Within about a dozen years a hundred and more new churches were built from resources supplied by government grants and voluntary contributions. While their architecture left much to be desired, they were at least capacious, and there was at the time a grave shortage of church accommodation. The pressing need for education, which was viewed with suspicion by many on the ground that it would make the working classes insolent, was to some extent met by the foundation of the National Society for Promoting the Education of the Poor in the Principles of the Established Church, the Anglican counterpart of the Dissenters' British and Foreign School Society.

'Liberal churchmen' by definition are or should be heterogeneous, and those in this period were certainly so. There was William Paley (1743–1805), lucid and skilful author of a commonsensical theology, famous for his watchmaker statement of the argument from design. His *Evidences of Christianity* (1794) continued to be a set-book for Little-go at Cambridge until early in the twentieth century. The utilitarianism of his Christian ethics – whatever is most expedient is right – was congenial to his contemporaries. A still more popular and independent clerical author was Sydney Smith (1771–1845), who was a liberal in politics as well as in religion, and one of the chief contributors to the *Edinburgh Review*, the organ of the Whigs. He used his

humour and his position in fashionable society in the cause
of the helpless and the persecuted.

The most distinguished *group* of Liberal churchmen was
that associated with Oriel College, Oxford. They were
known as the Noetics. They led a revival of academic life in
the university and made Oriel a centre of keen and critical
thought. Though not High Churchmen in the technical sense,
they had a high sense of the Church's mission. The group included Edward Copleston (1776–1849) and Richard Whately
(1787–1863), both of whom became bishops, and Thomas
Arnold (1795–1842), afterwards Headmaster of Rugby.

So much for the Church of England in this period. It was
not asleep, but it was only slowly and in parts rousing itself
into activity. It cannot be said that the other Christian
communities in England – the Dissenters, the Methodists,
and the Roman Catholics – were bursting with vitality, but
there was more ferment among them, if only because they
were minorities with disabilities and grievances that were
ripe for redress.

During the eighteenth century the dissenting bodies –
the Congregationalists or Independents, the Baptists, the
Presbyterians (who had for the most part become unitarian),
and the Quakers – had been in much the same condition as
the Established Church – dry, commonsensical, averse to
'enthusiasm', acclimatized to the Age of Reason. At first
they were less affected by the evangelical revival than the
Church of England. They did not approve of methodistical
enthusiasm, and Wesley for his part was as hostile as any of
the bishops to dissent. However, they could hardly fail in
the end to be affected by the awakening to a more vital
faith, and before the end of the century this had shown
itself in the initiation of foreign missionary work and in the
espousal of philanthropic causes.

In the first thirty years of the nineteenth century the
Dissenters were chiefly occupied with the campaign for
the removal of their disabilities, especially the repeal of the
Test Act. When at last it was repealed in 1828 and they were

free, as of right, to enter parliament and to hold other public offices, they still had many legitimate grievances, for example their exclusion from the ancient universities. Their own dissenting academies were often more intellectually alive than Oxford or Cambridge, but they did not rank as universities. London University was founded in the 1820s without any religious tests, though it did not receive its charter till 1836. The delay in according civic equality to Dissenters, and the virulent and contemptuous way in which they were treated by the Establishment, combined to embitter the relations between the Church and dissent throughout the century.[1]

At the beginning of the century the Wesleyan Methodists had little in common with the Dissenters. Their affiliation was rather with the Established Church from which the Wesleys themselves had never wanted to separate. Until his death in 1791, John Wesley, who maintained an autocratic control over the Connexion, was able to prevent a formal separation, but it had become inevitable long before that. After Wesley's death, most of the Methodists still regarded their interests as lying with the Establishment, and their Toryism prevented them from supporting the campaign for the repeal of the Test Act. Jabez Bunting (1779–1858), the dominant figure in Wesleyan Methodism during the first half of the century, was a thoroughgoing conservative and almost as much of an autocrat as Wesley himself.

But after Wesley's death, divisions began to make themselves felt in Methodism, and new Connexions were formed of those who broke away from the official Wesleyan Connexion. The Methodist New Connexion split off in 1797, the Primitive Methodists in 1810, and the Bible Christian Society was founded in 1815. There were further secessions and unions later. Eventually there were three principal Methodist denominations: the Wesleyan Methodists, the Primitive Methodists, and the United Methodists.

1. See Chapter 12.

The reasons for the early secessions were complex. Wesleyan Methodism became increasingly conservative not only politically but socially and ecclesiastically. The secessions sought to recover the more flexible, free, and democratic spirit which had marked the movement originally. The Wesleyans, for instance, refused to give laymen a place in their constitutional government, though they used them as preachers and class leaders. The constitution of the official Connexion was oligarchic and even sacerdotal. The Primitive Methodists, on the other hand, were democratic in spirit and gave equal status to laymen. They were also radical in politics, and in sympathy with the interests of the industrial workers, whereas the Wesleyans had become highly respectable and middle-class, and their chapels tended to be controlled by the wealthy. Nevertheless, despite the controversies which disrupted Methodism and its fluctuating fortunes, it became the strongest and most influential of the nonconformist communities.

At the end of the eighteenth century the Roman Catholics in England – commonly known as 'the Romish dissenters' or 'the papists' – were a tiny minority, about one per cent of the population. Their numbers had been sadly reduced as a result of the operation of the penal laws, their attachment to the Jacobite cause, and secessions to the Church of England. Newman, in his sermon 'The Second Spring', gave a classic description of their condition before emancipation:

No longer the Catholic Church in the country; nay, no longer, I may say, a Catholic community – but a few adherents of the Old Religion, moving silently and sorrowfully about, as memorials of what had been. 'The Roman Catholics' – not a sect, not even an interest, as men conceived it – not a body, however small, representative of the Great Communion abroad – but a mere handful of individuals, who might be counted, like the pebbles and *detritus* of the great deluge, and who, forsooth, merely happened to retain a creed which, in its day indeed, was the profession of a Church. Here a set of poor Irishmen, coming and going at harvest time, or a colony of them lodged in a miserable quarter of the vast metropolis. There, perhaps an elderly person, seen walking in the streets, grave and solitary. . . . An old-fashioned house of gloomy appearance, closed in with high walls, with an iron gate and yews, and the report attaching to it that 'Roman Catholics' lived there; but who they were, or what they did, or what was meant by calling them 'Roman Catholics', no one could tell – though it had an unpleasant sound, and told of form and superstition.

Nevertheless, though they were so small a body, they were at this time torn by violent controversy. It arose from a series of moves from some of their leading laymen to win relief from their disabilities. With this end in view, they proposed to repudiate subversive beliefs they were supposed to hold – the power of the pope to depose an excommunicated ruler or to approve his assassination, the doctrine that 'faith is not to be kept with heretics', and the infallibility of the pope; and they wanted a normal diocesan constitution to be restored with the election of bishops and even a royal veto. In the eyes of many of their co-religionists this was to concede too much, and there was the sorry spectacle of the papists roundly abusing one another.

Happier was the effect of the emigration to England of thousands of French Roman Catholics who fled from persecution in their own country. They were generously welcomed in England. Parliament made an annual grant of £200,000 for their support, and the sympathy they evoked should have hastened the process of full Catholic Emancipation. Indeed, in 1801 Pitt prepared a bill, but it could not be passed because King George III said his coronation oath would make it impossible for him to give his assent to it. So until 1829 the Roman Catholics could not sit in either house of parliament or occupy military, judicial, or administrative offices under the crown. The restrictions on them were not quite so severe in Ireland, where of course they were much more numerous. However, the pressure for Catholic Emancipation, espoused by the Whigs and opposed by the Tories, steadily gathered momentum. It was as a result of the Irish campaign, led by Daniel O'Connell (1775–1847), that even the Tory leaders in the end gave way, and a new chapter was opened in the prospects of Roman Catholicism in England as well as in Ireland.

4

The Anglican Revival, 1830–45

THE combined effect of the repeal of the Test Act and of Catholic Emancipation was to deal its death-blow to the old ideal, canonized by Hooker in his *Ecclesiastical Polity*, that Church and State in England were one society. The ideal had never been completely realized, and it had by now worn very thin. But so long as only members of the Church of England could hold public office, it seemed *in principle* to be maintained. In 1830 it was manifestly an anachronism.

There were other circumstances that pointed to the imminence of a crisis in the Church. In July 1830 the downfall of the Restoration monarchy in France sent a shudder of alarm through conservative circles everywhere. By this new revolution, which seemed to be directed against the Altar as well as against the Throne, all established institutions felt themselves to be threatened. 'The French are an awful people,' wrote Newman to Hurrell Froude. 'How the world is set upon calling evil good, good evil! This revolution seems to me the triumph of irreligion. . . . The effect of this miserable French affair will be great in England.' It was not in fact as great as Newman feared, but the position of the Church of England was to be sufficiently imperilled by events at home.

In 1830 the Whigs came into office after a long period of Tory ascendancy, and preparations began to be made for the passage of the Reform Act of 1832. Agitation for reform, not only of parliament, but of all national institutions, was mounting. No institution was more obviously in need of it than the Established Church. There were glaring abuses and inequalities in its system that had continued uncorrected since the time of feudalism, and would no longer be tolerated now that the middle classes were winning power. The fashionable utilitarian philosophy required that the Church like everything else should be submitted to the test of usefulness as an agency in contributing to the happiness of the nation. Its property should be reorganized and redistributed by this criterion. The scandals and anomalies in the ecclesiastical system were exposed to obloquy in *The Extraordinary Black Book* of 1831, and there was an outburst of articles in newspapers and periodicals, attacking much more than the Church's misuse of its property. A conservative churchman was hardly exaggerating when he described the temper of the time in these words:

Nothing was heard but dissatisfaction with the Church – with her abuses – her corruptions – her errors! Every sciolist presented his puny design for reconstructing this august temple built by no human hands. ... Reports, apparently well founded, were prevalent, that some of the prelates ... were favourable to alterations in the Liturgy. Pamphlets were in wide. circulation, recommending the abolition of the creeds. ... In fact, there was not a single stone of the sacred edifice of the Church which was not examined, shaken, undermined, by a meddling and ignorant curiosity.[1]

The Whigs had the support of the Dissenters, and many supposed that, when they had reformed parliament, they would proceed either to disestablish the Church or at least to impose high-handed changes in its order and forms of worship. They had a radical left wing which would gladly have gone to extreme lengths, being spurred on by the fact that the bishops as a whole were hostile even to parliamentary reform and were enveloped in unpopularity. They were mobbed or hooted at in church; the bishop's palace at Bristol was burnt down; the palace at Exeter had to be garrisoned by coastguards; in January 1832 a pamphleteer wrote: 'At this very moment there are new churches waiting till the bishop of the diocese can gain courage to consecrate them.' R. Southey was 'apprehensive that no human means

1. William Palmer. *A Narrative of Events.* 1883 ed., p. 99.

are likely to avert the threatened overthrow of the Establishment'.

But these were false alarms. The Whigs were moderate reformers, not wild revolutionaries. They had a mind to rationalize, but not to abolish, the Establishment. Their Irish Church Act of 1833, which dealt with the anomalous position of the Church of Ireland was a very reasonable measure.

The Irish Church had twenty-two Prelates, and 1,200 livings – fewer livings than the then Diocese of Lincoln. Of the 1,200 Incumbents forty-one had no Protestant parishioners. By the Act two Archbishoprics and eight Bishoprics were dealt with. The boundaries of the Sees were rearranged in relation to the Protestant population contained in them, and the revenues of the Bishoprics no longer needed applied to the benefit of the poorer livings, of which many were in great distress since Tithes could no longer be collected.[1]

However, it fell not to the Whigs but to the short-lived Tory government of Sir Robert Peel in 1835 to set in motion a practical reform of the Church of England, such as only parliament could then set in motion, since the Convocations of the Church had been suppressed for over a century. Peel did not originate the idea of an Ecclesiastical Commission. The appointment of commissions was a favourite Benthamite device, but whereas in the case of the Church the radicals would have used it as the prelude to an all-out attack, the Tories and the bishops, prompted by C. J. Blomfield (1786–1857), Bishop of London, were shrewd enough to adopt it as a means of promoting a reform of the Church by its well-wishers.

The Commission, appointed by Sir Robert Peel and continued under Lord Melbourne, had both episcopal and lay members and was, to begin with, a commission of inquiry. Blomfield's was the animating mind in its deliberations: the story is well known of how Vernon Harcourt, Archbishop of York, said of its meetings: 'Till Blomfield comes, we all

1. E. A. Knox. *The Tractarian Movement.* 1933, p. 121.

sit and mend our pens and talk about the weather.' The commissioners produced a series of reports with recommendations in 1835–6 which, notwithstanding some opposition from radicals, ultra-Tories, and High Churchmen, were translated into legislation in the succeeding years. As a result of these measures, the dioceses and episcopal revenues were reorganized, pluralism and non-residence were dealt with, cathedral chapters were drastically reduced, and the scandals of sinecures and nepotism were removed. The Ecclesiastical Commission was constituted a permanent body for the execution of the reforms. The consequence was not only that the Church of England could again hold up its head in the face of its critics and be provided with a tolerable working machinery, but its survival as an Established Church was in practice secured, though no one could say for certain on what principle, if any, its establishment now rested. It was a characteristic piece of English empirical adjustment. The young Gladstone, in his book *The State in its Relations with the Church*, tried to elaborate a principle that would justify their continued alliance, but he himself had soon to recognize that it would not hold water.[1]

The mechanics and economics of a Church are important. Unless they are reasonably efficient, and are felt to be workmanlike and just by those who have to operate the system and by those whom it seeks to serve, it can hardly be expected to realize its potentialities. But organization in itself is no more than dry bones. And in the 1830s the most serious question about the Church of England was: 'Can these bones live?' Indispensable therefore as were the reforms initiated by the Ecclesiastical Commission, for which Sir Robert Peel and Bishop Blomfield deserve most credit, they would not by themselves have added up to an 'Anglican revival'. The Church needed a new infusion of spiritual life if it was to recover anything like its traditional standing and influence among the English people. There was in fact a spiritual revival in the Church from the 1830s

1. See my book, *The Orb and the Cross* (1945).

onwards and it had a number of causes, of which the Oxford movement was the most conspicuous. The Church of England cannot be said to have renewed its youth, but it did at least get a new lease of life.

The Evangelical movement was far from being a spent force in the 1830s, although it had hardened into a party. It had, and continued to have, missionary zeal and moral fervour in abundance. It was in tune with, and indeed largely responsible for, the ethical earnestness of the Victorian middle classes. But its theology was narrow and naïve, and partly in reaction from the effects of the Oxford movement it became fanatically anti-Catholic as well as anti-liberal. After Simeon's death it had no equally commanding personalities, except for Lord Shaftesbury. Perhaps for this reason, its progress or decadence has not yet engaged the interest of historians to anything like the same extent as the Catholic side of the Anglican revival.

Anyhow, the Oxford movement dominated the scene until 1845. There was magic of one kind or another about its principal personalities – John Keble (1792–1866), John Henry Newman (1801–90), Richard Hurrell Froude (1803–36), and others too. It may be that there is magic in anything new that comes out of Oxford. Then, the movement was a response to a crisis: it was impelled by a threat of calamity and a sense of urgency. When Keble uttered his warning about 'National Apostasy', the expression bore its full weight; it was not pulpit rhetoric. The Tractarians really thought that for a civil government – and a Whig government at that! – to lay hands upon the Church, whether of Ireland or of England, was Erastian sacrilege, and it was being done at a time when the Church itself seemed to have lost all sense of its divine origin, mission, and authority.

One of the Tractarians, who in 1833 attended the conference at Hadleigh in Suffolk, where the movement was hatched, thus described the state of affairs by which they felt themselves to be confronted: there was '*no principle in the public mind to which we could appeal*; an utter ignorance of all rational grounds of attachment to the Church; an oblivion of its spiritual character as an institution not of man but of God; the grossest Erastianism most widely prevalent especially among all classes of politicians'.[1] It was this ignorance of the nature of the Church, among Englishmen generally and not least among the clergy, that the Tractarians set themselves to expose and to correct, while there was yet time to do so. (They were not of course the first people to disseminate *tracts*. Wesley had had his tracts: the Evangelicals had their Religious Tract Society. But there was novelty in the tracts of the Tractarians. They were products of the High Church, written and circulated by dons, and addressed not to the poor and simple, but to educated and fastidious minds.)

The method of the Tractarians was to concentrate attention on a single article of the Christian creed: 'I believe in one Catholic and Apostolic Church' – of which the meaning had been forgotten except in the few circles where the teaching of the Laudians or of the Non-jurors was still treasured. In fact, they began by nailing to the mast a single doctrine, and a provocative one at that – 'the apostolic succession', by which they meant the maintenance of apostolic order in the Church through the episcopate. 'There are some who rest their divine mission on their own unsupported assertion,' wrote Newman in Tract 1; 'others who rest it upon their popularity; others, on their success; and others, who rest it upon their temporal distinctions. This last case has, perhaps, been too much our own; I fear we have neglected the real ground on which our authority is built – OUR APOSTOLICAL DESCENT.' He also said that they could not wish their bishops, the 'SUCCESSORS OF THE APOSTLES', who would have 'to stand the brunt of the battle . . . a more blessed termination of their course, than the spoiling of their goods, and martyrdom'.

It was startling, not to say offensive, to bishops in the

1. W. Palmer, op. cit., pp. 99f.

reign of King William IV to be told that they ought to be welcoming the prospect of martyrdom, but such language was calculated to make Englishmen ask questions that had never before occurred to them, for there was little in the appearance of the Church of England in 1833 to suggest its identity with the Apostolic Church of the New Testament or of St Ignatius of Antioch.

It was as if the Tractarians were declaring that on the drab, dirty, and distempered walls within which English churchmen were accustomed to worship or to doze, there were wonderful pictures that, when uncovered, would transform the whole building into something mysterious and sublime. That such a transformation of the Church might take place was the possibility that began to haunt and charm the minds of many who read the Tracts for the Times. As the series advanced – ninety tracts in all were published – one aspect after another of the Church's rites and institutions that had seemed dead or obsolete began to glow with new meaning. It has been said of Keble's *Christian Year* that it made the spirit of the Book of Common Prayer living to men of his age, and of Newman's sermons in St Mary's, Oxford, that 'his power showed itself in the new and unlooked for way in which he touched into life old truths'. As they listened, men became strangely aware of the marvels of glory and awfulness amid which human life is passed.

The Tractarians then were much more than writers of tracts. Newman's sermons and Keble's verses and Pusey's consecrated learning made a far deeper and more lasting impression than the tracts, which indeed as they proceeded became more and more ponderous and less and less readable. Above all and animating all was the unobtrusive but intense spirituality which characterized the leaders of the movement and many of their followers. If it had a powerful effect on many who did not go along with it and who were repelled by its controversial tactics – for instance, in its persecution of poor Dr Hampden – it was because of the unmistakable holiness which it introduced into a society where standards of virtue had been of a very humdrum order. It was an austere holiness, but, unlike that of the Evangelicals, it was combined with a warm and refined appreciation of all human culture.

Nevertheless, the movement had limitations which it is importance to notice. Its being called the *Oxford* movement tells us more than that it originated in Oxford and radiated from there. It tells us also that the movement was academic, clerical, and conservative. Oxford in those days meant the university. So far from being an industrial city as it is today, with the university as a kind of Latin quarter, few places in England were more shut off from the industrialism that was rapidly stretching itself over many parts of the country. Dr Pusey might say, as he did: 'The Tracts found an echo everywhere. Friends started up like armed men from the ground. I only dreaded our becoming too popular.' But not many friends started up from the mills and factories and mines and workshops of England. There was no reason to fear that the Tractarians would become too popular there. The movement was academic, in that its appeal was restricted to the educated classes, not so much from deliberate intention as from the interests and sympathies of its protagonists. It was not until after 1845 that the Anglo-Catholic revival reached out to the poor and got a footing in the slums.

The movement was predominantly clerical like Oxford itself. Though it did acquire the support of some eminent laymen, the tracts were addressed primarily to the clergy. The movement had to be clerical to start with, since if the clergy did not accept its message it was certain no one else would. Its success in interesting the country clergy in theological questions and in church principles was a considerable achievement.

It was a graver limitation that the standpoint of the movement was backward-looking. As William Palmer of Worcester College put it (he was speaking of the original impetus of the movement from which he considered that it subsequently departed): 'Our effort . . . was wholly conservative. It was to maintain things that we believed and had been taught, not to introduce innovations in doctrine and discipline. . . . Our principle was traditional, the maintenance of that which had always been delivered. . . . Our appeal was to antiquity – to the doctrine which the Fathers and Councils and Church universal had taught from the creeds.'[1] Similarly, Dr Pusey wrote to a young clergyman in 1839: 'Do not think you have possession of any new thing (which is apt to puff people up). What you have which is true has been taught quietly and unostentatiously by many in all times before you: it is in the Catechism and Liturgy: it has only been brought out into open day and seems new to those who had forgotten it. Do not act or think as though you were the Apostle of some new doctrine.'[2]

All the same, we can now see that latent in the movement from the outset was another element, a dynamic, pragmatic, progressive element, which set more store by the spiritual vitality of a Church than by its title-deeds and prized the presence of holiness above even apostolicity of order. This was the case with Newman himself, and still more so with some of his younger disciples, notably William George Ward (1812–82), of whom it has been said that 'he had no distinctive affection for the Anglican Church. He disliked it in the present, and he knew nothing of its past. The study of primitive times was uncongenial to his unhistoric mind.'[3] Ward and those whom he influenced soon came to feel that the Church of Rome – which they may have seen through rose-tinted spectacles – possessed means of fostering the fruits of the Spirit which the Church of England had discarded and perhaps irretrievably lost.

It was for the sake of this Tractarian left wing that in 1841 Newman wrote Tract xc in which he argued that the

1. W. Palmer, op. cit., p. 44.
2. See Liddon. *Life of Pusey*. 1893, ii, pp. 144f.
3. See J. H. Overton. *The Anglican Revival*. 1897, p. 92.

Thirty-nine Articles did not condemn many Catholic practices and means of grace which they were generally supposed to condemn. The hostile reception of Tract xc – especially from the bishops for whose authority he had an almost superstitious veneration – increased Newman's suspicion that Anglicanism as a *via media* between Roman Catholicism and pure Protestantism was only a paper theory, and in the following years he worked out his theory of development in order to satisfy himself that the contemporary Church of Rome was the legitimate heir of the Church of the New Testament and of the Fathers. His secession in 1845, of which there had been many premonitions, marked the end of the Oxford movement proper.

Despite this devastating loss, the Tractarian ranks were steadied under the imperturbable leadership of Keble and Pusey, and a new phase of the movement, which was no longer concentrated in Oxford, contributed in ever widening circles to the Anglican revival that was to be consolidated in the second half of the century. The forces that were set in motion by the Oxford movement have left their impress on the teaching, the worship, the art, and architecture of the whole Church of England, and further afield too. It is a Free Churchman who recently said that 'the witness of the Anglo-Catholic section of the Church of England to a more spiritual view of the Church and an orderly form of worship has been taken up within the Free Churches and is now part of the witness of all the churches'.[1] Amid all the controversies in which Anglo-Catholicism became embroiled, it gave substance once again to the great idea of the Church of Christ as a divine society and a sacred mystery, both a home for sinners and a school for saints.

Newman – more than any other of the Oxford leaders – has attracted, and perhaps always will attract, biographers, psychologists, and theologians. Anglicans are naturally inclined to think that he misjudged the situation in 1845

1. A. Victor Murray. *The State and the Church in a Free Society.* 1958, p. 171.

and, in view of the later course of the revival in the Church of England, that he would have been happier, and would have had an altogether larger influence on the religion of his countrymen, if he had remained where he was. Or they may put the blame on the bishops of the time and say that, if they had shown more understanding of Newman and of the Tractarians generally, there need have been no secessions. On the other hand, it must be remembered that he never appears to have doubted the rightness of his decision in 1845, in spite of his unhappy experiences as a Roman Catholic and his lasting nostalgia for Oxford. A vast literature has grown up around his career and his personal history, and there is no lack of material for readers who seek to penetrate what has been called 'the mystery of Newman'.

Among those who also seceded in 1845, the most romantically fervent was F. W. Faber (1814–63).[1] He had been a latecomer into the Tractarian movement from Evangelicalism, and he had never shared Newman's deep affection for the Church of England. He was an enthusiast for Italian styles in devotion. His enduring memorial is the Brompton Oratory.

1. See Ronald Chapman. *Father Faber*. 1961.

5

Conflicts in Scotland

CONTEMPORANEOUSLY with, though quite independently of, the Oxford movement in the Church of England, there was a movement in the Church of Scotland which led to a graver crisis – not to a secession, but to a disruption. Both exemplify the new evaluation of the Church and its mission that was now emerging across Christendom. There were analogous movements, for instance, in Holland and Switzerland.[1] The Scottish movement was even more anti-Erastian than that in England: in this, as in other respects, it was conditioned by the different ecclesiastical history and circumstances of the nation. It was a Scots divine who once declared with some patriotic animus: 'Of all Protestant countries, England is the one where the claim of civil supremacy over the Church was most openly put forth, most fully conceded, and most injuriously exercised; while our own beloved land is that in which it had all along been most strenuously and successfully resisted.' The Disruption crisis is the supreme illustration of this resistance.

Ever since the Reformation, through the vicissitudes of Scottish history, the claim had been made that Christ was the sole head of the Church and that the civil magistrate had no rights of interference or control in ecclesiastical government. But it had been a recurring, if not a continual, source of controversy, especially in connection with the question of patronage, namely whether parish ministers should be 'presented' (i.e. nominated) by a lay patron or only 'called' (i.e. elected) by the Church itself. Patronage, abolished in 1690, had been restored in 1712, and thereafter

1. See J. H. S. Burleigh. *A Church History of Scotland.* 1960, p. 353.

was a constant disturber of the peace of the Church and the direct or indirect cause of several minor secessions.

At the end of the century there were two parties in the Church of Scotland, the Moderates and the Evangelicals, and the Moderates were in the ascendant. The two parties have been credited with various characteristics – for instance, with different styles of preaching, and even with different drinking habits – but the main ostensible cause of their differences was patronage, though behind this lay the contradiction between a cultured, rationalistic, somewhat worldly religious conformity and the zealous, astringent, missionary fervour of the strictest Calvinistic orthodoxy.

When lay patronage had been restored in 1712, there had still been a provision that the patron's nominee to a parish had to be called by the Church after due trials, so that, at least in theory, the right of the Church, that is of the presbytery, to accept or reject a nominee was safeguarded. The Moderates however came to treat this right as little more than a formality, some said as a solemn mockery (like the nominal right of cathedral chapters in England to elect a bishop when he has been nominated by the crown), whereas the Evangelicals wanted the right to be a reality.

During the long ascendancy of the Moderate party, the rights of patrons had come in effect to be regarded as absolute. But this was not the only cause of friction in the Church. The Moderates also stood for strict obedience to both civil and ecclesiastical law as they understood it; they were opposed to anything in the way of popular government or parochial liberty; and they were unfavourable to proposals for reform. In consequence the Evangelicals' ardour for church extension to serve the new centres of population was frustrated. The conflict which ensued became involved in extraordinary intricacies: only the main outline of the story can be given here.

The moving spirit in the Church of Scotland was now Thomas Chalmers (1780–1847), one of the greatest churchmen Scotland has produced, which is saying a great deal.

He was a man of commanding personality and presence, a splendid orator, with a range of interests unusual in a divine. He wrote and lectured on scientific subjects, on mathematics, and on political economy, as well as on divinity. While he spent most of his life in the occupancy of professorial chairs, he was first and foremost a man of action. His theology was practical, not speculative.

He became an Evangelical after he had been in the ministry for some years, as a result of an experience of conversion – of justification by faith. But in his case at all events it was a faith that issued in works: the Epistle of St James had nothing to teach him. Nor had Chalmers that narrowness of outlook which usually marked the Evangelical school. He was liberal, indeed ecumenical, in his ecclesiastical sympathies, though he drew the line at popery. Strong as was his belief in the establishment of national churches (he delivered a powerful course of lectures on the subject in London in 1838), he was also a genuine believer in religious liberty and toleration. He supported Catholic Emancipation, though admittedly on grounds that were not very flattering to Roman Catholics:

> Give the Catholics of Ireland their emancipation, give them a seat in the Parliament of their country; give them a free and equal participation in the politics of the realm; give them a place at the right hand of majesty and a voice in his counsels; and give me the circulation of the Bible, and with this mighty engine I will overthrow the tyranny of Antichrist, and establish the fair and original form of Christianity on its ruins.

Chalmers' overriding concern was that the Church should bring the Gospel and a Christian education to the whole Scottish nation, especially to the poor who were being caught in the toils of industrialism. From 1815 to 1819 he was minister of one of the chief city churches in Glasgow, where his preaching had an electrifying effect. But the parish included one of the most destitute districts in the city, and Chalmers was appalled by the fact that his congregation came from elsewhere. So, at the height of his success, he resigned and, in the face of astonished opposition, he got a new parish constituted, in which he worked out a system by which the Church could deal creatively not only with the irreligion, but with the illiteracy and pauperism, of the unchurched masses.

It must be borne in mind that, in the critical period that was to follow, Chalmers was impelled by this passion to bring Christian ministry and Christian community to the whole people. It was because he considered that the control of the Church by the Moderate party prevented the Church from fulfilling its mission that he fought the battle that issued in the Disruption.

The Ten Years' Conflict, as it is called, began with the attempt that was made in 1833 to pass in the General Assembly a Veto Act, which was designed to secure the right of parishioners (or, to be precise, 'the major part of the male heads of families in full communion with the Church') to reject a patron's nominee. The Moderates were able to stop this measure from being passed in 1833, but this was their last victory. In the following year the Veto Act was passed, and also a Chapels Act which would enable the Church to develop and adapt its parochial machinery to meet present and future needs.

In the years that followed, there was a series of complicated cases in which, under the Veto Act, the patron's nominee to a parish was rejected. The main point is that the opponents of the Act, that is the Moderates, then had recourse to the civil courts in order to get the rights of the patron enforced, and they were generally successful. Hence the issue became one of the relation between civil and ecclesiastical jurisdiction, or of the power of the State to control the Church in spiritualities as well as in temporalities.

Chalmers and the Evangelical leaders made repeated attempts to persuade both Whig and Tory governments in London to introduce a measure in parliament that would secure to the Church of Scotland the liberty it had always claimed, but their efforts were in vain. By 1842 it had become evident that, under the existing conditions of establishment, the Church would not be able to exercise the freedom that the Evangelicals regarded as essential. They had wide support among the laity as well as in the ministry and, convinced at last that no redress could be had from parliament, they made preparations to break with the State connection and to set up the Free Church.

When the General Assembly met in 1843, 451 ministers (out of 1203) left the Establishment. This entailed their giving up their parish churches, their manses, and their endowments, and starting afresh with no material resources. It was a magnificent, and perhaps an unparalleled, piece of renunciation in the cause of a great principle. A new General Assembly was constituted which, with Chalmers as Moderator, proceeded to make and execute plans for the upbuilding of the Free Church. Observe that they did not leave the Established Church because they had come to regard disestablishment and disendowment as a positive good. They had not been converted to voluntaryism, that is, the doctrine that churches ought to depend only on the voluntary support of their members, and not on State endowments.

The founding fathers of the Free Church left the Establishment because to have remained would have necessitated acquiescence in conditions of establishment which they looked upon as intolerable. Chalmers stated their position thus:

Though we quit the Establishment, we go out on the Establishment principle; we quit a vitiated Establishment, but would rejoice in returning to a pure one. To express it otherwise – we are the advocates for a national recognition and national support of religion – and we are not Voluntaries.

The Disruption in their view did not mean a disruption from the Church or the starting of a secession. It meant that the true Church of Scotland was severing or disrupting itself from the State. The Free Church therefore at once directed its energies to providing a national organization that would cover the whole of Scotland and be available for the whole people. Its achievements were amazing. Within two years, i.e. between 1843 and 1845, 500 places of worship were opened and a sum of £320,000 was contributed for their construction. £100,000 was raised for building new manses, and the sum contributed for foreign missions rose from £4,373 in 1843 to £9,518 in 1853. Thus the Ten Years' Conflict was followed by the Ten Years' Rebuilding. The Free Church was informed by an invigorating sense of mission both at home and abroad, and it is reckoned to have carried away about one third of the membership of the Established Church.

However, it does not follow that the Fathers of the Disruption were wholly justified, even on their own assumptions. It is a sound maxim that no church is ever one hundred per cent right in what it does. To split the Church of Scotland in twain was in itself a disaster. Nor was it only the Moderates who remained in the Establishment. Others, who shared the beliefs of the Free Church about the relation between civil and ecclesiastical jurisdiction, held that their object could be achieved if they were patient and allowed time for conciliatory measures, and they may have been right. Anyhow, there was, subsequent to the Disruption, a notable revival of church life in the Establishment itself, so that it can hardly have been so vitiated as was alleged. Moreover, in 1874 patronage was abolished by parliament, which was more than Chalmers himself had originally aimed at. But would these things have happened without the stimulus of the Disruption?

Another unhappy result of the Disruption was that the Free Church with all its vitality was separated from the main sources of Scottish culture, especially from the universities, and its theology remained narrowly and rigidly Calvinist. If Chalmers had lived on, it might have been otherwise. As it was, it did practically nothing to meet the intellectual challenge of the times. Nevertheless, it can be claimed that the religious life of Scotland gained more than it lost from the Disruption, and the Free Church set a noble example to all Christians who attach sovereign importance to the Church's integrity and independence in the ordering of its life and mission or, in a phrase that has hallowed associations, to the Crown Rights of the Redeemer.

*

We must not suppose that nothing else of interest was happening in this period. There was in fact a striking development in the field of theology, analogous to that initiated by Schleiermacher in Germany, though in Scotland it was coldly received. There were those in Scotland who began to look for the basis of theology not in external evidences and defined doctrines, but in the inner life of believers and of the Christian community. The outstanding names are those of Thomas Erskine of Linlathen (1788–1870), John McLeod Campbell (1800–72), and Edward Irving (1792–1834): in their different ways each was a herald of things to come.

Erskine was a country gentleman of ancient Scottish family, one of those lay theologians who have played a notable part in British divinity. He was thus free to depart from the strict Calvinism of the Kirk and the theological schools – the Calvinism that treated the Westminster Confession and the Shorter Catechism as virtually infallible and interpreted Scripture accordingly. If the official theology was to be believed, God had by an eternal decree predestined the elect, and only the elect, to salvation, and Christ had made atonement only for the elect, not for all mankind. One example of the current teaching may suffice: this was how a near neighbour of Erskine's was startling congregations out of their apathy:

What good will it do you in hell that you knew all the sciences in the world – all the events of history, and all the busy politics of your little day? Do you not know that your very knowledge will be turned into an instrument of torture in hell? . . . The place in hell is quite ready for every unconverted soul. . . . As when a man retires at night to his sleeping-room, so a place in hell is quite ready for every Christless person. . . . The fires are all quite ready and fully lighted and burning.[1]

Teaching of this kind was not of course peculiar to Scotland or to Calvinists. Erskine and those whom he influenced could not reconcile it with the love of God. Not that he turned against the whole Calvinist tradition or failed to acknowledge its virtues. He honoured Calvinism for the deep reverence it engendered before the holiness and majesty of God; its mistake lay in making power, instead of love, the paramount divine attribute.

He lived a quiet life of contemplation at Linlathen, making himself easily accessible to any who cared to consult and converse with him. Those who knew him found in him a wonderful witness to the reality of God. He believed that God was seeking to educate all men into a filial relationship with himself, and throughout his life he was himself a learner. It was said of him, as it was of Lessing, that if the truth had been offered him with one hand, and the pursuit of it with the other, he would have chosen the latter. The consequence was that men went to Erskine who would have been condemned out of hand if they had opened their doubts to the ordinary theologians and ministers. Here is a single instance of an answer he gave to a questioner:

I fall back more and more on first principles. The conscience in each man is the Christ in each man. It is the ray of light coming straight from the great Fountain of Light; or rather, it is the eye guided by the Sun; or it is the child's shell murmuring of its native ocean; or the cord let down by God into each man by which he leads each. Often the string lies quite slack; the man is not conscious of the guidance and the guide. Then the string becomes tight, and the man feels the drawing, he is conscious of God. The great thing is to identify duty and conscience hourly with God.[2]

1. See H. F. Henderson. *Erskine of Linlathen.* 1899, p. 76.
2. See W. Hannah. *Letters of Thomas Erskine 1840–1870.* 1877, p. 353.

This is reminiscent of the teaching of the Cambridge Platonists, with whom indeed Erskine had much in common. He worked out his ideas in a series of books in the 1820s and 1830s. Although they had a large sale and went through many editions, the theological climate was unfavourable to them, even more so in the Church of the Disruption than in the Established Church. It was not only in Scotland that his teaching was looked upon as dangerously subversive. In England too, one of the Tracts for the Times (No. LXXIII) was directed against Erskine as an example of the rationalism of the age, of which the orthodox should beware. Since however he was a layman, the Scottish Kirk was not able to take disciplinary measures against him.

It was otherwise with McLeod Campbell, who was minister of Row, near Cardross. He was a devout and devoted pastor. As he studied the Scriptures and visited his people, he was struck by their lack of vital faith. He came to the conclusion that it was because they were not really convinced of God's goodwill towards them as individuals. This led him to ask: How can any man in particular know that God loves him unless he can be assured that Christ has died for *all* men? He was thus brought to believe in a universal atonement, in defiance of Calvinistic orthodoxy. Campbell was a gifted preacher, and there was a small group of other ministers who also began to base their message on the doctrines of assurance and of a universal atonement. Theological inquisitors were soon on the track of what came to be known as the 'Row heresy'. Campbell and his confederates were summoned before the church courts, and in the General Assembly of 1831 the Moderate and Evangelical parties combined almost unanimously to condemn him, and he was expelled from the ministry. Thereafter he ministered to an independent congregation in Glasgow.

Later, in 1856, he published his book, *The Nature of the Atonement and its Relation to Remission of Sins and Eternal Life,* which is generally considered to be the greatest contribution to dogmatic theology made in Scotland in the nineteenth century. (A new edition was published in 1959.) Campbell criticized the forensic or legal, the substitutionary and penal, theories of the atonement, and sought to moralize the doctrine. Christ's work was to reveal the Father in humanity and for humanity, to be witness of a love that hates sin and seeks to save the sinner by converting him. The atonement wrought by Christ did not consist in the deliverance of men from future punishment and the obtaining of future happiness, but in communicating to them his own knowledge and love of the Father and putting them in possession of eternal life.

The same General Assembly of 1831, which expelled Campbell from the ministry, started proceedings against Edward Irving, though he was not finally deposed till 1833. Irving may have been more of a genius than Campbell or Erskine, but he was also more of a firebrand. After taking his degree at Edinburgh University he spent some years in teaching. Eventually he became assistant to Chalmers at St John's, Glasgow, which brought him into some prominence, but no church in Scotland called him to be its minister. He did however receive a call to the Caledonian Church in London, which was a struggling outpost of the Church of Scotland in the metropolis.

Here he quickly made a mark by the eloquence of his preaching, and attracted a large and eclectic congregation. Before long a much larger church had to be built for him. It was at this time (about 1827) that he became acquainted with McLeod Campbell, and like him arrived at a doctrine of the atonement which stressed the whole purpose of the incarnation, rather than the death of Christ alone. His teaching about Christ's identification of himself with humanity was taken to imply that Christ's own humanity was sinful, and it was on this ground that he fell under suspicion of heresy.

Meanwhile he had become associated with a development

in Campbell's parish at Row, where it was claimed that the gifts of the Spirit that had been manifested in the Apostolic Church were a permanent endowment of the Body of Christ, and were restrained only by the faithlessness of Christians. Both at Row and elsewhere there were outbreaks of apparently miraculous healing and speaking with tongues, which aroused widespread interest in Scotland.

Irving, who was a natural enthusiast, accepted them without hesitation, and in 1831 similar phenomena appeared in his congregation in London, where they were associated with an attitude to disease that was later to be characteristic of Christian Science. After Irving was deposed by his presbytery in Scotland in 1833, his ministry was in abeyance until one day a prophetic voice proclaimed his reinstatement, whereupon he was ordained again by the new apostolate which prophecy had established in his church in London. This was the beginning of the so-called Catholic Apostolic Church, commonly but misleadingly called 'the Irvingites'.

Irving himself died in 1834, and so had little to do with the formation of the Church. Its apocalyptic character was however derived from him. He regarded the reappearance of miraculous signs as evidence that the end of the world was approaching. The object of the Catholic Apostolic Church was to prepare believers for the imminent judgement and the glory that was to be revealed. 'Irvingism' was a forerunner of the numerous pentecostal sects that have been a feature of modern Christianity, and that raise the question whether the historic, institutionalized Churches have not lost something that was essential in apostolic Christianity.[1]

Irving was anything but liberal or progressive in his sympathies, but he too shows that there were already in Scotland, as well as elsewhere, the beginnings of a revolt against the hard and loveless rigidities of traditional orthodoxy. Though in his case the revolt took a different direction

1. Cf. Lesslie Newbigin. *The Household of God.* 1953, Chapter IV.

from that of Erskine and Campbell, they all represent anticipations of conflicts that were to become more and more serious. They all aspired after a larger conception of the Person of Christ, and a doctrine of the Holy Spirit as God presently active in human life, and a more vivid apprehension of the Church as the community of the Spirit.

6

Liberal Catholicism and Ultramontanism in France

WHEN the Empire of Napoleon I fell and the Bourbons returned, the Church of France was much relieved. Napoleon had given it a fresh start and healed its schism, but only too plainly his object had been to use it for his own purposes. The Bourbon Restoration brought with it a restoration of as much as possible of the *ancien régime*, but it was not possible to restore to the Church the vast endowments it had possessed before the Revolution or its monopoly of privilege. An attempt to negotiate a new concordat proved abortive, and so Church–State relations continued to be governed by the Napoleonic Concordat of 1801.

The outlook of the French hierarchy during the Restoration was thoroughly Gallican. That is to say, they regarded the Altar and the Throne as interdependent; they acknowledged the royal authority over the Church and minimized that of the papacy. Louis XVIII was a sagacious monarch. He realized that France was still deeply divided on the subject of religion and that it would be fatal for the Church to overplay its hand. Charles X, who succeeded him in 1824, was both more reactionary in his political ambitions and a fanatical Catholic. It was generally supposed that the Church had blessed in advance the unconstitutional measures he was contemplating when he was forced to abdicate in July 1830.

The Church had thus prepared trouble for itself, and it is not surprising that the July revolution had an anti-clerical character. The bishops were suspected, and justly suspected in most cases, of being attached to the cause of the Bourbons. Pope Pius VIII, however, wisely hastened to recognize the new regime of Louis-Philippe. In the new constitutional charter, although Catholicism was declared to be no longer the religion of the State, it was accepted as the religion of the majority of Frenchmen, and the clergy of the Catholic Church and of other denominations were still to be paid by the State. The new government, like its predecessors, was determined to maintain the traditional Gallican prerogatives, which included the nomination of bishops. Would the Church simply hanker after the good old days and look forward to another Bourbon restoration, or would it now learn the lessons of the revolution and adapt itself to the new state of affairs? That was the question.

It is against this background that the origins of the Liberal Catholic and ultramontane movements in the French Church must be seen. The key personality in the origin of both movements is Félicité de Lamennais (1782–1854). In all the phases of his career he was passionately concerned for the regeneration of society. In the first phase, he was associated with the traditionalism of Joseph de Maistre (1753–1821) and Louis de Bonald (1754–1840). These two writers attributed all the evils of the time to the French Revolution which had set everyone free to do what was right in his own eyes. The only hope for recovery lay in a return to dependence on authority: the authority of tradition; the authority of the Church, centred in the papacy; and authority in the State, of which legitimate monarchs were the bearers. Lamennais began by advocating similar ideas and by combining royalism with ultramontanism, though he was also from the start an advocate of church reform.

It was when he realized that the restored Bourbons were a broken reed that he turned against them and sought to identify the cause of Catholicism, and of the papacy in particular, with the cause of liberty. In other words, instead of trying to exorcize the Revolution, he decided to baptize it. Before 1830 he had come to the conclusion that this was the only hopeful line for the Church, and he had attacked the French hierarchy for their servile dependence on the throne. He wanted the Church to be independent of royal control, which restricted its freedom, and to depend on the papacy for leadership and direction in its mission to society. He was thus already both an ultramontane and a Liberal Catholic in the sense that he held that the Church should abandon its traditional policy of seeking to be exclusively privileged and patronized by civil governments, and instead should welcome a regime of liberty in which it would be free to develop its own spiritual resources. Also before 1830 Lamennais had drawn round him a group of able and enthusiastic disciples who shared his ideals and his aims. He had a magnetic capacity for inspiring devotion both by his personality and by his writings.

Another circumstance which encouraged Lamennais was the alliance that had been formed in Belgium of the Catholics with the Liberals in order to win their independence from Holland. When the July revolution took place in France, he and his friends were prepared and eager for a similar alliance in their own country. He never expected much from the bourgeois regime of Louis-Philippe, but it was a professedly Liberal regime. It promised to safeguard the constitutional liberties, including freedom of the press, and it was this that made it possible for the Mennaisians to launch their paper the *Avenir*.

Lamennais' collaborators included Henri Dominique Lacordaire (1802–61), Charles Montalembert (1810–70), and a number of other able writers who were more or less in sympathy with his policy. The *Avenir* rejected the divine right of kings (to which most of the bishops still clung) and embraced the doctrine of the sovereignty of the people. It advocated liberty of conscience, the separation of Church and State, the suppression of the payment of the clergy by the government, and liberty of education, of the press, and of association. During its short but exciting career – it lasted only thirteen months – the *Avenir* enlisted the support of a considerable section of the younger French priests and seminarists as well as a number of distinguished laymen.

It was an essential part of the Mennaisian plan that the papacy should abandon its dependence on temporal power and on the sovereigns of the Holy Alliance, and trusting only to its spiritual authority should lead the world into a new order based on constitutional liberty and moral regeneration. In his cooler moments Lamennais realized that there was little ground for hoping that the papacy would do anything of the kind, but the enthusiasm of the *Avenir*'s campaign sustained his hopes, and there was always a romantically apocalyptic strain in his expectations.

By November 1831, however, it was clear that the *Avenir* could not go on. The hostility of the bishops was reducing its circulation to the point of bankruptcy, nor was there any compensating support from the government of the Citizen King, which looked upon the paper's policy as dangerously revolutionary. At the instance of Lacordaire, it was decided to make a personal appeal to Pope Gregory XVI, but 'the pilgrims of God and of Liberty' were by no means welcome in the Eternal City. If anything, their action hastened the inevitable condemnation of the whole Liberal Catholic programme, which was accomplished in the Encyclical *Mirari vos* of August 1832. The papacy, so far from accepting the role Lamennais had cast for it, would have nothing to do with the liberties the *Avenir* had advocated: indeed, it treated them as monstrous innovations.

Gregory XVI was a devout and ascetic monk who would have liked to govern the Church as an abbot governs a monastery. His idea of riding the storm that was brewing in Europe was to sit still and play for safety, and in particular to strike the best bargain he could for the preservation of the papal states, which were at this time threatened by revolutionary movements. On account of his desire to appease both Metternich and the Tsar, he had political as well as doctrinal motives for condemning the *Avenir*.

In retrospect, it must seem that Lamennais' rupture with the Church was inevitable from this point, but it did not follow at once. As an ultramontane he at first made the submission that was required of him, but he did so in bitterness of spirit, for the bottom had been knocked out of all his hopes for Catholicism. In 1834 he burst out with *Paroles d'un croyant*, which was described in a further Encyclical (*Singulari nos*) as a book 'small in size but immense in perversity'. Henceforth he would devote himself to the cause of the people as a republican, a democrat, and a socialist, and he passes out of the history of the Church. On the other hand, his collaborators and associates in the *Avenir* sooner or later submitted and remained in the Church. While some of them abandoned what had been only a flirtation with Liberal Catholicism, others resolved to continue the quest for liberty within the limits imposed by the papacy.

*

The Liberal Catholic and ultramontane movements – which were at present one movement, though later they were to diverge and become opposed to each other – went on, notwithstanding the heavy reverse they had sustained. Even apart from the influence of Lamennais and the *Avenir*, the July regime was calculated to bring home to discerning Catholics that they could no longer depend on the government for support of the Church. The new situation required the Church to develop and deploy its own resources: it would have to take advantage of the liberty that was accorded to it, and to press for more. This was a task for Liberal Catholics. On the other hand, the removal of government support inclined the French Church to look more and more to the papacy as its stand-by. Now that the government was in effect non-Christian, the old Gallican case for asserting the claims of the French king, against the claims of the papacy to universal jurisdiction, had little to be said for it. The Church would have to trust to its own inherent spiritual authority, which ultramontanes held to be derived from that divinely guaranteed to Christ's Vicar on earth. Thus the motives to Liberal Catholicism and to ultramontanism still ran together.

Consequently, in the 1830s and 1840s there was a Catholic party in France that was both liberal and ultramontane – 'liberal' in the restricted sense of seeking to secure freedom for the Church to do its own work in a mixed society. The revival and extension of religious communities were encouraged. More attention was paid to the study of church history, and to finding arguments for Catholicism in the splendours of its past. Works on liturgy and moral theology were produced that were more in accord with the teaching and practice of Rome than those that had been in use in the Gallican Church. The younger French priests also acquired the habit of looking for guidance and protection to the Holy See instead of to their bishops, the older of whom were still impregnated with the Gallican spirit and disposed to treat their clergy in a high-handed and autocratic manner. In short, there was a general and steady trend in the ultramontane direction.

But the principal aim which the Catholic party set before itself in this period was to secure liberty of education, that is, freedom for the Church to have its own schools independently of the State University system which Napoleon had established. Even under the Restoration monarchy Lamennais had attacked the University's monopoly in the control of education. There were stronger grounds for objecting to it when the government ceased to be professedly Christian, and there was no assurance that a Christian, let alone a Catholic, education would be given in the schools. Catholic objections became stronger still when non-Christian philosophers like Victor Cousin became the chief luminaries in the University world.

In the old days when the Church had sought to remedy its grievances, the method had been for bishops to make private representations to the government. But now, partly inspired by the success of the Belgian Catholics in organizing a political movement and press campaign, the French also formed a Catholic party which engaged in systematic propaganda for educational liberty. What they claimed at this stage was educational liberty for all, that is for Protestants and Jews as well as for Catholics: they asked for no special privileges for the Church. This was equally the theme of Louis Veuillot (1813–83), the future ultramontane leader, in his daily paper the *Univers*, and of the Liberal Catholic monthly journal, the *Correspondant*, which were subsequently to fall foul of each other. By 1848, when the regime of Louis-Philippe fell, the militant Catholics in France were more united than they had ever been before – and, we may add, than they have ever been since. Lacordaire's biographer, recalling these days, wrote:

In face of the enemy (i.e. the University monopoly) we had organized ourselves. We had newspapers, reunions, programmes, doctrines; we asked for liberty in the name of the common law: that was the mast to which we all nailed our colours.[1]

The liberalizing honeymoon, with which Pope Pius IX began his pontificate in 1846, had also encouraged Catholics in France, as elsewhere, to believe that they were right to fight under the banner of liberty for all.

The 1848 revolution was as favourable to the Church as that of 1830 had been unfavourable. The Catholics, so far from having identified their fortunes with the July monarchy, had been actively opposed to it because it had refused to grant them the liberty they had demanded. Moreover, many of them were still legitimists at heart, which is to say that they still hoped for an eventual Bourbon restoration and looked upon any other regime as only provisionally acceptable.

It seemed at first that a marriage of religion with liberty might be consummated. The revolutionaries treated the clergy with great respect; the Archbishop of Paris at once gave his adhesion to the new government; and Pius IX shortly afterwards congratulated the people of Paris on the veneration they had shown for the Church.

1. See G. Weill. *Histoire du catholicisme libéral en France 1828–1908.* 1909, p. 77.

The Liberal Catholics founded a new journal, entitled the *New Era*, which seemed like a resuscitation of the *Avenir*. It proclaimed that there was no opposition of principle between Catholicism and democracy, and that the time had come for Catholics to adopt democratic institutions, following the example of Pius IX. Bishops made pronouncements to the same effect. For a month or two it seemed that in the new democratic State the Church would be given all the liberty that it asked for.

But the fair prospect was quickly clouded over. In June 1848 the violent proletarian insurrection in Paris, in the course of which the Archbishop lost his life on the barricades, was ruthlessly suppressed by the government forces, and all the conservative elements in the nation were appalled by the abyss of anarchy that had opened before them with its threat to property and to the preservation of law and order. The revolution abruptly changed its course, and henceforth was heading for the advent of Louis Napoleon, the *coup d'état*, and the second Empire.

These developments scattered to the winds the precarious unity of the Catholics. Most of them, including even Montalembert who was a natural patrician, reverted to their traditional conservatism, and would fall over one another in welcoming the dictatorial regime of Louis Napoleon – though Montalembert would quickly regret his folly in doing so. On the other hand, some of the Liberal Catholics remained steadfast in their democratic convictions. Here was one persisting source of division in the Catholic ranks.

But the most bitter source of division arose out of the culmination of the struggle for educational liberty and the establishment of Catholic secondary schools. The new constitution guaranteed liberty of education, but its provisions had yet to be carried out. Félix Dupanloup (1802–78), the future Bishop of Orleans, now came to the fore as an astute tactician on behalf of the Liberal Catholics. As a result of his initiative, Louis Napoleon accepted Count Falloux (1811–86), a devout Catholic and a skilful statesman, as minister of public instruction. Falloux appointed a commission to work out a new law about education, and succeeded in elaborating a compromise which would allow Catholics to have their own secondary schools without setting them entirely apart from the University system. It was passed into law in 1850 and is known as *la loi Falloux*.

While Catholics were permitted to have their own secondary schools, these were to be subject to government inspection, teachers were required to have degrees recognized by the University, and a new Council of Public Instruction was formed. On this Council there would be representatives of the University and the Church, and also of the Protestants and Jews, and it would have a certain supervisory control over free schools. At the same time, representatives of the Church were given a place on the Council that supervised government schools and colleges. It was an ingenious transaction which aimed at reconciling the interests of the University and the Church, and within a few years under its provisions a thousand Catholic secondary schools were established in France.

Unfortunately, *la loi Falloux* was fiercely assailed by the extreme ultramontanes, above all by Veuillot and the *Univers*, as a betrayal of the Catholic cause. They were sworn enemies of the whole system by which the University controlled education. They wanted Catholic schools to be entirely independent and free from any government inspection or interference whatever. They treated *la loi Falloux* as a surrender to the University, and they were horrified at the idea of Catholic prelates associating in the Council of Public Instruction with Protestant ministers and Jewish rabbis. In addition, Veuillot attacked the law on the ground that it had been negotiated by Falloux and Dupanloup without reference to the hierarchy in France and without being submitted to the Holy See for approval – which was quite true.

So intense was this controversy that the pope had to tell the French Catholics that they were to make the best of the new law. Veuillot was bound to submit, but the break between the authoritarian or intransigent ultramontanes who wanted all or nothing, and the Liberal Catholics who were prepared to get the best terms they could, was not healed. From now onwards the liberal and ultramontane streams in French Catholicism, which had hitherto flowed together, separated, and were engaged in continual controversy. (The controversies were complicated by the fact that some of the Liberal Catholics were Gallican and some ultramontane in principle, and also some of them were democrats and others conservative by disposition.)

The hostility between the two groups became more and more bitter. They disagreed politically, the ultramontanes being completely authoritarian, and praising Napoleon III for having abolished the liberties that they regarded as a baneful legacy of the revolutionary spirit. So we find Veuillot, who had gone right back on his earlier liberal statements, writing in the *Univers*: 'Provided one is not prevented from proving oneself a good son, a good husband, a good father, a good citizen, a good Catholic, we are not concerned about any other liberties.'

They differed also about educational policy: there was a fantastic and prolonged controversy about whether the pagan classics should be used in schools, the ultramontanes claiming that ancient languages should be taught only through Christian literature, such as the writings of the Church Fathers. Again, the ultramontanes emphasized the incompatibility of faith and reason, and urged that Catholics must wage war on all modern thought and philosophy. They also tied the faith of the Church up with the most improbable miracles and with legends such as the apostolic foundation of the principal French sees. The Liberal Catholics, on the other hand, sought to discriminate between what was true and false in contemporary thought and in the advance of knowledge: they wanted to keep at least on speaking terms with the intelligentsia. It is from this time that the terms 'clerical' and 'anti-clerical' came into common use, signifying a gulf that has harassed the French nation ever since.

Veuillot, it must be allowed, was a brilliant journalist, but the extravagance of the positions he occupied, and his lack of scruple in attacking those Catholics who were not as intransigent and authoritarian as he was, did immeasurable harm in the eyes of all who believed that some reconciliation was possible between Catholicism and new learning, and between the Church and free societies.

Meanwhile, in Rome itself the prospects of Liberal Catholicism had suffered a similar reverse. The revolutions of 1848 and the pope's enforced exile had abruptly killed his early enthusiasm for free institutions. Henceforth the pontificate of Pius IX was to be marked by the citadel mentality, which supposes that the only hope for the Church is to fortify itself against all new ideas and democratic reforms, and to wait for better days when the present tyranny shall be over. It is paradoxical that the movement which had received so strong an impulsion from Lamennais should have ended there.

7

Coleridge and Maurice

IT is as a philosopher and a theologian that Samuel Taylor Coleridge (1772–1834) has a place of his own in English church history. He stands at the starting-point of various lines of thought that were followed, and more carefully marked out, by a number of Christian thinkers whose minds he set in motion. He is said to have had a seminal mind himself: he supplied nothing like a rounded or coherent system, but scattered seed thoughts. His writings on religious subjects were fragmentary and unfinished, and some of them were published only posthumously. Two of them were aptly entitled *Aids to Reflection* and *Confessions of an Inquiring Spirit*.

He was not a philosopher or theologian in any professional or academic sense. He is best regarded as a seer, who was always trying to cast his perceptions into the moulds of philosophical thought which he could never fully master. It was well said of him that he was always learning things which eye hath not seen, nor ear heard, and which have not entered into the heart of man to conceive, and that 'what he thus learnt, though taught in a faltering voice, and with the mingled hurry and diffuseness with which we always fulfil the morning's task in the late afternoon, was yet enough to make him ... a teacher and seer such as the world has not often known'.[1] He has even been described as the British Plato. When A. P. Stanley first read Coleridge, he said that he felt as if he had got a new element into his mind.

Unlike most English theologians of his time Coleridge knew German and Germany, though he drew his inspiration

1. Julia Wedgwood. *Nineteenth-Century Teachers.* 1909, p. 27.

from many sources. He certainly had an affinity with philosophical idealism. He was convinced of the reality of an invisible world, upon which the visible world, the world of nature, is dependent. In this connection he drew a distinction between 'reason' and 'understanding'. Reason is 'the power distinctive of humanity': it is the eye of the spirit whereby spiritual reality is discerned. Understanding, on the other hand, is the faculty which deals with the objects of sense, analysing them, generalizing about them, with logic as its instrument. Understanding yields only abstract and superficial knowledge, whereas reason yields real knowledge and enables men to respond to what is real with their whole being. 'It is one thing', Coleridge said, 'to *apprehend*, and another to *comprehend*.' It is possible to apprehend the existence of another person, and above all of God, without comprehending, or at least with only a very limited measure of comprehension.

Understanding, in Coleridge's terminology, corresponds roughly to what we call 'scientific knowledge': knowledge 'which concerns itself exclusively with the quantities, qualities, and relations of particulars in time and space'. In the heyday of utilitarian empiricism, that is of a philosophy that based itself solely on sense-experience, and also at the dawn of the expanding age of modern science, Coleridge's teaching about the possibility, indeed the reality, of a higher kind of knowledge, delivered those who accepted it from a sense of inferiority, and gave them confidence to pursue the study of metaphysics and theology.

Coleridge also had a seminal influence through his attitude to the Bible. In Germany he had come into contact with some of the early essays in biblical criticism, and they had made him wonder whether the conventional assumptions that reigned in England were tolerable. The Bible was still accepted by nearly all Christians in England as a compendium of infallible oracles, equally inspired and authoritative in all its parts. It was used as a storehouse of external evidences for the truth of Christianity. Just as it was supposed that the existence of God could be demonstrated by Paley's watchmaker argument, so it was supposed that the truths of revelation could be proved from the fulfilment of prophecies regarded as predictions, and from miracles understood as interruptions of the laws of nature.

This entire attempt to treat Christianity as a matter of external evidences became anathema to Coleridge.

I more than fear the prevailing taste for books of natural theology, physico-theology, demonstrations of God from nature, and the like. Evidences of Christianity! I am weary of the word. Make a man feel the want of it; rouse him, if you can, to the self-knowledge of his need of it; and you may safety trust to its own evidence.

So with the Bible: he held that, if men would but read it without preconceived ideas about its plenary inspiration, and see whether it did not speak to them with convincing power, they would be assured of its authority. It should be read and studied like any other literature, and then it would be found to be unlike any other literature, a book in which deep answers to deep. The divinity of Scripture rested not in the letter but in the spirit: not in the infallibility of its statements, but in its power to evoke faith and penitence and hope and adoration. In this way, though few heeded his teaching at the time, Coleridge was preparing men for the inevitable shock which he saw the acceptance of critical methods of study would bring.

It must not be inferred that he made Christian truth purely a matter of private judgement or individual inspiration. On the contrary, the Church had an essential place in his teaching. 'My fixed Principle', he said, 'is: that a Christianity without a Church exercising spiritual authority is vanity and dissolution.' Individual judgement could be exercised rightly only if it took into account the judgement of the Church and its traditions and the fruits of competent learning. But loyalty to the truth itself was paramount. 'He, who begins by loving Christianity better than truth, will proceed by loving his own sect or church better than Christianity, and end in loving himself better than all.'

Coleridge's teaching about the *nature* of the Church was also at variance with the wooden notions of his time. Here too he started hares for others to follow. He distinguished between the Church of England considered, on the one hand, as the National Church and, on the other hand, as part of the universal or Catholic Church of Christ.

The National Church was an estate of the realm. Every nation requires for its health, in addition to those classes that serve its material well-being – for example soldiers, financiers, industrialists, traders, etc. – another estate or order which is responsible for the transmission and progress of its cultural inheritance – literature, learning, art, religion, etc. 'A permanent, nationalized, learned order, a national clerisy, or Church is an essential element of a rightly constituted nation.' The clerisy was not identical with the clergy: all clerks (in the archaic sense of the word) are included in it, not only clerks in holy orders. But the National Church had, as a matter of history, stood for the responsibilities of the whole clerisy. Seen in this light, it need not necessarily be Christian. The Church of England was established and endowed and treated as an essential part of the constitution, because its office was to serve the highest interests of the nation.

In contrast to the National Church, though intertwined with it where, as in England, it was Christian, was the Catholic or Christian Church. 'The Christian Church is no state, kingdom, or realm of this world; nor is it an estate of any such realm, kingdom, or state; but it is the appointed opposite to them all collectively – the sustaining, correcting, befriending opposite of the World; the compensating counterforce to the inherent and inevitable evils and defects of the State.'

Whereas the king is the head and protector of the National Church, the Christian Church has no head on earth and needs no earthly endowment: Christ himself is its only head. The Christian Church is universal, 'neither Anglican, Gallican, nor Roman, neither Latin, nor Greek', but it is not invisible. It consists of 'visible and public communities'.

It must be confessed that Coleridge did not clearly work out the relation between the Catholic Church and the National Church. In both sides of his teaching there was pregnancy, though there must have been tension between these twins even in the ample womb of his own mind. In this case too, his ideas would bear fruit in the future, though few who came after him were able to compass the full range of his thought.

*

Principal John Tulloch, in his valuable book on *Movements of Religious Thought in Britain During the Nineteenth Century* (1885), said of Coleridge that 'the later streams of religious thought in England are all more or less coloured by his influence'. But his influence was of a kind that is not easily traced with precision, partly because those who were indebted to him did not want to give the impression that they approved of all his speculations. For instance, it is likely that his essay *On the Constitution of the Church and State*, which first appeared in 1830, affected Tractarian teaching about the Catholic Church (not the National Church!), but there is not much identifiable evidence that it did so. There were however a number of English theologians who left their readers in no doubt about their debt to Coleridge. For example, Julius Charles Hare (1795–1855), who said that 'to those who knew Coleridge, to those ... whose hearts glow with gratitude and love towards him, as their teacher and master, the establisher of their faith, and the emancipator of their spiritual life from the bondage of the carnal understanding – to such persons a Vatican all libels against him would be of no moment'; Arthur Penrhyn Stanley (1815–81), who became Dean of Westminster and was the quintessential Broad Churchman; Rowland Williams (1817–70), one of the contributors to *Essays and Reviews*; and Frederick Denison Maurice (1805–72).[1] We

1. To this list might be added John Sterling, R. W. Church, F. J. A. Hort.

must confine our attention to Maurice, who himself exercised an influence comparable with that of Coleridge and was the most originating of Victorian theologians.

In his lifetime Maurice was variously estimated, and very contradictory things were said about him by his contemporaries. Many people found him difficult to understand, maybe because he did not fit into any of the schools of thought or ecclesiastical parties that they were familiar with. He was the son of a unitarian minister. All the members of the family were deeply devout and highly intelligent. They broke away from their father's faith in different directions, some being drawn to Calvinistic nonconformity, others to the Church of England. This distressing state of division in his own family drove Maurice to seek for a ground of unity between men other than that of their religious opinions. He entered the Church of England, because he had become convinced that in the historic Catholic Church with its God-given constitution men could be brought together and held together in a unity and a community which were already provided for them, instead of having to fabricate a ground of unity out of their own ideas or notions. The Church was a deliverance from all sects and parties. This was the theme of his first major work, *The Kingdom of Christ*. He held to the Coleridgean maxim that men are mostly right in what they affirm and wrong in what they deny. So he maintained that each of the main divisions in Christendom, and each of the parties in the Church of England, and indeed each secular philosophy and movement too, stood at bottom for a true principle or at least a valid quest: their mistake was to assert their own truth exclusively against others. This has become almost a commonplace today in ecumenical circles, but it was not at all a popular view in the nineteenth century.

There was nothing facile or shallow about Maurice's teaching. He dug down to the theological roots of every question. Most of his books were in the form of sermons or expositions of the Bible. It was in the Bible that he saw the witness to the unfolding of God's purpose for a universal community. For Maurice, as for Coleridge, the Bible shone in its own light, or rather with the light of divine revelation. Therefore he did not panic about the higher criticism. He was not himself well-versed in critical study, and he had little patience with what seemed to him block-headed critics like Bishop Colenso (1814–83) who were so concerned about numerical blunders in the Pentateuch – 'doing sums on Mount Sinai', as someone said. At the same time, Maurice professed himself not only willing but bound to accept whatever conclusions were established by critical study.

The most serious episode in Maurice's career was his expulsion from his professorship at King's College, London. He had been an undergraduate at Cambridge and a pupil of J. C. Hare, but he had not been able to take his degree because he was then still a nonconformist who could not conscientiously subscribe to the Thirty-nine Articles. When subsequently he entered the Church of England and decided to seek holy orders, he went to Oxford and took his degree there. After a short time in a country parish, he became Chaplain of Guy's Hospital (1836). The Tractarians had hitherto looked upon Maurice as an ally. They were pleased that he had written in support of retaining subscription to the Thirty-nine Articles at Oxford, though he had done so on quite different grounds from those commonly advanced. He shared of course their high conception of the nature of the Church. It was when Pusey published a tract on baptism that Maurice realized he could not go along with them. For Maurice held that all men are born into a race of which Christ is the Head and baptism is the sign that they are, whereas Pusey's teaching seemed to him to mean that the race is given over to the devil except for those individuals who are rescued out of it by a sacramental change of nature.

In 1840 he was elected to a professorship at King's College, London, and in 1846 he became Chaplain of Lincoln's Inn, an office which he could combine with his

professorship. The crisis at King's College arose out of the
publication of his *Theological Essays*. The essays were
ostensibly addressed to unitarians with a view to meeting
their objections to the traditional theology of the Church,
but they could be construed as an attack on conventional
Christian orthodoxy. For instance, Maurice rejected the
view of the atonement as an appeasing by Christ of the
anger of God. But it was the essay on 'Eternal Life and
Eternal Death' upon which his critics fastened. Here
Maurice touched one of the most sensitive spots in Victorian
orthodoxy. Belief in the everlasting punishment of the wicked
and of infidels was regarded as absolutely fundamental to
the Christian faith. It was supposed that, if this belief was
weakened or abandoned, morality would lose its most
powerful sanction, namely the fear of hell, understood as a
place or state of endless torment.

Maurice did not revolt against this belief on sentimental
or humanitarian grounds. He maintained that it was in
contradiction to the revelation in the Bible, where 'eternal'
does not mean 'of endless duration'. Eternal life means to
know God and his Son Jesus Christ, eternal death means
to be separated from God, and both are present realities.
Maurice knew what he was doing when he threw down this
challenge. 'When I wrote the sentences about eternal
death,' he said, 'I was writing my sentence at King's
College.'

The prophecy was quickly fulfilled. A hubbub of protest
started at once, and the religious press demanded that drastic action be taken. It was intolerable that the sons of
Christian parents should be receiving such teaching. The
Principal of the College, R. W. Jelf (1798–1871), an
amiable but weak and accommodating man, tried to persuade Maurice to resign, but he was ever a fighter when he
was convinced he was standing for a righteous cause. At
length on 27 October 1853 the Council of the College met
to decide what should be done, and by a large majority it
was resolved that the opinions set forth in the essay on

Eternal Life, especially those referring to 'the future punishment of the wicked and the final issues of the day of Judgement, are of a dangerous tendency, and calculated to
unsettle the minds of the theological students of King's
College'. Maurice was dismissed.

The other outstanding theological controversy in which he
engaged – and this was on his own initiative – was about the
meaning of revelation. In 1858 H. L. Mansel (1820–71),
afterwards Dean of St Paul's, delivered the Bampton Lectures at Oxford on *The Limits of Religious Thought*. He was a
brilliant logician, a lucid writer, and a master of style. His
philosophy he derived from Kant through Sir William
Hamilton. He held that Absolute and Infinite Being cannot
be known by the human mind which is finite and capable of
understanding only finite objects. If men make statements
about the Infinite, they land themselves in impossible
contradictions. It should therefore be acknowledged that
they cannot by reasoning know anything about God. Both
the confident assertions of Dogmatists and the brash denials
of Rationalists are equally ruled out of court: both are
transgressing the limits of human thought.

But, Mansel went on to say, although, so far as metaphysics or speculation goes, men must be resolutely agnostic,
the Christian revelation supplies what he called 'regulative
truths', that is truths which, while they do not reveal what
God is really like, nevertheless tell men how to regulate
their thought and their lives with regard to him. The Bible
was throughout a miraculously guaranteed body of information of this kind. It was presumptuous to question it or to
examine its reasonableness. Mansel based the case for the
plenary inspiration of Scripture on the old arguments from
the fulfilment of prophecies and from miracles.

Obviously Mansel's teaching completely contradicted the
theology that stemmed from Coleridge and that Maurice
stood for. The fact that Mansel was being enthusiastically
applauded by both Evangelicals and High Churchmen as a
champion of the faith decided Maurice that he must assert

his own fundamental convictions. He therefore published a long book entitled *What is Revelation?* and, after Mansel had replied to it, followed it up with a *Sequel*. It seemed to Maurice that on Mansel's view Christianity tells men just enough to keep them right with a God whom they cannot really know, whereas the heart of his own faith was that the only way men can be kept right is by a direct and conscious participation in the very life of God. He appealed to the Bible which speaks of eternal life as already available and as consisting in the knowledge of God himself, not of mere regulative truths. He appealed also to the Fathers, the Schoolmen, and the language of the Prayer Book, to corroborate this conviction.

He did not appear at his best in this controversy. Even his warmest friends and admirers regretted the violence and asperity with which he attacked Mansel. The contestants never got anywhere near to understanding one another. Even if it be thought that Maurice was contending for what is basic to the Christian Gospel and that Mansel's position was an impossible one for orthodoxy to rest in, yet there can be no doubt that he was facing a real problem which needed to be discussed calmly and philosophically, not with the white-hot passion that Maurice felt and displayed. Is it not the case that the language which is used in speaking about God never is and never can be adequate to the truth about God? It can never be more than analogically true. On the other hand, that does not make it necessary to deny that men can have a real, personal knowledge of God in this life. The proper conclusion may be that Maurice and Mansel were battling in a fog, but that, if the fog could be cleared away, there would be much to be learned from both of them.

Although Maurice wrote a *History of Moral and Metaphysical Philosophy* and was towards the end of his life appointed to the Knightsbridge Professorship at Cambridge, which was then known as a Professorship of 'Casuistry, Moral Theology, and Moral Philosophy', he was not a philosopher in the academic sense, but a theologian, first, last, and all the time. But he was never a narrow theologian. He saw theology as having connections with all other subjects of study, just as the Bible is concerned with the life of mankind in its totality, and not only with religion. He was also a practical theologian, as was shown in his lifelong devotion to educational enterprises and in his participation in the Christian social movement.

8

The Christian Social Movement

NONE of the eminent Victorians had a stronger dislike of both Christianity and Socialism than Herbert Spencer. The Christian Socialist movement of 1848 to 1854 seems to have made no impression on him, although at the time he was sub-editor of the *Economist*. All we know is that in 1852 he met Charles Kingsley at a picnic, found him delightfully unclerical, and could not make head or tail of his opinions. But in his *Autobiography* Spencer, with a measure of gratification, gives some account of one of his uncles, the Rev. Thomas Spencer, a severely evangelical clergyman, who combined with personal asceticism not only much practical philanthropy but also a passion for social justice. Herbert Spencer, before recording that his uncle said grace at the first Anti-Corn Law banquet, pays him this warm tribute:

Differing profoundly from those Church-of-England priests who think their duty consists in performing ceremonies, conducting praises, offering prayers, and uttering such injunctions as do not offend the influential members of their flocks, his conception of the clerical office was more like that of the old Hebrew prophets, who denounced the wrong-doings of both people and rulers. He held that it came within his function to expose political injustices and insist on equitable laws.

Full credit should be given to the Rev. T. Spencer, though his nephew's claim cannot be strictly true that at the time of the Anti-Corn Law agitation there was beside him only one other avowed Free-Trader among what he calls 'the State-appointed teachers of rectitude'. There were in fact in the 1830s and 1840s quite a number of clergymen of Thomas Spencer's stamp, though they were no doubt exceptional.

The attitude of churchmen as a whole to political and social change during the first half of the nineteenth century was indubitably negative. To the Reform Bill of 1832 it has been said that 'there was but one class opposed ... with anything like unanimity – the clergy of the Church of England'. The Dissenters were of course favourable to political reform, since it was in their interest to be so. But as regards economic reform, or remedying the evils of pauperism that were consequent on the industrial revolution, the Dissenters and the Wesleyan Methodists of this period have much the same record as the Established Church. Only the Primitive Methodists were an exception to the rule.[1]

In 1825 the subject of the Bampton Lectures at Oxford was *The Scheme of Divine Revelation considered principally in its Connexion with the Progress and Improvement of Human Society.* The outlook of the lecturer was by contemporary standards liberal and humane, but he showed no awareness of the terrible evils that in the industrial areas of England were crying aloud to heaven, although they were unheeded by the professed representatives of heaven on earth. 'We know', he elegantly remarked, 'the tendency of charity, in its enlarged signification, to humanize society, to sweeten ordinary life, to mitigate, almost to subdue every calamity that can afflict our nature.' Such pious sentiments were an inadequate response to the gross inhumanity of the society in which multitudes of Englishmen had then to exist, or to the bitterness of ordinary life in the hovels where they had to live and in the factories and mines where women and children as well as men had to work for insufferable hours.

There is, we know now, a long story behind the failure of Christian people to wake up not only at the onset of the industrial revolution but also when it was far advanced. The remoter causes have been traced by Professor Tawney in *Religion and the Rise of Capitalism.* He shows how in the centuries that followed the Renaissance and the Reformation,

1. See R. F. Wearmouth. *Methodism and Working Class Movements 1800–1850.* 1937.

the Churches became narrower and narrower in their interests, until almost everything that was not ostensibly spiritual or ecclesiastical was left free from criticism in the name of God and his commandments. 'The social teaching of the Church', he says, 'had ceased to count, because the Church had ceased to think. . . . An institution which possesses no philosophy of its own accepts that which happens to be fashionable.'

The social philosophy that was fashionable at the beginning of the nineteenth century was a crude utilitarianism. Uncontrolled commercialism was the order of the day and, as we have seen, Paley, the Church's most fashionable divine, was frankly utilitarian in his ethics. 'The laws of commerce', Burke has said, 'are the laws of Nature and consequently the laws of God.' There must therefore be no tampering with them. *Laissez faire*. Every individual must be left free to pursue his own interests; then everything will work out for the greatest happiness of the greatest number. This was axiomatic, at least to the upper and middle classes – to the pillars of the Church, as well as to the pundits of political economy. It would be unwise to blame them, for it may be that we today take for granted notions and practices that will seem equally outrageous to posterity.

All the same, surprise has been felt that not even the religious revivals of the period were sensitive to the hellish accompaniments of the rising industrialism. The Evangelicals had more of a social conscience than the Tractarians, but neither were able to read the signs of the times. Lord Shaftesbury, however, was not the first Christian to take up the question of child labour. It was in fact an Evangelical clergyman who induced him to do so,[1] and it would appear that there was a good deal more support for the cause of the workers among churchmen, not only among Evangelicals, than has commonly been supposed.

1. See J. C. Gill. *The Ten Hours Parson: Christian Social Action in the 1830s.* 1959.

One reason why churchmen were frightened of proposals for social change was that Robert Owen, the founder of Socialism and Cooperation in Britain, was anti-clerical, if not anti-Christian, as well as wildly utopian. In 1817 he had published a 'Denunciation of All Religions', which sounded terribly shocking to ecclesiastics, but his real target was the church systems and theologies with which he was acquainted and which certainly invited plenty of denunciation. Owen professed a 'consistent practical religion, based on different ideas of the Great Creating Power of the Universe'. There was a lot of practical Christianity in his teaching, and Christians made in his case the mistake they often make of judging men and movements by their labels and their slogans.

This was also the case with Christian reactions to the Chartists. The Chartist movement came into being because, although the working class as well as the middle class had agitated for the passing of the Reform Act of 1832, the Act benefited only the middle class. Not only were the workers still without any voting rights and representation in parliament, but the reformed House of Commons consisted of members of the nobility, of the army and navy, of lawyers, and of the moneyed classes, and naturally represented the interests of property. When the smoke of the struggle cleared away, the proletariat realized that they had reaped no benefit from the reform which they had helped to secure, and that there was no prospect of an amelioration of their conditions of life and work from a parliament that was dominated by the doctrine of *laissez faire*. Chartism was an agitation for more extensive political reforms in a fully democratic direction.

The movement gathered impetus until about 1842, after which the high tide receded, but during these two decades Chartism was regarded by all the conservative forces in the country as an awful menace, threatening revolution and the overthrow of established institutions. (In point of fact, most of the demands of the Charter were eventually granted without the revolutionary consequences that had been apprehended.)

As regards the attitude of the Chartists themselves to the Church, the following retrospective statement by one of their leaders sums it up:

None of us had any great love for 'the cloth'. Not that we had any bad feelings towards them, but I believe we mostly thought the whole Church Establishment was a matter of money, and that all clergymen did and said their doings and sayings merely to get paid. So that we had rather a feeling of contempt for them because we thought them so uncommonly like hypocrites. The same with regard to religion generally. There was very little real enmity against it, as far as I could see, among working men. We only thought it a humbug, and not worth a sensible man's troubling his head about.

How any professing Christian could remain indifferent to the wretched conditions prevalent among the manufacturing and agricultural poor was to the Chartists a mystery. What they looked for was some practical demonstration of the social teachings of Christ which, they supposed, should take the form of an effort to improve their lot. They could make nothing of the doctrine, which was widely held in the Churches, that it was wrong for a Christian to meddle in political matters, especially when they observed that both Churchmen and Dissenters did not hesitate to use political means when their own interests were at stake.

The few clergymen, whether anglican or nonconformist, who did identify themselves with the Chartist movement were immensely popular with the workers, though they outraged ordinary church opinion. *The Christian Remembrancer*, a High Church periodical, asked how the Rev. Thomas Spencer could 'be allowed to propagate such pestilential opinions . . . without being made to feel the just punishment for his apostasy by being degraded and excommunicated'. Sermons denouncing Chartism were frequently preached, here are a few extracts from one entitled *Chartism Unmasked*, which, when published, went through nineteen editions:

The doctrines taught and urged by the Chartist leaders are as diametrically opposed to the doctrines revealed in the eternal word of God, as the North is to the South.

The Chartist leaders preach and teach the doctrine of 'equality'; but we have no such doctrine taught in the Book of Nature or the Book of God. . . .

Another Chartist doctrine opposed to the Word of God is that poverty is not the result of the everlasting purpose of a Sovereign God but is only the result of unjust human laws. . . . This is disproved by the Bible which says 'The poor shall never cease out of the land'.

The Unitarians were the only denomination of which a considerable section was in sympathy with the Chartist movement.

*

The Christian Socialist movement of 1848–54 was in a sense born out of Chartism. John Malcolm Ludlow (1821–1911), Charles Kingsley (1819–75), F. D. Maurice, Thomas Hughes (1822–96), and the rest, were a group of churchmen who realized that the Gospel of Christ must have something better to say to the working people of England than what the official Church was saying. It used to be said that Thomas Carlyle was the inspirer of the Christian Socialists. He had indeed thundered against the doctrine of *laissez faire*, and he made a deep impression on Maurice and Kingsley, but the real impetus of the movement came from Ludlow. He was a layman who had been educated in France and had got to know some of the groups of French socialists and social Catholics.[1] He had studied the case for democracy and shared the aspirations of the French revolution of 1848. He was in Paris at the time and wrote to Maurice 'to express his conviction that Socialism was a real and very great

1. On the continent, Christian reactions to the consequences of the industrial revolution were similar to those in England, but there were interesting variations and mutations, especially in France. See my Scott Holland lectures, *A Century of Social Catholicism 1820–1920*, 1964.

power which had acquired an unmistakable hold, not merely on the fancies but on the consciences of the Parisian workmen, and that it must be Christianized or it would shake Christianity to its foundation, precisely because it appealed to the higher and not to the lower instincts of the men'.[1]

Maurice was deeply moved by this communication, and wrote to Ludlow: 'The necessity of an English theological reformation, as the means of averting an English political revolution and of bringing what is good in foreign revolutions to know itself, has been more and more pressing upon my mind.' Maurice, Kingsley, and Ludlow got together, and decided to issue a new series of 'tracts for the times', entitled *Politics for the People*. The series lasted for only a few months, but the articles are full of interest and variety. Kingsley, who had a special flair for this kind of writing, wrote 'Letters to the Chartists' over the signature 'Parson Lot'; Ludlow reported on developments in France; Maurice tried his hand at composing dialogues; and they got some come-back in the way of letters from working men.

If Kingsley knew best how to talk the language of the people, his ideas were based on the theology he had learned from Maurice. For Maurice attacked the whole *laissez faire*, competitive, commercialist outlook in the name of theology. Men, he insisted, are not in their true nature, as created by God and redeemed by Christ, mere self-contained individuals who are bound to compete with one another, each in pursuit of his own interests. 'Competition', he wrote to Kingsley, 'is put forth as the law of the universe. That is a lie. The time is come for us to declare that it is a lie by word and deed.' The true law of the universe is that man is made to live in community: men realize their true nature when they cooperate with one another as children of God and brothers in Christ.

There is really no such thing as a single life. Men are so constituted that they must live in families, tribes, nations,

1. See F. Maurice. *Life of F. D. Maurice.* 1884, 1, p. 458.

and at last in a universal brotherhood. They are not truly human if they do not live and work interdependently. Maurice did not say that this was an ideal which, it was to be hoped, might one day be realized. He asserted that it was an already existing fact. 'You are brothers,' he would say, 'whether you acknowledge the fact or not, even when you behave as if you are not. You must become what you are.' The Church was the society which was called to bear witness to this truth both in its teaching and in the character and quality of its own corporate life.

The adoption of the word 'socialism' was meant to be provocative, to stir people up and make them think. 'The mere word of Socialism . . . means nothing of itself but the science of making men partners, the science of partnership.' It was because they believed that Christianity stood for a structure of society which would enable men to work with one another, instead of against one another, that they called themselves 'Christian Socialists'. They did not adopt any particular economic doctrine, and they acknowledged that Tories, Whigs, and Radicals all had some truth to contribute to the right understanding of social order.

Politics for the People brought the original group new friends and collaborators. Before long Maurice was holding meetings for discussion with groups of Chartists. But they felt that more was needed than talking and writing. After a good deal of hesitation – for Maurice dreaded the formation of a party organization – it was resolved to form cooperative associations, e.g. for tailors, builders, printers, etc. These associations never met with more than a small measure of success, but they played a significant part in the origins of the Cooperative movement. Although their particular enterprises ended in failure, these Christian Socialists had in a few years done much to rouse public opinion and even to influence legislation. Maurice himself was driven to the conclusion that working men would not be qualified to manage their own affairs until they had received fuller opportunities of education: so he turned his efforts to the foundation of the Working Men's College, of which he became the first Principal.

The movement received little sympathy or support from churchmen who at this time were in a fever of excitement caused by the long drawn out Gorham controversy about baptismal regeneration and the so-called Papal Aggression. The first phase of the Christian Socialist movement in England may be said to have come to an end in 1854, and from then until 1877 there was no organized group within the Church of England that concerned itself with the social implications of the faith. In the interval the Church of England had acquired organs through which it could express its mind, in so far as it had a mind to express. Convocation started meeting again in 1852; the Church Congress was held annually from 1861, and diocesan conferences began to meet; in 1867 the Lambeth Conference met for the first time. But these bodies were chiefly concerned with religious questions, and had little to say about social problems. Some individual churchmen were active in promoting social reforms, but on grounds of charity rather than of justice. It was supposed that the ills of society could be cured by voluntary action, either by stimulating the benevolent sentiments of the rich and powerful, or by persuading the poor to help themselves. The Trade Union movement was left to develop without any assistance from the Established Church.

It was not until 1877 that a new generation, particularly of High Churchmen, began to organize themselves in the cause of social reform. In that year the Guild of St Matthew was founded. It represented a fusion of the original Tractarian movement with the theology of Maurice and the Christian Socialists. Its founder, a young priest named Stewart Duckworth Headlam (1847–1924), had derived from Maurice a theological outlook that was altogether more liberal than that of the Tractarians and also the passion for social righteousness which was the distinguishing mark of his life. Headlam was often in trouble with his bishop, whether for attacking conventional teaching about everlasting punishment, or for championing the stage. In a lecture on 'Theatres and Music-halls' he advised young ladies 'whose name was *Dull* to see these young women who are so full of life and mirth'. Later he created a sensation by his courage in standing bail for Oscar Wilde.

The members of the G.S.M. attacked injustice wherever they detected it, and were seldom at a loss to suggest how abuses should be remedied. Headlam was as contemptuous of plutocrats as he was of the officials of a Church who tolerated things which were plainly iniquitous. A typical remark of his was: 'It is absurd to say Convocation is the voice of the Church; it is hardly the squeak of the Church.' The Guild was never a large body: it was a ginger-group in the Church, which deliberately adopted shock tactics in order to arouse the Christian conscience to its responsibility for the well-being of the workers. It pressed for government legislation about such matters as hours of work, housing, taxation, and free education. John Morley said of its magazine, *The Church Reformer*, that 'there was enough matter in it to stock five ordinary newspapers'. Among its members were C. W. Stubbs (who became Dean of Ely and Bishop of Truro), H. C. Shuttleworth, the first priest to combine 'chasubles before the altar with flannels before the stumps', and Father Stanton of St Alban's, Holborn, who was content to remain an assistant curate all his life. At a later stage Frank Weston, the future Bishop of Zanzibar, was a member, and it was entirely in the spirit of the Guild that at the end of the First World War he led a campaign against forced labour in East Africa and wrote a pamphlet entitled *The Serfs of Great Britain*.

Another organization, founded in 1889, was the Christian Social Union. It was more respectable and more academic and had a larger membership. The C.S.U., like the G.S.M., represented a fusion of the Tractarian and Maurician traditions, but there were other intellectual tendencies at work in it too. The idealist philosophy of T. H. Green (1836–82) had given his disciples a system of social ethics and a zeal to

fulfil the obligations of citizenship. Again, the old political
economy, which had treated the laws of economics as having
so cosmic an authority that they must be left to operate
themselves, was giving way to new theories which recognized
that the economic order could be directed and controlled.

Instead of going into action like the G.S.M. with flamboyant denunciations, the C.S.U. concentrated at first on
establishing the principle that the Christian faith had to do
with the whole ordering of the life of man in society, and on
organizing study groups about the application of this principle. It had a decisive influence in acclimatizing in the
Church of England the idea that Christians ought to be
outward-looking in their concern for human well-being
everywhere. From this time onwards it became quite usual
for Church Congresses and diocesan conferences to pass
resolutions about matters of social justice. For instance, in
1895 the Newcastle diocesan conference passed a resolution
that a decent wage 'should be the first charge upon products', which was then a fairly novel notion in church circles.

Although the C.S.U. had a good many lay members, the
clergy, and even church dignitaries, predominated in it,
and this encouraged the questionable idea that the Church
has done something about industry or politics when the
clergy have said something. But the C.S.U. did do some
things of a quite practical nature. Its branches made
inquiries about the conditions of work in the firms and factories in the neighbourhood with a view to eradicating
sweated labour. White lists were published of firms that
passed the test and members of the public were called on to
transfer their custom to them so that recalcitrant tradesmen
might be forced to reform. This may have been little more
than ambulance action, but it was a step towards a more
realistic perception of what is involved in responsibility for
social justice. Much the same can be said of the enterprising
works that were initiated by the Salvation Army. It was not
until well on in the twentieth century that Christian social
thinking would get to closer grips with this responsibility.

9

From Strauss to Ritschl

HEGELIANISM, as we have noted (p. 31), fascinated the nineteenth century whether by attraction or repulsion. This was especially the case with German theologians. Of those to be considered in this chapter, two – D. F. Strauss (1808–74) and F. C. Baur (1792–1860) – bear the positive impress of Hegelianism, whereas the third – Albert Ritschl (1822–89) – was in violent reaction not only against Hegelianism but against the association of Christianity with any form of metaphysics.

Strauss was considerably younger than Baur, and in fact was at one time his pupil, but he precedes Baur both chronologically and theologically. When Strauss's *Life of Jesus* was published in 1835, Baur was only beginning to work out his interpretation of Christian origins, and his work represents a definite advance on Strauss. The *Life of Jesus*, which made an unknown young man well-known in a moment, gave a signal impetus to reconstructions of early Christian history and to the study of the four Gospels.

It was as a teacher of philosophy and as an apostle of Hegelianism that Strauss started his career. He had been to Berlin to sit at the feet of Hegel and Schleiermacher, but it was Hegel who really drew him. Hegel, however, died within a few weeks of his arrival. Strauss heard the news in Schleiermacher's house, and exclaimed – somewhat tactlessly – 'And it was to hear him that I came to Berlin!' He became a faithful Hegelian in that he saw Christianity as an expression of eternal truths: the historical setting was of secondary interest.

Christ for him was only incidentally an individual person. He stood for an idea: the idea of humanity moving towards the perfection in which the process of history was to be fulfilled. Since the universe is a process that is developing by its own immanent powers, it is inconceivable that its end should be reached at some point in the process by a transcendent incursion, or that the infinite should be embodied in the finite. The ideal can be realized only in the outcome of the whole process: no single point or person in the course of it could possess finality.

With these assumptions in mind, Strauss approached the life of Jesus. He rejected both the orthodox and the rationalist interpretations that were current in his day. The orthodox accepted the records as they stood, the supernatural elements along with the natural, and contrived somehow to harmonize the Gospel narratives. The rationalists accepted the records as in principle historical, and then sought to make them intelligible by distinguishing the core of fact from its miraculous embellishments, explaining how these had arisen from magnifying or misunderstanding what had actually occurred. In Strauss's view, argument between orthodoxy and rationalism led to an impasse. The antagonism between them could be overcome only by a new interpretation of the life of Jesus: the mythological. This was a typical example of the Hegelian rhythm of affirmation, negation, and a synthesis of opposites.

The concept of myth had been applied to the biblical records before Strauss took it up. But, whereas his predecessors had introduced the notion to account only for the stories of Jesus's entry into the world and of his departure from it, Strauss applied it to the Gospel narratives as a whole. He held that myth was not the invention of an individual mind but the product of communal imagination.

Conceive [he says] a recently established community, revering its founder with all the more enthusiasm on account of his unexpected and tragic removal from his work; a community impregnated with a mass of new ideas which were destined to transform the world; a community of orientals, chiefly unlearned people, who therefore could not appropriate and express those ideas in the abstract conceptual forms of the understanding, but only as symbols and stories in the concrete fashion of the imagination. When all this is remembered, one can perceive that in these circumstances there must necessarily have arisen what actually did arise, viz. a series of sacred narratives fitted to bring vividly before the mind the whole mass of new ideas, started by Jesus, and of old ones, applied to him, cast in the form of particular incidents in his life.

Strauss did not deny that Jesus had been a historical person. Myths are not manufactured out of nothing. Jesus was a purely human person who came to believe himself to be the Messiah, and who made so profound an impression on his followers that their myth-making imagination transformed him into the divine and supernatural Christ. The materials for this transformation lay ready to hand in the Old Testament, notably in its messianic prophecies and its miraculous legends: for example, the story of the Transfiguration had to find a place in the life of Jesus because of the precedent of the shining of Moses' face. Strauss showed great ingenuity in discovering in the Old Testament detailed sources that had suggested the miraculous deeds that were ascribed to Jesus in the Gospel narratives. It was not his intention to undermine or dissolve the Christian faith. In true Hegelian fashion, he conceived himself to be reinterpreting it in a way that would make it acceptable to reasonable men.

The strength of his work lay in its being a consistent interpretation of the *narratives*: its weakness was that it was not based on a critical study of the *documents*. He contributed little, if anything, to an understanding of the literary relationship between the Synoptic Gospels. He supposed that Mark was dependent on Matthew and Luke. He did however break with a tradition that had been taken for granted by orthodoxy and rationalism alike, namely that the Fourth Gospel was the record of an eyewitness.

*

Baur perceived the weakness in Strauss's book. He had attempted a criticism of the Gospel history without any proper criticism of the Gospels themselves. His concern had been to interpret the sacred history as a sensuous form of the absolute philosophy. Baur, on the other hand, wanted to discover what the history really had been. He was as much a Hegelian as Strauss, but there was more of the genuine historian in him. It was the virtue of Baur that he saw that there could be little progress in the study of Christian origins until a more scientific investigation had been made of the character of the New Testament literature: the origin, composition, and date of the various books, the relations between them, and their setting in the development of the Church.

He did not suppose – like the orthodox and the rationalists and indeed like Strauss – that the Christian movement had been homogeneous from the outset. On the contrary, the Hegelian dialectic predisposed him to look in primitive Christianity for signs of conflict and the resolution of conflict: thesis, antithesis, and synthesis. The synthesis was to be seen in the doctrine and constitution of the Catholic Church as it clearly appeared in the latter part of the second century. He asked himself what process of development by antagonism lay behind that fully-fledged apparition.

His conclusions, which were tied up with a radical reconstruction of the literary evolution of the New Testament documents, were in outline as follows. The outstanding fact about the Christianity of the apostolic age was a deep division of opinion about the character and object of the new religion. The church was divided into two parties, the Judaists and the Universalists. The original apostles were all Judaists, who insisted that the obligation to keep the Jewish law was perpetual. Jesus the Messiah had re-established Judaism. The Universalists, on the other hand, who were headed by the Apostle Paul, held that the Gospel was addressed to Jews and Gentiles alike on equal terms. It proclaimed a liberation from Jewish law and traditions. All the antitheses to be found in Paul's authentic Epistles (Galatians, Romans, I and II Corinthians) – grace and law, faith and works, the spirit and the letter, etc. – reflect the antagonism between these contrary beliefs.

According to Baur, Paul understood Jesus better than the original disciples. The religion of Jesus had been spiritual and universalist; he had discerned the highest elements in the religious movements of the past, out of which the religion of the future might be fashioned. But in order to get a footing for it in the world, he had to claim to be the Messiah of Jewish expectation, a claim which could be understood – or misunderstood – in a narrowly Jewish sense. It was so taken by the original disciples, but the germs of the dialectical conflict between Universalism and Judaism were latent in the teaching of Jesus himself.

The conflict between these antithetical forms of early Christianity was not only intense but prolonged. It was not until after A.D. 150 that they were definitely reconciled in a synthesis. From a Hegelian point of view, it was a fine example of the way in which unity is evolved out of contradiction. The Catholic synthesis *was* a synthesis, and not a complete victory for either side. It was Pauline in its Universalism, but also Petrine since it found a place for a new law, a new priesthood, and a new ritual.

All the New Testament documents bore the marks of this dialectical process. The more eirenic the tone of any document, the more obviously did it belong to the latest or synthesizing phase of the process. Thus the incompatibility of the Acts of the Apostles with the authentic Epistles of Paul is due to the fact that Acts was a work of fiction, written about the middle of the second century with the intention of covering over the conflict that had divided Christians in the apostolic age and of promoting the harmony that was now being reached. Hence Acts suppresses all mention of the conflict between Peter and Paul at Antioch, and represents Paul as zealously fulfilling the Jewish ceremonial law and as addressing himself primarily to Jews, while at the same time it attributes a universalist attitude to the earliest disciples who are said to be the first to declare that the Torah was not binding on Gentile converts. By such means Acts produces its synthesis.

Each of the four Gospels was likewise written with a purpose that reflected a different phase of the dialectical process. In the Fourth Gospel, which Baur dated late in the second century, the culmination of the synthesis was reached. The identification of Jesus with the Logos of Greek philosophy made possible the elaboration of a Christian gnosis that could embrace all the metaphysical and ethical ideas that had been present in the Christian movement.

Baur was the chief light in a school of theologians that was centred in Tübingen; it was of course quite distinct from the earlier Tübingen school of Roman Catholic theologians (see p. 31). But Baur – a man of immense industry and patriarchal stature – was its founder and pre-eminent mouthpiece, and his death marked its dissolution. Although as a systematic whole his reconstruction of Christian origins became outmoded, he had asked many of the right questions even if he had given wrong or improbable answers. Whereas Strauss had attributed the Gospel narratives to the unconscious, mythologizing activity of the collective Christian imagination, Baur explained their variety as a result of a conscious and purposeful interpretation of the life of Jesus. He was also more historically realistic than Strauss in that, in his account of Christian origins, powerful personalities, especially St Paul, played an influential part. He saw that more was at work than the operation of immanent ideas, even if the more that he saw was out of focus. Nevertheless, at bottom both Strauss and Baur saw Christianity not as the outcome of particular, concrete events, but as part of an ideal, evolutionary process, and their handling of the historical data seems to have been controlled by their philosophical presuppositions. It was a perception of this state of affairs that provoked the Ritschlian reaction.

*

Albert Ritschl was the son of a bishop in the Lutheran Church. Perhaps it was this circumstance, together with his earnest disposition and his restless intelligence, that led to his seeing the work of a theologian as his life's vocation. His mind was so powerful and independent that he was not likely to be a faithful disciple of any master or a member of any school of thought except his own. On the other hand, he was a lifelong learner, and his teaching never reached the finality of a finished system. For this reason, and because of his cumbrous way of expressing himself, he has often been charged with inconsistency, but whatever disagreements there may be among those who have studied his works, there is general agreement that during the last quarter of the nineteenth century no one had a stronger or more wide-spread influence on Protestant theology in Germany and indeed beyond Germany. We must therefore take note of the principal features of his teaching.

(1) *The separation of theology from metaphysics.* It has been justly said that as a result of Ritschl's work Christianity was saved from degenerating into a historical illustration of Hegelian principles. Ritschl did not look upon the Hegelianism of the Tübingen school merely as an outsider. At the start of his career he was one of its most promising recruits. But he very soon reacted, and reacted violently, against the intrusion not only of Hegelianism but of any metaphysics whatever into Christian theology. He was determined to distinguish the Christian revelation from all forms of speculative theism.

He considered that the traditional arguments for the existence of God yielded at best no more than a First Cause, a Supreme Being, or the Absolute, which was something quite different from the God and Father of Jesus Christ. Immense harm had been done to theology by its alliance with philosophies, whether Platonic, Aristotelian, Hegelian, or any other. The consequence had been to force the data of divine revelation into the mould of alien intellectual systems. This mistaken course had had a long history. A bad precedent had been set by the hellenizing of ecclesiastical dogma in the early centuries. This was a theme that Adolf Harnack

(1851–1930), a younger Ritschlian, was to enlarge upon in his *History of Dogma* (1886–9).

While Ritschl expelled metaphysics from theology, he certainly had his own epistemology or theory of knowledge, which was different from Kant's. Kant had maintained that things-in-themselves are unknowable; only appearances can be known by pure reason. Ritschl accepted the distinction, and agreed that things-in-themselves, that is things at rest and apart from their activities and appearances, are not subjects of knowledge. But he held that things-in-themselves can be known through their action upon us and through our response to them. Thus, while God in abstraction from the world cannot be proved by reasoning in the way that was attempted by the traditional arguments for theism, yet he can be known through the revelation in which he makes a personal impact upon men.

'Every claim', Ritschl said, 'to teach something concerning God in himself apart from some real revelation on his part, felt and perceived on our part, is baseless.' Christian faith is a matter not of intellectual assent to argument, but of a response of person to person, in which the will plays a larger part than the intellect. Religion has a character of its own and can stand on its own feet. It does not need to be buttressed, or given a right of way, by other forms of human thought or experience. This claim was obviously attractive at a time when it was being alleged that Christian faith was being rendered untenable by philosophical criticism or by scientific discovery. Ritschlianism offered an unshakeable, independent basis for religion. One way in which the Ritschlians stated their case was by drawing a sharp distinction between judgements of fact and judgements of value.

(2) *Value-judgements*. Ritschl did not adopt this term till towards the end of his life, but once it had been adopted it seemed to crystallize the positive aspects of his theory of religious knowledge. Whereas the scientist and the philosopher make theoretical or factual judgements about objects as they exist in themselves or on their own, and about the

causal or other relations between them, the religious man *qua* religious is drawn to make value-judgements by objects that evoke in him feelings of pleasure or pain, of satisfaction or dissatisfaction. The distinction is not absolute, for there can be no judgement of fact without some valuation, and there can be no value-judgement which does not imply that the object evaluated exists.

The Ritschlians certainly did not mean that value-judgements are purely subjective, though that suspicion lay against them. Both judgements of fact and value-judgements are concerned with what is really there, but whereas science and philosophy try to explain objects as disinterestedly as possible, religion evaluates them as regards their practical worth, that is by whether they satisfy or frustrate the highest purposes of human life. The Ritschlians vehemently denied that value-judgements yielded an inferior kind of knowledge, a point that comes out in their attitude to the person of Jesus.

(3) *The Jesus of history.* Where Schleiermacher had taken the datum of theology to be the religious consciousness, Ritschl insisted that it was historic fact – the historical revelation of God in Jesus Christ. Everything in Christianity depended on that. Ritschl would not allow that Christians, in so far as their faith was concerned, had anything to learn from other religions, any more than from science or philosophy. Hence he was against the appeal to mystical experience. There was nothing specifically Christian in it, and it sat loose to the historic revelation in Christ.

Unlike Strauss, Ritschl was confident that the reality of Jesus was faithfully transmitted through the Scriptures. He had broken with Baur's theory which dated most of the New Testament documents in the second century and treated them as a collection of tendentious and conflicting interpretations of the mission of Christ. Ritschl dated the Gospels in the first century; he recognized the priority of Mark; and he accepted nearly all the Pauline Epistles as authentic. He held that the documents provided a united and historically dependable testimony to the work of Christ. Otherwise, he could not have rested his whole system on the revelation in the historic person of Jesus.

All the same, faith in Christ was for him a value-judgement, not an inference from the study of history. The historical facts become the revelation of God to every believer, in so far as Jesus appears to him, lays hold of him, and sets him free, enabling him to share in the divine lordship over the world, and emancipating him from being a slave of a mechanical system of causation. The following passage shows Ritschl's characteristic way of affirming the Godhead of Christ:

> If by trusting for my salvation to the power of what he has done for me, I honour him as my God, then that is a value-judgement of a direct kind. It is not a judgement which belongs to the sphere of disinterested scientific knowledge, like the formula of Chalcedon. ... The nature of God and the Divine we can only know in its essence by determining its value for our salvation. ... We know God only by revelation, and therefore also must understand the Godhead of Christ, if it is to be understood at all, as an attribute revealed to us in his saving influence upon ourselves.

This is to say that Ritschl saw the Godhead of Christ in his *work*, and his work was the founding and building of the Kingdom of God.

(4) *The Kingdom of God and the Redemption.* In his emphasis on the Kingdom of God, Ritschl was unearthing a central element in the Synoptic Gospels. There is a celebrated saying of his that Christianity is 'an ellipse with two foci', namely the Kingdom of God and personal redemption or justification by faith, but his interpreters agree that he subordinates the doctrine of redemption to the doctrine of the Kingdom.

God is love, and the purpose of God for the world is the building up of a kingdom of free spirits of every nationality and race who are bound together in a moral community and in brotherly love. It was the vocation of Christ to set the Kingdom in motion, and he gave his life for this end. For

Ritschl the Kingdom of God was ethical, rather than eschatological. He had little to say about eschatology or the last things. It was the progressive establishing of the Kingdom of God in history that absorbed all his interest.

Believers are redeemed by Christ from sin, that is from the self-assertion that spreads ruin through the social order, by being brought into the Kingdom of God so that they may participate in the work of the Kingdom. The object of Christ's redemption is not the individual, but the community. The Church consists of the members of the Kingdom united in prayer and worship. It has been well said that, for Ritschl, the Church was the Kingdom on its knees with hands folded in prayer, and that the Kingdom was the Church on its feet with tools for work and weapons for warfare in its hands. One of his reasons for condemning mysticism was that it made for individualistic detachment from the moral and social tasks of the Kingdom of God.

*

Such were the chief notes struck by Ritschl and his followers, and they had a stirring effect. A French writer gave these reasons for the manifold appeal of Ritschlianism:

To those who are disheartened by the attacks of criticism it affirms that faith and salvation are independent of the results of our historical researches. To theologians weary of dogmatic controversies it presents a Christianity free from all foreign metaphysics. To scholars trembling to see theology fall before the attacks of the natural sciences, it shows a way by which all collision with the natural sciences becomes impossible. To students devoted to history, it unfolds the development of the primitive Church. To timid Christians, it says, God has never been angry with you: he declares to you that you may return to him. To worn-out pessimists, it cries: Work for the advancement of the Kingdom.[1]

1. H. Schoen. *Les Origines historiques de la théologie de Ritschl.* 1893, quoted by 'E. A. Edghill. *Faith and Fact: a Study of Ritschlianism.* 1910, pp. 59ff.

10

Science and Christian Belief in England

IT is commonly supposed that the Victorian age was an age of religious faith, and at first sight it is a supposition that has much to support it. Churches and chapels were crowded with worshippers. In the middle classes and upwards you were not quite respectable if you did not go regularly to church. It was an age of much church building and restoration. The Evangelical and Tractarian movements had many adherents and nonconformity was thriving. There was a tremendous output of religious and theological literature in the form of books, pamphlets, tracts, sermons, periodicals, and newspapers. It was a time of notable missionary zeal and expansion. Certainly, there were multitudes of people who had a simple and unshaken confidence in the faith of their fathers, and who were devoted to its practice and its propagation. Surely these are all evidences of an age of faith.

But on a more discriminating view there is reason to question this characterization of the Victorian era. Beneath the surface of respectable religious conformity was a turmoil of doubt and uncertainty. Nearly all the representatives of Victorian thought, nearly all the intellectuals, had to struggle with the problem of belief. Most of the influential teachers of the age were either unbelievers or professed a faith more or less far removed from conventional Christian orthodoxy. Thomas Carlyle, John Stuart Mill, George Eliot, James Anthony Froude, Francis Newman, John Morley, Matthew Arnold, Leslie Stephen, Thomas Hill Green, George Meredith – the teaching of all these was calculated to unsettle, if not to destroy, traditional Christian belief. 'Never has any age in history produced such a detailed literature of lost faith, or so many great men and women of

religious temperament standing outside organized religion.'[1]
Moreover, those teachers who did not themselves renounce
Christian belief bore witness to the insistent pressure of
doubt.

It may also be surmised that the strident tones and
the proclivity to heresy-hunting that were characteristic of
many orthodox Victorian divines may have hidden, from
themselves as well as from others, an uncertainty or anxiety
about the grounds of their own faith. Men talk with shrill
excitement when they are least sure of themselves and most
fearful that those who disagree with them may be right. It
would be truer to say that the age was one of religious
seriousness than of faith. No considering man felt able to
ignore the question of religious belief, as is easily done
today. There is the great difference between that age and
this.

The authority of traditional Christianity was threatened
from many sides. When the debate was fully joined, the
discoveries of the natural science and the literary and
historical criticism of the Bible figured most prominently,
and these are topics that will engage our attention in
this and the next chapter. But it should be borne in mind
that doubt and unbelief had other sources as well. In particular, what caused many to revolt from Evangelical or
Catholic orthodoxy was the apparent immorality and
inhumanity of the Christian scheme of salvation (divine
favouritism, the substitutionary atonement, everlasting torment in hell, etc.) and also its bare-faced next-worldliness
which seemed to deny both the possibility and the duty of
improving conditions of life in this world. For example,
it was on these grounds, not on account of natural science
or the Bible, that Francis Newman, J. A. Froude, and George
Eliot first turned their backs on orthodoxy.[2] What it called
upon them to believe, with such confidence of its superiority,

1. Margaret Maison, *Search your Soul, Eustace.* 1961, p. 209.
2. See H. R. Murphy. 'The Ethical Revolt against Christian Orthodoxy in Early Victorian England'. *American Historical Review,* July 1955.

struck them as morally inferior to their own ethical ideals and standards.

Nevertheless, the discoveries of natural science offered a more sensational challenge to belief. British Christianity was more ill-prepared for the impact of Darwinism than was the case in Germany. With rare exceptions theologians had remained impervious to the ferment that had been going on there since the time of Kant; and for the first half of the nineteenth century religious belief in England was comparatively little disturbed by new knowledge. There was much religious agitation but it had to do with such questions as the apostolic succession, the claims of the papacy, baptismal regeneration, and the relations of Church and State, not with the fundamental grounds of belief.

Christians in Britain continued to suppose that the Bible was unlike all other books: a divinely guaranteed repository of knowledge about God and the world, true in all its parts, and qualified, when its right meaning was ascertained, to settle any controversy. Not only the Bible itself was accepted as completely dependable, but the framework of ideas that had come to be associated with it. F. D. Maurice, for example, in the 1850s was still talking about the world's being only 6,000 years old. The world had been created by a sudden divine fiat, and all the species of animals as well as man were ready-made. It was assumed that the stories at the beginning of Genesis about Adam and Eve and the patriarchs were fully historical, and that Adam had been created in a state not only of innocence but of marvellous blessedness and wisdom which he had lost in consequence of a single act of disobedience, known as the Fall.

The first rumblings of trouble ahead, for all who were fixed in these beliefs, came from the science of geology. In the 1830s books by Sir Charles Lyell and Dean Buckland established the geological succession of rocks and fossils, and showed the world to be much older than the accepted date for the Garden of Eden. It was, however, possible for traditionalists to meet this difficulty by maintaining either (as P. Gosse, himself a scientist, did in 1857) that God had put misleading fossils into the rocks in order to test the faith of mankind, or that the 'days' in Genesis 1 really meant long periods of time. Not only theologians, but scientists themselves, were willing to approve such ways of meeting the difficulty.

Other difficulties could be got round with a little ingenuity. The Bampton Lecturer in 1833 explained the longevity of the patriarchs on the hypothesis that Moses had used an Egyptian scheme of chronology in which, instead of a year of twelve months, seasons of three months were computed as a year. The ages given in Genesis could thus be reduced to a quarter of the figures given. Methuselah's real age was 242, and if allowance was made for the relative simplicity and purity of the lives of the patriarchs and the unhurried nature of their existence it was easy to believe that they had lived longer than the normal span of human life.

Orthodoxy did however receive a serious shock fifteen years before the appearance of Darwin's *Origin of Species*, when in 1844 *Vestiges of the Natural History of Creation* was published. It had an enormous sale, going through four editions in its first six months, and eleven editions by 1860. The book was all the more exciting or infuriating because it was anonymous and no one could say who had written it. For months it provided a favourite subject of conversation at dinner parties. Names of possible authors were eagerly canvassed, including Thackeray, Prince Albert, and Byron's daughter. The secret was not released till forty years later. The author was a Scotsman, named Robert Chambers (1802–71), not a professional scientist but a man of wide interests and a prolific author and editor. *Chambers's Encyclopaedia* takes its name from him.

The *Vestiges* was a survey of the findings of the physical and biological sciences, based on the view that the whole of nature was subject to a uniform law. 'It being admitted that the system of the Universe is one under the dominion of natural law, it follows that the introduction of species into the world must have been brought about in the manner of law also.' The book called in question not the divine creation of the world, but the received opinion about the manner of creation. The belief that 'the Almighty Author produced the progenitors of all existing species by some sort of personal or immediate exertion' was absurd and superstitious. 'The Eternal One arranged for everything beforehand, and trusted all to the operation of the laws of his appointment.'

Although the *Vestiges* theory of the development of species was in principle the same as Darwin's and raised the same problems for traditional orthodoxy, the crisis of belief was postponed. It was not even necessary for the theologians to refute the book, since the scientists did so for them. The fact is Chambers was only an amateur and often misunderstood what he was writing about. The professional scientists were quick to fasten on his mistakes and they went to great pains in exposing them. Around 1850 few scientists of any note had a good word to say for the idea of evolution. The dismissal of the *Vestiges* by the scientists gave religious believers a false sense of security. It was left to Darwin to get evolution taken with real seriousness.

While Lamarck and Erasmus Darwin, and others such as the author of the *Vestiges*, had advanced theories of biological evolution, their theories had been in the nature of brilliant guesses, and on the evidence available it had seemed just as reasonable to believe in the doctrine of sudden creation. What Charles Darwin did was to assemble such a mass of data that could be convincingly explained only by a theory of evolution as to make it impossible to dismiss the idea as no more than a wild guess. His theory that natural selection was the cause of the origin of species made his work appear additionally shocking.

The conclusion that the higher animals and man had evolved from lower forms of life as a result of the struggle for existence was obviously fatal to the literal accuracy of the

Book of Genesis, and, what is more, it seemed that the traditional Christian doctrines about the creation and fall of man would have to go by the board. Man appeared to owe his origin to the operation of impersonal and natural forces or laws instead of to the direct, personal action of God. The whole scheme of Christian belief, which was based on the supposition that man had all at once been created with a fully formed capacity for communion with God, a capacity that the human race had lost through the disobedience of the first human pair, was thrown into disarray. The work of Christ had been to redress this primordial catastrophe. If that had not happened, then the doctrines of redemption and atonement stood in jeopardy too. As Dr Pusey put it: 'It lies as the basis of our faith that man was created in the perfection of our nature, endowed with supernatural grace, with a full freedom of choice such as man, until restored by Christ, has not had since.'

We can see then why Darwin's work caused so much alarm. Samuel Wilberforce (1805–73), the most eloquent and cultivated of the bishops, took upon himself to lead the attack in an article in the *Quarterly Review*, and also in a speech at the meeting of the British Association which was held at Oxford in 1860. In the *Quarterly* he declared that Darwin was guilty of 'a tendency to limit God's glory in creation'; that 'the principle of natural selection is absolutely incompatible with the word of God'; that it 'contradicts the revealed relations of creation to its Creator'; that it is 'a dishonouring view of nature', and so on. The reports of the British Association meeting are not altogether clear. What Wilberforce appears to have said to Huxley is: 'If anyone were to be willing to trace his descent through an ape as his *grandfather*, would he be equally willing to trace his descent similarly on the side of his *grandmother*?' – a way of putting the case that reflects the sentimental attitude of the Victorians to women. Thereupon Huxley murmured to his neighbour, 'The Lord hath delivered him into mine hands,' and he concluded his reply by saying in effect: 'If I had to choose, I would prefer to be a descendant of a humble monkey than of a man who employs his knowledge and eloquence in misrepresenting those who are wearing out their lives in the search for truth.'

Another defender of traditional belief ended an impassioned discourse with the words: 'Leave me my ancestors in Paradise and I will allow you yours in the Zoological Gardens.' Similarly Archbishop Manning, soon to be a cardinal, described the new view of nature as 'a brutal philosophy – to wit, there is no God, and the ape is our Adam'. These examples of outraged reaction could be multiplied. They continued for a considerable time. As late as 1886, J. W. Burgon (1813–88), Dean of Chichester – a die-hard conservative if ever there was one – wrote:

When the Natural Philosopher claims that MAN shall be held to be the product of EVOLUTION – and to be descended from an ape – . . . we are constrained to reject his hypothesis with derision. It is plainly irreconcilable with the fundamental revelations of Scripture. . . . An hypothesis is gratuitously put forth utterly destitute of scientific proof, and flouted by such a first-rate Naturalist as Sir Richard Owen.

It is true that there were still scientists like Owen who refused to acknowledge the cogency of the evolutionary theory, and theologians were naturally tempted to make the most of this circumstance. Indeed the obtuseness of scientists may be held to afford considerable excuse for the obtuseness of theologians, who were not so well qualified to assess the relevant evidence.

All the same, there were from the first some Christian believers, both scientists and theologians, who were not panic-stricken by Darwin. They perceived the force of his discoveries, and saw that they must reckon with them. Such was the eminent American botanist, Asa Gray (1810–88), a friend of Darwin, who combined acceptance of the theory of evolution with belief in orthodox Christianity. Such on the theological side was Richard William Church (1815–90), the future Dean of St Paul's and a friend of Asa Gray. When

The Origin of Species was published, he reviewed it respectfully and without alarm, and he wrote to Gray: 'It is wonderful "shortness of thought" to treat the theory itself as incompatible with ideas of a higher and spiritual order.' Years before, he had said: 'I most assuredly should *not* give up the faith in God which [the biblical writers] have cherished in me, if I found they had made mistakes.' Likewise, in March 1860 F. J. A. Hort wrote to B. F. Westcott: 'Have you read Darwin? How I should like a talk with you about it! In spite of difficulties, I am inclined to think it unanswerable. In any case it is a treat to read such a book.'

Gradually, it was borne in upon thoughtful Christians that, instead of fearing advances in science, they should welcome them. On a popular level this was the attitude of the members of the Guild of St Matthew (see pp. 98f.). In their attempts to commend the faith to secularists, they found they had to deal with this question. So, for example, we find Stewart Headlam saying in the course of a sermon preached in 1879:

> Thank God that the scientific men have . . . shattered the idol of an infallible book, broken the fetters of a supposed divine code of rules; for so they have helped to reveal Jesus Christ in his majesty. . . . He, we say, is the Word of God; he is inspiring you, encouraging you, strengthening you in your scientific studies; he is the *wisdom* in Lyell or in Darwin. . . .
> It gives us far grander notions of God to think of him making the world by his Spirit through the ages, than to think of him making it in a few days.

Even the veteran Dr Pusey, towards the end of his life, in a university sermon entitled *Unscience, not Science, Adverse to Faith*, went as far as he could to meet the theory of evolution. He did not allow that the Darwinian theory was proven, but he denied that genuine theology invests any physical theory with the sacredness of divine truth or had to exclude the evolutionary hypothesis *in toto*. It would be possible to acknowledge, if the case were made out, that man had evolved from lower forms of life, though the emergence of a rational being from a non-rational ancestry would involve a stupendous miracle. Anyhow the soul was no subject of physical science. Pusey was depending on the impossibility of *proving* that man had evolved from the lower animals. This was a hazardous position to take up, for it was always possible that science might discover the missing link.

Christian apologetic at this time was inclined to grant that there might well have been a natural process of evolution, and to suppose that the creative action of God should be seen in the gaps or lacunae in the scientific theory, especially the gap between inorganic matter and life, and the gap between man as a rational being and irrational animals. This was to pin the Christian faith to the belief that the gaps never would be closed.

There was a young Oxford theologian in the Tractarian tradition who saw the weakness of that position; indeed, he went further and said that it involved a heretical conception of God's relation to the world. This was Aubrey Moore (1848-90), whose early death was a grave loss to English theology. Moore called attention to A. R. Wallace's theory of evolution which was similar to Darwin's, except that he left a loophole for direct divine intervention. Wallace maintained the evolution of man out of a lower form but contended – he called this his 'heresy' – that natural selection should have given man a brain only a little superior to that of the apes, whereas in fact it was very much larger. It could therefore be held that a higher intelligence may at this point have supervened on natural selection to produce man. But Moore would have nothing to do with this idea.

Whether [he wrote] from the scientific side this is rightly called a heresy or not, it is not necessary to decide; but certainly from the religious side it is a strangely unorthodox view. If, as the Christian believes, the 'higher intelligence', who used these laws for the creation of man, was the same God, who worked by these laws in creating the lower forms of life, Mr Wallace's distinction, as a distinction of cause, disappears; and if it is not the same God, we contradict the first article of the Creed. Whatever be the line which

Christianity draws between man and the rest of the visible creation, it certainly does not claim man as the work of God and leave the rest to 'unaided nature'.

Nor was Moore favourable to the idea of 'special creations', which he said were not part of the faith, but a product of the seventeenth century that owed its popularity largely to Milton.

Apart from the scientific evidence in favour of evolution, *as a theory* it is infinitely more Christian than the theory of 'special creation'. . . . *A theory of occasional intervention implies as its correlative a theory of ordinary absence.* . . . This fitted in well with the Deism of the last century. For Deism . . . constantly spoke of God as we might speak of an absentee landlord. . . . Yet another more opposed to the language of the Bible and the Fathers can scarcely be imagined. With St Athanasius, the immanence of the divine Logos is the explanation of the adaptations and unity in nature. . . . Special creation [is] the scientific analogue of Deism. Order, development, and law are the analogue of the Christian view of God.

Moore said he looked forward keenly to the time when, in the progress of science, the 'breaks' or gaps, on which some people based their theology, would disappear by being made intelligible to reason. He also reinterpreted the doctrine of the Fall by making it dependent on inferences about the disorder in human nature as it has appeared in history, instead of on some prehistoric event like that narrated in Genesis. About the same time a Cambridge theologian (A. J. Mason) said: 'If it can be shown that the human mind is only a development from the analogous faculties in other animals, the Christian, so far from being staggered, will only find fresh matter for adoring the power and wisdom of God.' And Hort said that the early chapters of Genesis were 'a divinely appointed parable or apologue setting forth important practical truths on subjects which, as a matter of history, lie outside our present ken'.

So about 1890 theologians, at least in the universities, were no longer making reluctant concessions to advances in natural science but were claiming them almost as a godsend. This change of front was doubtless wise but perhaps it was too facile, for there is a deeper cleavage between the scientific and theological ways of looking at the world than became clearly visible in the controversies about the Book of Genesis. It was possible to reach an accommodation there, while leaving profounder conflicts of attitude and presupposition unresolved. However, as we shall see in due course, more comprehensive attempts were to be made by theologians to reinterpret the Christian faith with regard to the advances that had been made not only in scientific thought but in biblical criticism. But we have still to reckon with the repercussions of the storm that was started by a publication that appeared a few months after *The Origin of Species.*

11

The Bible and the Broad Church

THE nineteenth century in England abounded in religious crises. That occasioned by the publication in February 1860 of the volume entitled *Essays and Reviews* surpassed them all. The controversy raged for four or five years in the first instance and then, like thunderstorms that return when you think they are over, led to another violent explosion in 1869. The whole affair throws much light on the Victorian religious scene, and in particular on the condition of the Church of England, but it is not an edifying story. Here, to preface it, is a typical piece of the scurrility that attended it.

In 1860 the Master of Wellington College was Edward White Benson (1829–96), a future Archbishop of Canterbury. He presented a copy of *Essays and Reviews*, soon after its publication, to the assistant masters' library. A contributor to *The Record*, an organ of militant Evangelicalism, got wind of this, and wrote to the paper a scandalized letter to the effect that the Master had presented a copy of the obnoxious book to the *boys'* library. Benson thereupon wrote to say that it was to the masters' library he had given it, which was in a room inaccessible to the boys, and he considered the nature of the masters' profession made it desirable that they should study works of very various tendencies. The editor of *The Record* replied that a Christian public would certainly not accept this evasion.

The idea of producing a volume of essays originated in the mind of H. B. Wilson (1803–88), a former Oxford tutor, who had taken the Liberal side in the Tractarian controversy. He put the idea to Benjamin Jowett (1817–93), Tutor and later Master of Balliol, the most influential of Liberal Anglican divines, who welcomed it. He had himself for some time been working on an essay about the critical study of

Scripture which he wanted an opportunity of publishing. Jowett, who tried without success to rope in A. P. Stanley, explained the project to him in these terms:

> The object is to say what we think freely within the limits of the Church of England. A notice will be prefixed that no one is responsible for any notions but his own. It is, however, an essential part of the plan that names shall be given. . . . We do not wish to do anything rash or irritating to the public or the University, but we are determined not to submit to this abominable system of terrorism, which prevents the statement of the plainest facts, and makes true theology or theological education impossible.

In the event, seven contributors were enlisted. Frederick Temple (1821–1902), Headmaster of Rugby, wrote on 'The Education of the World'; most of his essay would strike a reader now as commonplace pulpit rhetoric, but it led up to a plea for fearless study of the Bible and for readiness to revise received opinions. The essay by Rowland Williams (1817–70), Professor of Hebrew at Lampeter, was ostensibly a review of 'Bunsen's Biblical Researches'. Baron von Bunsen was a Prussian diplomat who had been ambassador in London and was well-known in English society as a man of great learning and an ardent Christian. The subject enabled Williams to commend the critical approach to the Bible, already well-established in Germany, and to suggest a more acceptable interpretation of some Christian doctrines, for example the atonement should be taken to mean 'salvation from evil through sharing the Saviour's spirit', not a 'purchase from God through the price of his bodily pangs'. The argument of the essay by Baden Powell (1796–1860), Professor of Geometry at Oxford, was that Christianity no longer depends for its verification on external evidences, especially miracles, but on the appeal to moral and spiritual experience. He and other essayists acknowledged the debt they owed to Coleridge.

H. B. Wilson wrote on 'The National Church'. It should aim at embracing all the elements of spiritual life in the nation and allow the greatest possible flexibility in the interpretation of its formularies. He also questioned the belief that non-Christians would be eternally lost. The essay by C. W. Goodwin (1817–78), a Cambridge man, on 'The Mosaic Cosmogony', said that the story of creation should be regarded as a simple Hebrew myth adapted to the needs of those for whom it was written. There followed an essay by Mark Pattison (1813–84) on 'Tendencies of Religious Thought in England 1688–1750' which implied that, since theology had grown in the past, it should be expected to do so in the future. Jowett wound up the series with a careful argument for the use of reason in the interpretation of Scripture. Students should seek to ascertain what the authors actually meant, instead of starting with *a priori* notions about inspiration. So interpreted, the Bible would be found to witness to a progressive revelation of God. The Christian religion, he said, is in a false position when all the tendencies of knowledge are opposed to it. 'The time has come when it is no longer possible to ignore the results of criticism.'

And that was the theme of the whole volume – in so far as it had a single theme. It was an attempt to acclimatize in the Church of England the critical and historical study of the Bible, which had been actively engaging the minds of German thinkers for fifty years and more. It was high time the attempt was made, if English theology was not to be left in a back-water. But now for the sequel.

The first serious attack on *Essays and Reviews* was launched in October 1860, and it came from an unexpected quarter. It was an anoymous article entitled 'Neo-Christianity' in the *Westminster Review*. It was in fact written by Frederic Harrison (1831–1923), who had been a High Anglican until his faith was undermined by science and biblical criticism; he then became the leading representative in England of Comte's positivism and religion of humanity. He agreed of course with the concessions to modern thought that were made in *Essays and Reviews*, but in effect he said to the essayists: 'You have no business to adopt this reasonable view of the Bible and to remain in the Church.' It was folly to suppose that the Church, which was irrevocably bound up with the traditional system of orthodoxy and biblical infallibility, could come to terms with new knowledge. The essayists should have come out of the crumbling ruins of orthodoxy and not pretend that the ancient faith could be modernized.

This article provoked an even more violent attack from an opposite quarter. Samuel Wilberforce, who had lately been busy with Darwinism, came forth again in the *Quarterly Review* as the champion of orthodoxy. Himself an accomplished writer, he began by making light of the literary merits of *Essays and Reviews*; then he suggested that there was little in the volume that was really new and that it would not have attracted attention but for its authors' position in the Church. He agreed with Harrison that their teaching was entirely inconsistent with the Christian tradition and with holding office in the Church. Scarcely veiled atheism, open scepticism, laxity, and daring flippancy were charges that he brought against some of the essayists. He was a little gentler with Temple and Jowett whom he regretted to see led away by such bad company. 'We earnestly trust, and we believe', he said, 'that the Head Master of Rugby is above the theories of the essayist Dr Temple, or we should tremble, not only for the faith, but for the morals of his pupils.'

After this, A. P. Stanley tried to pour some oil on the troubled waters in the *Edinburgh Review*. While he did not take his stand with the essayists, he protested against the attempt to silence them and to drive them out of the Church. Stanley had always come to the defence of men who were attacked by ecclesiastical agitators, whatever their complexion. He was opposed to any attempt to narrow the borders of the Church of England, and he endorsed Jowett's remark that 'doubt comes in at the window when inquiry is denied at the door'.

But by now there was a gathering outcry, especially among the clergy, that something drastic should be done: in consequence *Essays and Reviews*, which had made a quiet start, was selling like hot cakes. Disraeli remarked that it was convulsing Christendom and seemed 'to have shaken down the towers of Chichester Cathedral' (the piers of the central tower did in fact collapse in February 1861).

Addresses and appeals had been pouring in upon the bishops. They held an urgent, private meeting. The Archbishop of Canterbury, J. B. Sumner (1780–1862), was an old and failing man, and Samuel Wilberforce succeeded in taking the lead, but all the bishops were greatly rattled. Even Bishop Hampden of Hereford, who in earlier days had been hunted by the Tractarians as a heretic, now emerged as an extreme champion of orthodoxy. He said that it was a question between Infidelity and Christianity, and that they ought to prosecute. To begin with, an episcopal letter was issued which was intended to reassure the faithful.

One of its signatories was A. C. Tait (1811–82), Bishop of London. It happened that Temple, Jowett, and Stanley, all of whom were old friends of his, had each separately visited him at Fulham Palace not long before, and had got the impression that he more or less agreed with *Essays and Reviews*. They could not understand how he had brought himself to sign a letter which seemed quite inconsistent with all that they knew of him. A long and painful correspondence ensued, particularly between Temple and Tait: it looked as though Tait, who had preceded Temple as Headmaster of Rugby, was lending his name to a public and official censure of his successor.

The bishops held a further meeting and decided to prosecute, but this was more easily said than done. Only Williams and Wilson could be got at in the church courts. Both were accused of denying the inspiration of Scripture, and Wilson was further charged with denying the doctrine of eternal punishment. The two cases were long drawn out, and, to the dismay of conservative churchmen, the sentence of the Court of Arches against Williams and Wilson was reversed on appeal to the Judicial Committee of the Privy

Council. It was of this judgement in February 1864 that a wit remarked that the Lord Chancellor (Westbury) 'dismissed Hell with costs, and took away from orthodox members of the Church of England their last hopes of everlasting damnation'.

Wilberforce now persuaded the bishops to condemn *Essays and Reviews* synodically in Convocation. Of the only two dissentients one was Tait, who by now had recovered some of his independence. Meanwhile, Dr Pusey had entered into an unholy alliance with Lord Shaftesbury and *The Record* newspaper, and had prevailed upon 11,000 clergymen and 137,000 laymen to sign an address in which they declared their

firm belief that the Church of England and Ireland, in common with the whole Catholic Church, maintains without reserve or qualification, the Inspiration and Divine Authority of the whole Canonical Scriptures, as not only containing but being the Word of God; and further teaches, in the Words of our Blessed Lord, that the 'punishment' of the 'cursed' equally with the 'life' of the 'righteous' is 'everlasting'.

The final outcry in this controversy came five years later when Temple was nominated by Mr Gladstone to the bishopric of Exeter. Pusey and Shaftesbury were again united in action to resist the appointment. The whole country was agitated. A bishop wrote to *The Times* newspaper that Temple's appointment was 'a blow from which [the Church of England] may rally for a time, but after which she can never be the same'. Most of the bishops shrank from taking part in Temple's consecration, though Tait, who was now Archbishop, would have done so if he had not been seriously ill at the time.

Temple was no sooner enthroned at Exeter than the storm began to abate. He proved to be an admirable bishop, and before the end of the century became Archbishop of Canterbury. The whole story is a parable of the folly and injustice of reckless ecclesiastical agitations. It should be added that the *Essays and Reviews* controversy had been crossed and intensified by the contemporaneous and complicated case of Bishop Colenso of Natal. So far as the Bible was concerned, the question at issue was much the same, and Colenso's views on the Pentateuch simply added fuel to the flames of a fire that would have blazed away anyhow.

*

The contributors to *Essays and Reviews*, Stanley, and Colenso might all be classified as 'Broad Churchmen', but the term 'Broad Church' is even less specific than High Church or Low Church. Broad Churchmen were not organized as a party, as the Anglo-Catholics and the Evangelicals were. Moreover, for lack of a better word it could be used as a description of any churchmen who did not line up with either of those parties, for example the Cambridge Triumvirate to be mentioned presently.

Stanley was the archetypal Broad Churchman who rejoiced in the title. When he became Dean of Westminster he made it his object to counteract the narrow partisanship which, he thought, was poisoning the life of the Church of England and thwarting its mission to the nation. So, for instance, he invited representatives of all schools of thought to preach in the Abbey, but the High Church leaders – Keble, Pusey, and Liddon – refused, though Pusey with more hesitation than the other two. In their eyes Stanley was damned, because he had befriended Colenso and spoken out against the condemnation of *Essays and Reviews*. He was deemed, in Liddon's words, to have cast in his lot 'with men who are labouring to destroy and blot out the faith of Jesus Christ from the hearts of the English people'.

To say that was certainly unjust to the Broad Church divines. At the same time, there was point in a private note made by Tait, who combined liberality of outlook with deep evangelical conviction:

What is wanted is a deeply religious liberal party. . . . The great evil is that the liberals are deficient in religion, and the religious are deficient in liberality.

But such generalizations are subject to qualification. Stanley, for example, was on any showing a genuinely religious man, but in the case of others like Jowett it did appear that their Christianity was almost entirely moral and intellectual. This consideration goes some way to explain the panic that beset so many devout churchmen.

The most serious attempt made at the time to provide a refutation of *Essays and Reviews* could not command much intellectual respect. It was a symposium entitled *Aids to Faith*, edited by W. Thomson (1819–90), afterwards Archbishop of York. It was a last-ditch endeavour to defend the traditional view of the Bible, the Mosaic authorship and historicity of the Pentateuch, the unity of the creation stories in Genesis I and II, etc. It was left to others to respond to the very reasonable request that had been made by Henry Sidgwick (1838–1900), in a letter to *The Times* newspaper (20 February 1861):

> May I address you a few words, on behalf of the thinking laity of England, upon the much-vexed question of *Essays and Reviews*?
>
> What we all want is, briefly, not a condemnation, but a refutation. The age when ecclesiastical censures were sufficient in such cases has passed away. A large portion of the laity now, though unqualified for abstruse theological investigations, are yet competent to hear and decide on theological arguments. These men will not be satisfied by an *ex cathedra* shelving of the question, nor terrified by a deduction of awful consequences from the new speculations. For philosophy and history alike have taught them to seek not what is 'safe', but what is true.

He cited Westcott as a divine who appreciated this. Of course Pusey and Liddon were not blind to the need to answer the arguments of the biblical critics. Pusey laboured away at a vast work on the Book of Daniel, in order to vindicate its historical character. Liddon delivered his eloquent and impressive Bampton Lectures on *The Divinity of Our Lord* in 1866. But they were both really pre-critical.

Even before the appearance of *Essays and Reviews*, the Cambridge friends, Westcott, Lightfoot, and Hort, had been making plans, at the instance of Macmillan the publisher, for the production of a series of commentaries on the whole of the New Testament with a view to meeting the critics on their own ground. They had hoped that Benson would join them, but he became absorbed in other interests. Lightfoot was to deal with the Pauline Epistles, Hort with the Synoptic Gospels and the Epistles of James, Peter, and Jude, and Westcott with the Johannine literature. This scheme was never completely carried out. Hort, who was an extremely fastidious worker, produced only fragments of his share. But Lightfoot's commentaries on several of St Paul's Epistles, and Westcott's on the Fourth Gospel and also on Hebrews, stand as commentaries of outstanding excellence, though they need now in the nature of the case to be supplemented by the fruits of later knowledge.

The characteristics of their work on the New Testament can be gleaned from a tribute that was paid to Westcott when he succeeded Lightfoot as Bishop of Durham in 1890:

Before all things a Biblical student, bringing to the text of the Bible all the habits and resources of most accurate linguistic scholarship, along with a reverential affection to which no detail, however slight, was insignificant; unsurpassed in his command of all the statistics of text and matter, yet never mastered by them, never mechanical nor dry; resolute in insisting that exegesis must be, first and foremost, historical, yet never content with history as an end in itself; free from all verbal or mechanical ideas of inspiration, yet treating every syllable of Scripture with a reverent care which no maintainer of verbal inspiration could excel.[1]

When *Essays and Reviews* appeared, Westcott was much concerned. He was not sure which he disliked most, the volume itself or the attacks upon it. He was then a master at Harrow, and he wrote to Hort: 'I have not spoken to Lightfoot yet, but I think it is needful to show that there is a mean between *Essays and Reviews* and Traditionalism.' And later he wrote: 'As far as I have seen, those who have written

1. *Durham University Journal.* 10 May 1890. See C. K. Barrett, *Westcott as Commentator.* 1959, p. 2.

against the Essayists have been profoundly ignorant of the difficulties out of which the Essays have sprung.'

Westcott wanted Lightfoot and Hort to collaborate with him in preparing a volume of theological essays, which would serve as an introduction to their projected commentaries, and at the same time would meet the immediate crisis. They would have the incarnation as the centre of theology, and 'on either side the preparation for it, and the apprehension of it in history'. But Lightfoot was unfavourable to this proposal, wanting to get on with his commentaries; so it was abandoned. Westcott approached the Bible not only critically but as witnessing to the whole course of God's self-revelation. 'From first to last,' he said, 'God is seen in the Bible conversing with man.'

He agreed with Jowett that the Bible should be studied and interpreted like any other book, but the phrase meant something different to Westcott. 'It meant that the minutest attention must be paid to every detail, every syllable of the text. All the resources of scholarship must be employed and focused upon each sentence, each clause, each word.'[1] That was not Jowett's method. He did not consider that the language of the New Testament was a precise medium like classical Greek, and his strength did not lie in the minutiae of scholarship. Westcott may have gone to the other extreme: he found so much meaning in every word and phrase that he was reluctant to allow that there were errors in Scripture. Here he differed from Hort whose perception was more acute and who had a greater willingness to acknowledge the human elements in the Bible.

But Westcott differed from Liddon and the Traditionalists in that he did not adhere to the old idea of prophecy as miraculous prediction of long future events. He saw it as the gradual preparation of the world for the revelation of God in Christ. Nor for Westcott were miracles *proofs* of Christ's divinity: they were the natural concomitants of it.

As for Lightfoot, his commentary on Galatians virtually

1. Barrett, op. cit., pp. 13ff.

demolished the theory of Baur and the Tübingen school, which had dated most of the New Testament documents in the second century. He showed that a severely critical and historical study led to conclusions quite different from those that the German critics reached because they started with a theory into which they made the facts fit.

Hort, though he produced little in comparison, is generally reckoned today to have been the greatest theologian of the three. He was without Westcott's timidity, and he was more of a theologian than Lightfoot who was primarily a historian. Hort had the larger reponsibility for Westcott's and Hort's work on the text of the New Testament, destroying the conservative attachment to the *Textus receptus* embodied in the so-called Authorized Version of the Bible, which was still being defended by Dean Burgon.

It was a weakness of the Cambridge Triumvirate that they were so absorbed in New Testament studies that they did not attempt to grapple with the problems raised by the critical study of the Old Testament. Their work on the New Testament represented, of course, only a transitional stage. They did not anticipate future lines of study on the literary relationship and historical character of the Gospels. But they prepared another generation of scholars to proceed further with their methods. In October 1881 a writer in the *Church Quarterly Review* said that the Cambridge school of theology was 'exercising a profound modifying influence upon many of the younger generation of High Churchmen at Cambridge', but it was at Oxford that the most striking attempt was to be made at reconciling this new approach to theology with the Catholic tradition of Anglican churchmanship – as we shall see when we come to 'Lux Mundi'.

12

The English Free Churches

WHAT in England are now known as 'the Free Churches'
have been so called only since the latter part of the nineteenth century. Previously, the terms 'Dissenters' and
'Nonconformists' were most in use. But any generic name
for these Christian communities can obscure the fact that
there are important differences between them: were it not
so, they would doubtless have become fully united. There
is the difference between the Methodists who derive from
the eighteenth-century evangelical revival and the old nonconformists whose separation from the Church of England
stems from the Reformation and the events of the sixteenth
and seventeenth centuries. These comprise the Congregationalists or Independents, the Baptists, and the Presbyterians, with the Quakers and the Unitarians to their left.
There are obvious differences between these bodies which
are signified by their names.

There is also a difference between those nonconformists
who are opposed to a connection between Church and State
on principle, and those who, while not objecting to such a
connection on principle, in practice cannot conscientiously
conform to the actual Church that is established in their
country. The Congregationalists and Baptists belong to the
former class, while the Presbyterians and Methodists, at
least according to their original tradition, are in the latter
case, as is shown, for instance, by the fact that a Presbyterian Church is established in Scotland.

The history of the English Free Churches in the nineteenth
century can be considered under the heads of (1) their
emancipation, (2) their expansion, and (3) their organization. The combined effect of the developments we are to

notice was greatly to enhance their impact on the religious and social life of the nation.

*

The repeal of the Test and Corporation Acts in 1828, while it allowed the right of Dissenters to participate in the government of the country, was only a first step towards the acquisition of the full civil and religious equality which they desired and were justly determined to achieve. The ancient universities were still closed to them. They could not be married in their own chapels, or buried except in church-yards with the rites of the Church of England. They were compelled to pay church rates for the support of the Established Church of which they conscientiously disapproved. The measures of 1828 opened a door which could lead to the removal of these disabilities, but did no more than open a door.

Again, it might be supposed that the repeal of the Test and Corporation Acts would have improved the relations between the Dissenters and the Established Church, but it was the contrary that happened. It was rightly apprehended by the Dissenters that the Established Church would cling tenaciously to its other traditional privileges and resist further concessions. On the other hand, now that the Dissenters had won the first round in their struggle for emancipation, they had no disposition to pull their punches, or any longer to conceal or play down their hostility to the Church by law established. Moreover, the Reform Act of 1832, which was carried by their allies the Whigs, gave them substantial representation in parliament and encouraged them to press on hard and quickly for the redress of their other grievances. Since the Established Church was the chief obstacle in the way, it was natural that a strong attack should be made on the Establishment itself which, as we have seen, was on other counts in an exceedingly vulnerable position at this time, i.e. before the reforms that were initiated by the Ecclesiastical Commission. Without those reforms, it is more than probable that the Establishment would have been overthrown.

But, once church reform had been set in motion, the Church itself was in a stronger position to withstand attacks. The conservatism of the English, which is always tougher than eager radicals expect, reasserted itself, and anyhow conservative forces were still firmly entrenched in the centres of power. The hostility that had been shown to the Establishment was calculated to rally churchmen to a dogged defence of their remaining privileges and traditions. These circumstances explain why the relations between the Church and dissent, so far from being improved, were embittered, and why the granting of full equality was so long delayed. While sheer attachment to power and privilege was doubtless the most potent cause of the reluctance of churchmen to recognize the rights of nonconformity, it should also be remembered that the old idea or principle that unity of religion is a requisite for the moral health and social cohesion of a nation retained its hold on many Anglican minds: nonconformity was an evil that might be tolerated if need be, but it remained an evil that should not be countenanced any more than was necessary.

Now let us briefly notice how nonconformist disabilities were removed or, to put it positively, the stages by which religious equality was realized. The only grievance to be redressed with comparative ease and promptitude was the requirement that marriages should be solemnized only in the Church of England. The effect of two Bills, passed into law without a division in 1836, was to permit marriages to be celebrated in duly licensed chapels: indeed provision was also made for purely civil marriage. The other matters gave rise to protracted contention.

Church rates. As the law stood, every parish was bound to maintain the fabric of the parish church, and the churchwardens and parishioners, in vestry assembled, were entitled from time to time to levy a rate which all rate-payers were bound to pay – not only for the upkeep of the fabric, but for the maintenance of church services, and the payment of officials, e.g. the parish clerk. The first Bill to abolish church rates was brought forward in 1834, but, though a whole series of Bills was introduced in the intervening years, it was not till *thirty-four* years later, in 1868, that compulsory church rates were abolished. Various compromises had been suggested from time to time, but the conservatives always treated any concession as though it would be a move in the direction of disestablishing the Church. Where the Dissenters were strong enough to do so, they forced the injustice of their position on public attention by frustrating the operation of the law and taking the consequences. One notorious case at Braintree in Essex resulted in legal proceedings that went on for sixteen years! There were other cases in which nonconformists were sent to prison for contempt of court.

Burials. Until 1852 there were no public burial grounds except the churchyards. In that year an Act was passed which enabled Corporations to provide municipal cemeteries. But this relieved the situation only in populous or urban districts. Nothing was done to remove the grievance that was felt by nonconformists in all the villages of England. Year after year a Bill was brought forward in parliament that would allow Dissenters to be buried in churchyards by one of their own ministers. But it was again and again defeated. The parish clergy were violently hostile to the proposal. Not until 1880 was an Act passed which gave the desired permission. Archbishop Tait supported the Bill and incurred the wrath of the clergy for doing so. A bishop wrote to him that 'a general reign of sacrilege and confusion would result'; and a clergyman wrote:

The measure looks simple, but is an artful, treacherous, and insidious blow at Episcopacy, abolishing the consecration of the Bishops, the Holy Orders of the clergy, and the authority of the Book of Common Prayer. I am astonished to think that your Grace can expect an honest measure from infidels and heretics, and I implore you, as your Grace would tender the love of the great

Head of the Church, to pluck up courage and strangle this young viper of heresy and schism.

This is not an exceptional illustration of the acrimony that this very reasonable reform aroused.

Education. The quest for religious equality in the field of education has a more complicated history, and one may say that it is not yet complete. In the early part of the nineteenth century it was common ground to both churchmen and non-conformists that it was the task not of the State, but of the Church and voluntary agencies, to provide education. But eventually both had to acknowledge that the education of the whole people was beyond their resources, and that the State would have to undertake the responsibility. The Forster Education Act of 1870 set up Board Schools, side by side with existing voluntary schools. What religious instruction, if any, was to be given in them? Anglicans wanted definite church teaching, while nonconformists would have preferred a secular system leaving religious instruction to be given outside school. A compromise had to be accepted which allowed undenominational religious instruction or 'simple Bible teaching' and forbade the use of any distinctive formulary, for example the Church Catechism. This arrangement, which was strengthened by the Butler Education Act of 1944, has continued to be a feature of the English educational system, although it is constantly being called in question.

In 1902, when a Conservative government favoured the Church of England, which owned the great majority of voluntary schools, by putting them on the rates, Free Churchmen not only protested but launched a movement of passive resistance to the payment of rates that were to be used for denominational purposes, and sympathy for their cause certainly contributed to the sweeping victory of the Liberal party in the General Election of 1906.

Proposals to admit nonconformists to the ancient universities by the abolition of religious tests met with prolonged opposition. Dreadful prognostications were entertained about the results of throwing the universities open to men of any religion or none. When in 1854 parliament passed the first of the measures that were to terminate the Church of England's monopoly of Oxford and Cambridge (religious tests for college fellowships were not abolished till 1871), Burgon expressed in extravagant terms what more sober divines like Pusey and Liddon felt no less keenly:

Oxford, I fear, has seen her best days. Her sun has set and for ever. She never more can be what she has been – the great nursery of the Church. She will become a cage of unclean beasts at last. Of course we shall not live to see it; but *our great-grandchildren will :* and the Church (and Oxford itself) will rue the day when its liberties and its birthright were lost by a licentious vote of a *no longer Christian* House of Commons.[1]

It will be readily understood that the manifestation of such sentiments (for they were not only whispered in the closet), in conjunction with the long refusal of churchmen to concede what seemed to be the logical corollaries of the measures of 1828, sharpened and inflamed the will of militant dissent to bring about the downfall of the Establishment. The body that was most active in this campaign was 'The British Anti-State Church Association', which was formed in 1844, and was renamed in 1853 'The Society for the Liberation of Religion from State Patronage and Control'; it became known simply as 'The Liberation Society'. Its moving spirit was Edward Miall (1809–81) who edited a paper called *The Nonconformist* and took care that the demand for disestablishment was constantly before the public. The paper kept up a highly effective exposure of abuses in the Establishment.

There were times when the disestablishment of the Church of England looked like coming to the front in politics, notably when Mr Gladstone carried the disestablishment of the Church of Ireland in 1869 – regarded by many of his followers and of his opponents as only a

1. See E. M. Goulburn. *Life of Dean Burgon.* 1892, 1, 283.

beginning. Joseph Chamberlain and Sir Charles Dilke, who seemed likely to succeed to the leadership of the Liberal party, were both keen disestablishmentarians, and in the 1870s and early 1880s there was growing pressure in that direction. But thereafter it was never so strong again. Chamberlain broke with the Liberal party over Irish Home Rule and Dilke's career was ruined by a notorious divorce case. When the Liberal party was returned with an overwhelming majority in 1906, it proceeded no further than to disestablish the Welsh Church, and there the matter has rested. In the twentieth century some Anglicans have been more urgent advocates of the disestablishment of the Church of England than Free Churchmen: but it has never been a live political issue. The bitterness that beset the road to religious equality in the nineteenth century has to a large extent been replaced by cordiality, mutual sympathy, and cooperation.

*

About the expansion of the Free Churches in the nineteenth century less need be said, though it was of course more important. They all shared in the general religious prosperity of the Victorian age. Chapels were built in profusion in town and country and they were thronged with worshippers. For instance, between 1812 and 1836 the number of both Independent and Baptist congregations in England and Wales more than doubled. The repeal of the Test and Corporation Acts, the campaign for the removal of their other disabilities, and the after-effects of the evangelical revival, all stimulated the zeal of the nonconformists. It was an age of great nonconformist preaching: Charles Haddon Spurgeon (1834–92) was the greatest in a great galaxy. Then, the larger scope that the Free Churches gave to lay participation and responsibility and to individual enterprise geared in better with the temper of the times than the conservative clericalism of the Established Church. The nonconformists were more in tune with the advancing liberalism of the period, and they were a political, as well as a religious and moral, power to be reckoned with.

*

This will become clearer if we turn to the development of their organizations. This was a feature even of Congregationalism, which was naturally suspicious of any organization beyond that of the local church itself. Each local church depended directly on Christ its Head. But as the Independent churches grew in number, the question inevitably arose how they were to cherish their fellowship with one another and to combine in witnessing to their principles. Before 1830 some steps had been taken to meet these objects through County Associations. The growing complexity of industrial society and the evident advantages of organization in other Christian bodies pointed to the need for closer unity and cooperation. So the Congregational Union of England and Wales was founded, though it was not at first assured of anything like general support.

However, it proved its utility, e.g. by publishing a hymn book and other literature that would be beyond the capacity of any local congregation, also in organizing home and foreign missions, promoting the building of new chapels, etc. The headquarters of the Union were eventually established in an imposing building in the City of London, known as the Memorial Hall, where the Secretary of the Union acquired a status similar to that of the principal officers of other denominations. Congregationalists sometimes lament that, notwithstanding the obvious advantages of this development, they are now hardly less immune than other Churches from the concomitants of a centralized bureaucracy.

The Baptists stood nearest to the Congregationalists: both stemmed from the left wing of the Reformation. They differed obviously about the doctrine and practice of baptism, and the Baptists tended to be connectional rather than independent in their church order. In the eighteenth century they had been weakened by internal divisions, but from the beginning of the nineteenth they steadily advanced. Whereas in 1801 they had only 652 buildings, by 1851 they had 2,789. But there was still a division between the General and Particular Baptists, the former being Arminians and the latter high Calvinists. Nevertheless, as the century drew on they were drawn together. The Baptist Union was founded in 1813, and served as a meeting-ground for both denominations. With the decline of high Calvinism their views about predestination ceased to diverge, and the question of open or closed communion (that is, should all believers be welcomed to communion, or only those who had been baptized by immersion?) was no longer an obstacle to unity. Open communion steadily gained ground among the Particular Baptists, though a minority dissented and formed a sect known as the Strict and Particular Baptists. In 1891 the General and Particular Baptists were fused in one organization and since 1903 there has been a Baptist Church House in London, the counterpart of the Congregationalists' Memorial Hall and the Anglicans' Church House, Westminster.

As regards the Presbyterians, who had been a powerful force in the seventeenth century but had declined in numbers and become unitarians for the most part in the eighteenth, there were very few of them at the beginning of our period. The present-day Presbyterian Church of England, which has close associations with the Church of Scotland, was constituted in 1876. Though much smaller in membership than the other Free Churches, it enjoys a high prestige, not least because of the quality of its ministerial education. In Wales Presbyterianism received a new lease of life through the Calvinistic Methodist wing of the evangelical revival.

During the nineteenth century the fortunes of Methodism fluctuated. At first the almost despotic control which Jabez Bunting[1] exercised over the Wesleyans had a consolidating

1. See p. 41.

effect. He was the virtual founder of the Methodist Missionary Society and he did much to improve the education of
ministers. But after 1830 his autocratic methods began to
be resented, and in the 1840s there was a violent feud
between his supporters and his critics. This was known as
the Fly-sheets controversy, and it had discrediting and
disastrous consequences. It is estimated that Wesleyanism
lost 100,000 members at this time, and there was a legacy
of bitterness that was not easily lived down.

However, the second half of the century produced a new
leader, equal in stature to Bunting but very different in
character and policy. This was Hugh Price Hughes (1847–
1902), a Welshman, who combined with Celtic fervour
natural gifts of the first order. He had prophetic passion,
was fluent and courageous in speech and debate, and an
accomplished journalist. His paper *The Methodist Times* had
a weekly circulation of 24,000. He played a leading part in
the 'Forward Movement' by means of which Methodism
rallied its forces and made fresh conquests.

Perhaps his principal achievement was to convince
Methodists that Christianity was a *social* gospel. He assimilated and extended the teaching of the Christian Socialists.
He and those who worked with him weaned Wesleyanism
from its original Toryism, and aligned the Methodists with
the other nonconformists behind Gladstonian Liberalism.
He also espoused the cause of Methodist unity and was the
herald of the union of the Wesleyan, Primitive, and United
Methodists which finally came into being in 1932. More
than anyone else he was the mouthpiece of 'the nonconformist conscience', which had as its principle the maxim
that what is morally wrong cannot be politically right. The
nonconformist conscience made itself felt as a power in the
land in regard to such matters as temperance and the drink
trade, standards of moral purity, educational equality,
horse-racing and gambling. It was Hughes who said of Lord
Rosebery that the nonconformist conscience would not
tolerate a racing premier.

The most conspicuous instance of its power was seen in its sealing the fate of Parnell, the leader of the Irish Home Rule party. When in 1890 he was found guilty of adultery, the Irish party wanted to stand by him and he himself was determined to stay on. But Hughes made up his mind that Parnell must go. He considered it intolerable that a morally compromised leader should be retained. So he launched a campaign to bring about his downfall, and it is said that it was the pressure of the nonconformists that made Mr Gladstone, who had at first thought Parnell should stay at his post, change his mind.

Whether Hughes was justified in this case is another question. This may be an illustration of the fact that the formula 'what is morally wrong can never be politically right' is too simple. The essence of politics is largely the art of compromise. The point is however that for good or ill the nonconformist conscience was a potent influence in British politics in the late nineteenth and early twentieth centuries when the power of the Free Churches was at its height.

Hughes also did much to promote closer fellowship between all the Free Churches. There had previously been some abortive attempts to bring nonconformists together on a more positive basis than that of the Liberation Society. In the 1860s the success of the Anglican Church Congresses suggested that nonconformity might adopt the same method of combining for witness to the Gospel. But nothing then came of it.

Not until 1892 was the first Free Church Congress held. It had 370 members drawn from ten nonconformist bodies. Many leading nonconformists however were conspicuous by their absence, in particular Robert William Dale (1829–95), the revered Congregationalist leader, who feared that nonconformists were going to organize themselves for political purposes, and even as a political party, whereas he held that it was the task of the Churches to make individual Christians who would be socially and politically responsible. But Hughes and others tirelessly advocated the cause of Free

Church unity with a view to wider hopes of Christian reunion, and the movement gathered momentum.

The Free Church Congress was transformed in 1896 into
a more permanent organization, known as the National
Council of Evangelical Free Churches. Its declared aim was
positive, not negative, that is it was not identified with the
Liberation Society's attack on the establishment of the
Church of England. It was not *against* the Establishment
but *for* the Evangel. The definite adoption of the title
'Evangelical Free Churches' was evidence of this. From now
onwards, there was a steady increase in collaboration
between the Free Churches, not only nationally but also
locally through the formation of Local Free Church Councils.
In 1919 a further step forward was taken when the Federal
Council of the Evangelical Free Churches was formed. But
by that time the movement towards Free Church unity
in England was coming to be bound up with something
altogether larger – what is now called the Ecumenical
Movement.

13

The Pontificate of Pius IX

ON New Year's Day 1860, Mr Disraeli wrote to Mrs Brydges Willyams: 'Only think of our living to see the Pope on his last legs – and to be betrayed, too, by "the eldest son of the Church"! A great Roman Catholic lady told me yesterday that the truth was too obvious; mankind would no longer endure clerical authority.' It did look as though the papacy was on its last legs. In the previous year most of the papal states had been overrun by the army of Victor Emmanuel II, King of Sardinia, with the connivance of Napoleon III, 'the eldest son of the Church', and in the following year Victor Emmanuel was proclaimed King of Italy. The pope's temporal power seemed to be doomed, and in fact it was doomed, though the final act did not take place till 1870.

It must be remembered that in the nineteenth century the pope himself, and the vast majority of Roman Catholics, regarded the temporal power as vitally necessary to the proper functioning of the papacy as a spiritual authority. Pius IX used to describe the papal states as 'the robe of Jesus Christ'. If he had to preside over their liquidation, it would be with the dispositions of a martyr. It is difficult even for Roman Catholics to recapture now the feelings of that time, and this is one circumstance that makes a sympathetic judgement of Pio Nono difficult.

It has been generally supposed that after a rash flirtation with liberal ideas he became for the rest of his life a blind and obstinate opponent of every kind of reform, and left the papacy to his successor at the nadir of its fortunes. On the other hand, Cardinal Manning predicted that 'when the history of the Pontificate of Pius IX shall be written, it will be found to have been one of the most resplendent, majestic, and powerful – one that has reached over the whole extent of the Church with greater power than that of any other Pope in the whole succession'. Where lies the truth?

About one thing there is little room for disagreement, the charm of Pio Nono's character. This tribute from Newman, who had no great opinion of his sagacity, seems to have been thoroughly deserved:

His personal presence was of a kind that no one could withstand. . . . The main cause of his popularity was the magic of his presence. . . . His uncompromising faith, his courage, the graceful mingling in him of the human and the divine, the humour, the wit, the playfulness with which he tempered his severity, his naturalness, and then his true eloquence.

One of Pio Nono's most engaging characteristics was the personal affection and solicitude he showed towards those whom officially he could not help looking upon as his worst enemies, for example Cavour, Victor Emmanuel, and Napoleon III.

As regards the pope's intelligence and the wisdom of his policies during his long and eventful reign (he had a longer tenure of the papal throne than any of his predecessors), few now would dissent from Metternich's opinion that he was warm-hearted but of poor intelligence. Unlike many of the popes, he had had no political or diplomatic training worth mentioning; he knew little of the world; he had only once been outside the papal states. These were serious handicaps for a pope who had to guide the Church in a time of revolutionary change and through an epoch-making political crisis.

The policies of Pius IX can be considered under three heads, though they are interrelated: his attitude to the *risorgimento*, that is, the movement for the unification of Italy; his reaction to European liberalism generally; and his promotion of ultramontanism in the Church.

*

It is conceivable that Pio Nono might have become the first President of a democratic federation of Italian States. This

..a was in the air during the first two years of his pontificate and it was advocated by the influential liberal Catholic, Vincenzo Gioberti (1801–52). From 1846 to 1848 Pius IX appeared in the guise of a reforming pope and was the idol of the Italian nationalists. 'A pretty state we are in altogether,' wrote Robert Wilberforce to J. B. Mozley in 1848, 'with a Radical Pope teaching all Europe rebellion.' R. W. Church, on a visit to Italy at this time, noted: 'the enthusiasm of the population for Pio Nono is quite medieval: they can talk of nothing else; "Viva Pio Nono" was written over almost every door in the little towns I passed through – and there is no title too grand for him in the various inscriptions in his honour.' But the dream of an Italian federation under the pope was shattered by the events of 1848, when Rome fell into the hands of the revolutionaries and Pio Nono had to flee. In any case it is hard to believe that he could have collaborated for long with the more extreme Italian liberals like Mazzini and Garibaldi. Their religious positions were irreconcilable, and Pio Nono was above all things a man of religion.

The pope's attitude to the *risorgimento* thus runs out into the larger question of his attitude to liberalism generally, to all the reforming and radical ideas and movements of the age, to all the forces in Europe that had sprung from the French Revolution. The word 'liberalism' has many shades of meaning. Broadly speaking, in the nineteenth century Liberals were those people who were in favour of the new kind of state and society that had issued from the Revolution. They were in favour of constitutional and representative governments, of religious toleration, and of the separation of Church and State ('a free Church in a free State' was the slogan of both Cavour and Montalembert). Liberals were in fact for liberty all round: liberty of the press, of association, of education, etc.

At the opposite pole were those who, like de Maistre and his disciples, regarded all these libertarian ideas as subversive of law and order, as bound to lead to anarchy and tyranny, and as the outcome of rejecting the Christian doctrine of authority in Church and State. These anti-Liberals wanted to restore the firm alliance of Church and State, with its supervision of morals and its suppression of error. Christianity and Liberalism, therefore, appeared to be fundamentally incompatible, and the Christians and the Liberals ranged themselves in opposite camps. Having done so, they naturally became more and more hostile and uncomprehending in their attitude to each other. The battle between clericalism and anti-clericalism was joined. It did not occur to either side to inquire whether its opponents might not be standing for some principles that were vital for social and political health.

If it be allowed that the Liberals were right in standing for free institutions and in attacking authoritarianism, it must be said that they were too optimistic and idealistic – though they were not all as simple-minded as they are often now made out to be. But they did tend to assume that, once men had been set free and given an opportunity of education, everything in the garden would be lovely. The natural perfectibility of human nature, the inevitability of progress, a vaguely conceived utopia on earth, and romantic notions about nationality – such ideas captivated their imaginations. The Christian tradition had something to teach them with its sombre realism about the finitude of earthly existence and the egotism that is native to mankind, with its witness to a God, who is transcendent over the world and not merely immanent in the process of evolution, and to a moral authority, to which all nations and earthly potentates – democratic majorities as well as absolute kings – are subject at last.

On the other hand, the Church had much to learn from the Liberals, for they realized that man was coming of age and that the time for keeping him in political and ecclesiastical tutelage was passing. The Church needed to learn that liberty was a more wholesome air for Christianity itself to breathe than authoritarianism. It would be unjust to put all, or most, of the blame for the conflict between the Church and Liberalism on the shoulders of Pius IX. He maintained the tradition he had inherited. It would have been a miracle if he had suddenly reconciled the Church with the cause of freedom for all. Churches do not change their outlook or their orientation overnight, nor do they usually give up positions of power and privilege, however obsolete these may be, until they are compelled to do so.

What Pius IX can be blamed for is that he failed to read the signs of the times. He failed to perceive that the Church had got to adjust itself to new political realities, and also that it would be in a stronger position without the exclusive privileges and archaic institutions to which it had clung for too long. A wise pope would have set himself prudently to educate the Church into an understanding of its new historic environment, and he would have encouraged those groups in the Church, the so-called Liberal Catholics, who were seeking to reconcile what was best in the old order with what was best in the new.

As it was, Pius IX treated the Liberal Catholics as traitors in the camp and thwarted their endeavours all along the line. In France, for example, he supported the fanatical authoritarianism of Louis Veuillot and the *Univers* against the attempts of Montalembert, Lacordaire, Dupanloup, and others to identify the cause of the Church with that of liberty. It was in France that the conflict between the ultra-montane or integrist Catholics and the Liberal Catholics was most conspicuous and persistent. In Italy there were some Liberal Catholics even after 1848, but they were regarded by Pius IX as being willing to abandon the temporal power of the papacy and therefore as being accomplices of his most dangerous foes.

Liberal Catholicism in Germany and England was more intellectual than political. It was concerned with meeting the need for a new presentation of the Catholic faith in the light of philosophical and scientific thought and for a more critical reckoning with the facts of history. Dr Döllinger

(1799–1890) was the centre of a school of Catholic theologians and historians at Munich who sought to apply the same critical standards in their work as their Protestant neighbours did. In England the group of Roman Catholics associated with Lord Acton (1834–1902), in the conduct of a journal called *The Rambler*, and subsequently *The Home and Foreign Review*, took an advanced and independent line on many subjects. But they were always under suspicion at Rome.

All these Liberal Catholic groups and tendencies were sharply condemned in 1864 in the encyclical *Quanta cura* and the *Syllabus Errorum*, in which Pius summed up the teaching of his pontificate against modern errors. He had contemplated the issue of such a document for a long time, in fact ever since his definition of the dogma of the Immaculate Conception of the Blessed Virgin in 1854, but for various reasons the project had hung fire. Two events in 1863 helped to precipitate matters. One was an outspoken Liberal Catholic oration by Montalembert at an international congress organized by the Belgian Catholics at Malines, which was enthusiastically received there, but infuriated the intransigents and greatly annoyed the pope. The other was the appearance in France of Renan's *Vie de Jésus* which the intransigents declared to be a scandalous publication that ought to have been suppressed by the government.

The encyclical and Syllabus were promulgated in December 1864. The Syllabus was based on a selection of Pius IX's previous allocutions. It was an over-all condemnation in the most unqualified terms of rationalism, indifferentism, socialism, communism, naturalism, freemasonry, separation of Church and State, liberty of the press, liberty of religion, culminating in the famous denial that 'the Roman pontiff can and ought to reconcile himself and reach agreement with progress, liberalism and modern civilization'. It seemed that the pope had declared war on modern society in all its aspects. While the extreme ultramontanes were enchanted, most Catholics were disconcerted and did not know what to make of it, while the anti-clerical press did not conceal its delight at this manifestation of what Catholicism was really like. Diplomatic protests poured into Rome, and also requests from Catholics that some reassuring explanation should be forthcoming, since they found themselves unable to justify what the pope had said.

It was at this juncture that Mgr Dupanloup produced a brochure in which he explained away the *prima facie* impression that the Syllabus gave. He drew upon the distinction that was just coming into use between the *thesis* and the *hypothesis*. The thesis was what was ideally desirable in the abstract: the hypothesis was the right thing to do in the actual circumstances. The Syllabus, Dupanloup argued, had to do with the thesis: it was not dealing with the actual state of affairs or with the policy of Catholics in the modern world. This ingenious theory was received with much relief by puzzled Catholics, and the pope himself, who had been taken aback by the violent reactions he had provoked, allowed it to pass as a legitimate construction. The Parisian intellectuals, however, made fun of it: asked what was the distinction between the thesis and the hypothesis, they replied – alluding to the worldly manner of life of the papal nuncio in Paris – 'It is the thesis when the nuncio says that the Jews ought to be burnt; it is the hypothesis when he goes out to dinner with M. de Rothschild!'

The true explanation of the extreme language of the Syllabus is that the pope and his advisers had their attention fixed on the threat to the temporal power of the papacy and on the Italian Liberals who were the spearhead of the attack upon it. The pope wanted to condemn in unequivocal terms the doctrines on which he conceived this threat to be based. If some of the denunciations are studied in their original context, their effect is somewhat mitigated. All the same, the general public was to be pardoned if it could not make allowances of that kind. The Syllabus is the supreme instance of Pio Nono's ineptitude and of his failure to discriminate between what was true and false in 'Liberalism'.

It is only fair to add that at the end of his life he had the candour to admit his limitations: shortly before his death he is reported to have made this confession:

I hope my successor will be as much attached to the Church as I have been and will have as keen a desire to do good: beyond that, I can see that everything has changed; my system and my policies have had their day, but I am too old to change my course; that will be the task of my successor.

But we have still to consider the positive side of his policy, which was the promotion of ultramontanism. Since in Pio Nono's view there could be no reconciliation between the Church and the modern world, the Church had evidently to close its ranks and to brace itself for a long struggle. It must be made capable of defending itself against all the encroachments of Liberalism and what have since been called the acids of modernity. Wilfrid Ward put the case thus: 'Pius IX took up the position that Christendom had apostatized. The appropriate action of Catholics was intense loyalty to the central power, unity among themselves, and separation from the outside world.'

Pio Nono was peculiarly qualified to promote loyalty to the papacy as the centre of the Church. He was, as we have seen, personally most attractive and, unlike many popes, he enjoyed social life and made himself easily accessible to all who visited Rome. He spent many hours a day in giving audiences to individuals and to groups. His charm and spontaneity won him passionate affection, all the more so on account of his sufferings and political adversities which gave him the halo of a martyr. The mystique about the Holy Father, and what often seems an unwholesome adulation of his person, date from Pius IX. When a French priest visited Rome in 1842, he had been struck by the fact that when the pope went by, you need not even bother to raise your hat. It was Pio Nono who created and encouraged that intense veneration for the Vicar of Christ which has been until recently such a striking feature of modern Roman Catholicism.

The devotion to the pope went to such lengths that an

Archbishop of Reims described it as 'an idolatry of the papacy'. The pope was spoken of as 'the vice-God of humanity'. Hymns, which in the breviary were addressed to God, were addressed to Pius IX. A Jesuit review, which he patronized, explained that when the pope meditated God was thinking in him, and a leading French ultramontane bishop spoke of him as the continuation of the Incarnate Word. The prevalence of these sentiments explains in part the ease with which the clergy and the faithful rallied to Pio Nono's leadership and accepted his teaching.

But there were of course many propagators of ultramontanism. Outside Italy, there were Louis Veuillot and those for whom he spoke in France, and Manning and W. G. Ward in England. It was Ward who said he would like to have a papal bull every day with his *Times* at breakfast. These ardent ultramontanes denounced all who did not go along with them as disloyal and as minimizers. Considerable courage was required to resist this kind of pressure. In any attempt to understand the first Vatican Council which was the climax of the ultramontane movement, it is important to bear in mind that this extravagant cult of the Holy Father was being widely cultivated in the Church, and that anyone who criticized it was liable to be pilloried in the ultramontane press as faithless and no true Catholic.

*

When, soon after the promulgation of the Syllabus in 1864, Pius announced that he was contemplating the summoning of a General Council, the Liberal Catholics were pleased: indeed, they had urged the holding of a Council before the pope had shown his hand. They thought that the pope would be shown not to be the sole authority in the Church and that the bishops in council would check the advance of ultramontanism. But they soon saw reason for alarm, especially when in February 1869 a quasi-official organ of the Holy See published an article in which these words occurred:

All genuine Catholics believe that the Council will be quite short. . . . They will receive with joy the proclamation of the dogmatic infallibility of the sovereign pontiff. It is not at all surprising that, from a feeling of proper reserve, Pius IX does not want to take the initiative himself in proposing what seems to concern him directly, but it is hoped that the unanimous revelation of the Holy Spirit, by the mouth of the Fathers of the ecumenical council, will define it by acclamation.

This was the first plain indication that the dogma of papal infallibility was going to be brought forward. There were three main parties in the Roman Church as regards this question: first, there were the ultramontanes who wanted as extreme a definition as could be compassed; secondly, there were those like Döllinger who were opposed to the doctrine on historical and theological grounds; and thirdly, there were those described as 'inopportunists': they did not deny the doctrine if it were properly qualified, but they considered that it was inopportune to define it under existing conditions. This last was the position of the minority at Vatican I; the anti-infallibilists were hardly represented at it.

The inopportunists forced the organizers of the Council to realize that any project for carrying papal infallibility by acclamation would not be feasible. When the Council met at the end of 1869, it was given the task of preparing a comprehensive statement of Roman Catholic teaching, which would be debated and take a long time. When however the prospect of completing this task became very uncertain by reason of the political situation, the question of papal infallibility was brought forward so that the controversy which was now raging about it could be settled before the Council had to adjourn.

The inopportunist minority put up a stout resistance. While they did not succeed in preventing the definition, they did succeed in getting it qualified in a manner that was not at all to the liking of the extreme ultramontanes. Even so, they refused to vote for the decree, but rather than cause scandal by voting against it they left Rome the day before: about sixty bishops did this. Thus when the final voting took place in St Peter's on 18 July 1870, amid a terrific thunder-storm, 533 voted for the decree, and only two against.

On the following day war was declared between France and Prussia. At the beginning of August the French troops were withdrawn from Rome. Early in September the Italian armies invaded the pope's territory, and later in the month the city capitulated, the kingdom of Italy was established, and the temporal power of the papacy was at an end. In these circumstances it was impossible for the Council to continue its work, so it was adjourned *sine die*.

The Vatican decrees were violently attacked after the Council, not least by Mr Gladstone. Many controversialists spread the idea that it had been conducted in a most unscrupulous fashion. But it is now clear that there was ample scope for free discussion, and that the minority was not brow-beaten. No doubt there was much intrigue behind the scenes, but no more than is customary, and perhaps inevitable, in ecclesiastical assemblies. It is true that the pope himself did before the end make the mistake of bring-ing his personal influence to bear, but the outcome would probably have been what it was without his intervention.

What Pio Nono will have to answer for at the bar of his-tory is not his conduct at the Vatican Council but his reading or misreading of the signs of the times. His whole policy was calculated to make the Roman Church a close corporation. As J. B. Mozley said, 'Close corporations are proverbially inaccessible to new ideas, and blind to new facts; they are averse to any enlargement of mind from without, and their natural tendency is to be the whole world to themselves.'

It is not so much the decree about papal infallibility, which is susceptible of varying interpretations, but the whole strategy of Pius IX's pontificate that left its impress on the Roman Church for generations to come. Some of his successors, notably Leo XIII, had a more open or friendly attitude to the modern world, but there was no substantial change in the authoritarian pattern which he had canonized until the dramatic reign of John XXIII.

14

Ritualism and Prayer Book Revision

In 1863 Dean Stanley on a visit to Rome had a private
interview with Pio Nono. As they parted, the Pope said to
him: 'You know Pusey? When you meet him, give him this
message from me – that I compare him to a bell, which
always sounds to invite the faithful to Church, and itself
always remains outside.' Many Englishmen would have
relished this remark, for there was a widespread suspicion
that Puseyism or Anglo-Catholicism or Ritualism (as it was
now commonly called) was an attempt to romanize the
Church of England. While much of the excitement that was
engendered by this suspicion seems in retrospect to have been
occasioned by trivialities, it played a large part in English
church history during much of the nineteenth and the early
twentieth centuries, and it is necessary to understand what
all the commotion was about.

The Oxford movement in its first phase was not ritualistic,
i.e. concerned to introduce new forms of service or ceremonial. The original Tractarians were quite content with
the Book of Common Prayer, and were punctilious in
observing its directions. They appeared as restorers of the
old ways, not as innovators. It was not until about 1840
that Tractarianism began to have a startling impact on the
worship and adornment of parish churches by the introduction of unfamiliar rites and ceremonies. Only a handful of
churches was affected at first, but as time went on, the con-
tagion of Ritualism spread to most parts of the country and
became a source of hotter and hotter controversy. Ritualism
had many degrees or gradations, and only comparatively
few High Churchmen went all the way with it. Its outward
and visible manifestations can be listed as follows: altar
lights, vestments, wafer bread, the mixed chalice (mixing a

little water with the wine at the communion), making the sign of the cross, incense, genuflexions, preaching in a surplice instead of a black gown, surpliced choirs, much singing and chanting, the use of holy water, fixed stone altars instead of movable wooden ones, crucifixes and statues, cultus of the Virgin Mary and Saints, reservation and adoration of the eucharistic sacrament, and auricular confession. Some of these, for example surpliced choirs, were eventually adopted almost universally in the Church of England, but most continued to be peculiar marks of Anglo-Catholicism.

It would be tedious to trace in detail the controversies about Ritualism and the measures that were used to attempt its suppression. It is more worthwhile to distinguish the causes that gave rise to it and then the motives that prompted the opposition to it.

In the first place, the Oxford movement had brought to life the idea of the Church as a sacred mystery, a holy fellowship, and in particular the seriousness and solemnity of its worship and sacramental ordinances. It was almost inevitable that those who had learned this lesson from the Tractarians should want to enact it in the form and manner of the church services and to revive as much as possible of traditional Catholic worship. This might take the form either of recovering the ceremonial of the pre-Reformation Church in England or of appropriating or adapting the ceremonial of the modern Roman Church in the spirit of W. G. Ward. Some Anglo-Catholics favoured one of these courses, and some the other, and the difference between them persisted until the second half of the twentieth century when Rome itself threw its imitators into disarray.

A second cause of the extension of Ritualism was that many priests in the Tractarian tradition went to work in the slums, where the conditions of life were terribly drab, colourless, and depressing. The conventional worship of the Church of England seemed much too dull and cold and reserved to appeal to, or to mean much to, people living in those conditions. Anyhow they were people who could learn much more through the eye than through the ear. It was common sense to bring home to them the meaning of the Church and sacraments through every artifice of colour, music, and dramatic action. The Ritualist slum priests were often men of wonderful devotion and heroic sanctity, who burned themselves out in the service of the poor and outcast. Their flocks responded warmly to the kind of churchmanship that was commended to them by lives of such disinterested service.

Thirdly, it was found to be arguable that many ritualistic practices, although they seemed unfamiliar and unanglican, were in fact legal – not only permissible but actually ordered in the formularies of the Church rightly understood, for example by the so-called Ornaments Rubric in the Book of Common Prayer. The legal decisions that were given on this subject varied, and it was easy for the Ritualists to believe that the decisions unfavourable to themselves were due to Protestant prejudice. The persuasion that the law, properly understood, was on their side, enabled them with a good conscience to persist with ritualistic practices, when bishops and others tried to stop them.

Fourthly, the archaeological element in the Oxford movement, which in fact owed more to Cambridge, favoured the spread of Ritualism. The revived interest in church architecture and furnishing, and the desire to restore the parish churches of England to what was supposed to be more or less their original state, had the effect of making people want to adorn churches as they had been adorned in the Middle Ages and to use them for the rites and ceremonies for which they had been designed.

A fifth circumstance that played a part in the growth of Ritualism was the revival of religious communities for men and women in the Church of England.[1] One of their primary works was the daily worship of God in a round of liturgical offices. It was soon found that the Prayer Book

1. See P. F. Anson. *The Call of the Cloister.* 1955; A. M. Allchin. *The Silent Rebellion.* 1958.

made inadequate provision for the worship of a monastic community, so the tendency was to enrich it with material that could be borrowed from pre-Reformation or Roman Catholic sources.

It must be emphasized that Ritualism was not merely a matter of external rites and ceremonies. It was felt to symbolize and safeguard deep doctrinal convictions, especially about the presence of Christ in the eucharist. The strength of Ritualism lay in its devout sacramentalism and its encouragement of a disciplined and winning spirituality that seemed to be lacking in ordinary, conventional Anglicanism.

But now we must look at the causes of the opposition or hostility to Ritualism. To begin with, whatever may be the case with other peoples, the English are conservative in their attitude to the Church, and inclined to resent innovations whether they are good, bad, or indifferent. Their natural reaction to a new hymn tune or to a red Dean is negative. A lot of anti-ritualist feeling can be accounted for in this way, as is shown by the fact that once a congregation had become familiar with ritual innovations it became equally tenacious of what it was used to.

Secondly, the ordinary Englishman likes, or thinks he likes, simplicity in religion, and dislikes elaboration and sophistication. Ritualism seemed to be both elaborate and sophisticated. There is an incongruity here, for the English have always been much wedded to elaborate ceremonial and pageantry on royal, civic, and academic occasions. In the nineteenth century, however, they drew the line when it came to religion.

Thirdly, the English are a law-abiding people, and the Ritualists, especially in the early days, appeared in the guise of law-breakers. Though, as has been pointed out, there was a good deal of confusion in the decisions that were given by the courts, they were predominantly against Ritualism, and Ritualist priests lay under the suspicion of breaking their oaths of canonical obedience to their bishops.

But an altogether more serious cause of the hostility to Ritualism was the fear that it was heading for Romanism. This fear was a compound of blind prejudice and reasonable apprehension. Ever since the Reformation 'no popery' had been a cry to which the English were ready to rally, and at times it had driven them almost frantic, for example the Spanish Armada, the Gunpowder and Popish Plots, the Gordon Riots. Much of this was irrational, but mixed up with it was a rational perception that Roman Catholicism made assertions and claims that were not only incompatible with the liberty and independence which England prized, but were also heavy with the threat of a spiritual, if not a political, tyranny.

Things happened around the middle of the nineteenth century that could hardly fail to excite both the blind prejudice and the reasonable apprehension. When the Oxford movement began to issue in secessions to Rome, above all in Newman's secession, there was a sense of horror about what might be going to happen next, and what did happen next was, in the words of *The Times* newspaper, 'an audacious and conspicuous display of pretensions to resume the absolute spiritual dominion of this island which Rome has never abandoned'. This was the famous 'Papal Aggression' of 1850, when Pius IX set up a Roman Catholic hierarchy and dioceses in England, and Cardinal Nicholas Wiseman (1802–65), appointed Archbishop of Westminster, issued his flamboyant pastoral letter 'From out the Flaminian Gate of Rome'. Lord John Russell, the Prime Minister, wrote an open letter to the Bishop of Durham, which was opportunely sent on the eve of Guy Fawkes day. 'My dear Lord, I agree with you in considering "the late aggression of the Pope upon our Protestantism" as "insolent and insidious", and I therefore feel as indignant as you can do upon the subject. . . .' He went on to promise legislative action, and then to attack the Ritualists. 'Clergymen of our own Church, who have subscribed the Thirty-nine Articles, and acknowledged in explicit terms the Queen's supremacy, have been the most forward in leading their flocks, step by step, to the very verge of the precipice.' But he was confident that the great mass of the nation looked 'with contempt on the mummeries of superstition, and with scorn at the laborious endeavours which are now making to confine the intellect and enslave the soul'. The hubbub about the Papal Aggression subsided fairly soon, but the flames of hostility to Ritualism had been briskly fanned.

A further cause of this hostility was the fact that Ritualism was predominantly a clerical movement. Often clergymen introduced unfamiliar rites and ceremonies on their own initiative in the face of lay opposition and protests, and imposed the ritual for which they had a predilection on congregations that were entirely unprepared for it. More than anything else, this kind of proceeding made, and continued to make, Anglo-Catholicism unpopular.

Such was the atmosphere in which a whole series of attempts was made to suppress Ritualism – by the bishops, Royal Commissions, Acts of Parliament, legal proceedings, organized petitions and agitations, not to mention the anxieties of Queen Victoria herself. The tide to some extent turned when under the Public Worship Regulation Act of 1874 a number of Ritualist priests were sent to prison. This measure, so far from putting down Ritualism, made martyrs of the Ritualists, and advanced their cause. For public opinion, hostile as it was to what they stood for, would not tolerate for long good and faithful men being treated as criminals because they would not abandon their conscientious convictions. In due course the Public Worship Regulation Act became a dead letter, but attacks upon Ritualism continued, and even the saintly Bishop of Lincoln, Edward King (1829–1910), was tried in the court of the Archbishop of Canterbury (Benson) on account of a number of alleged illegalities.

*

When Randall Davidson (1848–1930) became Archbishop of Canterbury in 1903, his first public action was to receive at Lambeth Palace a hundred members of parliament who came to urge upon him effective action against Ritualism. Since it was clear that a fresh attempt must be made to tackle the problem, Davidson persuaded the Prime Minister, A. J. Balfour, to appoint another Royal Commission. It was known as the Royal Commission on Ecclesiastical Discipline. Most of its members were laymen but they were all churchmen. It sat for two years and made a thorough investigation of the whole subject from a historical point of view. Davidson, who was a member, observed that never since the Reformation had there been uniformity in practice in the conduct of divine service in the Church of England and that wide varieties had prevailed.

The Commission reached two main conclusions, which, since they went to the root of the matter, are worth quoting:

First, the law of public worship in the Church of England is too narrow for the religious life of the present generation. It needlessly condemns much which a great section of Church people, including many of her most devoted members, value; and modern thought and feeling are characterized by a care for ceremonial, a sense of dignity in worship, and an appreciation of the continuity of the Church, which were not similarly felt when the law took its present shape. In an age which has witnessed an extraordinary revival of spiritual life and activity, the Church has had to work under regulations fitted for a different condition of things, without that power of self-adjustment which is inherent in the conception of a living Church. . . .

Secondly, the machinery for discipline has broken down. The means of enforcing the law in the Ecclesiastical Courts, even in matters which touch the Church's faith and teaching, are defective and in some respects unsuitable. . . .

The Commission accordingly recommended that the Convocations should be authorized to consider what changes were needed in the Church's law of worship, and made proposals for new Ecclesiastical Courts with a new final court of appeal other than the Judicial Committee of the Privy Council, to which much objection had been taken on account of its allegedly secular character.

The Convocations therefore embarked on what proved to be the long and involved process of revising the Book of Common Prayer, which had not been revised since 1661. The wheels of Convocation grind slowly at the best of times. At first, it was thought that very few changes were called for, and that an interpretation of the Ornaments Rubric which would allow variety of use was the principal need. But as the discussions went on it began to look as though a larger revision would emerge. Then came the First World War which both held matters up and changed the situation.

Convocations were of course purely clerical bodies, and a promise had been given that the House of Laity in the Representative Church Council should be consulted before the revision was completed. But there was no prospect of being able to consult a representative House of Laity till after the war. At the same time, the war itself led to a demand for greater freedom in worship. For instance, the reservation of the sacrament and its extra-liturgical cultus became a good deal more common during the war, and there was a widespread desire for prayers for the dead, which were not provided for in the Prayer Book. Moreover, army chaplains found that they wanted much more freedom in liturgical experiment. Consequently, after the war, at least among a considerable proportion of the clergy, a more extensive revision than had previously been contemplated was viewed with favour.

Another circumstance that altered the situation after the war was the passing in 1919 of the Enabling Act which brought into existence the Church Assembly. This included a House of Laity, and was in future to be the principal organ of government in the Church, subject to the overriding control of parliament. The Church Assembly showed from the outset that it intended to take a hand in the work of Prayer Book revision.

So during the years from 1920 to 1927 the Church Assembly, especially the House of Bishops, spent a great deal of time in putting into shape proposals for a revised Prayer Book. It was to be an alternative to, not a replacement of, the old Prayer Book. Many groups and individuals also had much to say about what sort of revision was needed. In particular, three sets of proposals were published known as the Green, Grey, and Orange books. The Green book contained the proposals of the English Church Union, the body that spoke for many Anglo-Catholics. The Grey book expressed the wishes of a group of central or liberal churchmen, headed by William Temple (1881–1944). The Orange book was the work of the Alcuin Club which stood for a more moderate and traditionally English type of Anglo-Catholicism. The Evangelicals did not produce yet another coloured book because they professed to be content with the old Prayer Book or to want only a few minor modifications in it.

In the end, after much discussion and amendment, a revision was approved by large majorities in all three Houses of the Church Assembly, and it remained for the measure to be accepted by parliament. Unfortunately, there were two groups in the Church that were strongly opposed to the measure, the extreme Evangelicals and the extreme Anglo-Catholics – the former because it went too far in a catholicizing direction, the latter because it did not go far enough. Both felt so strongly that they did not scruple to lobby M.P.s with a view to persuading them to vote against the measure. This may have given M.P.s the impression that there was much more division in the Church about the Revised Prayer Book than was in fact the case, for those who were for the Book were not animated by the same enthusiasm as its opponents.

The Prayer Book measure came at last before the House of Lords on 12 December 1927 and was debated for three days, at the end of which it was approved by 241 votes to 88. All seemed to be going well, and it was expected that it would pass the House of Commons too. But there everything went wrong. The speeches of those who proposed the measure were ineffective, whereas the speeches against the measure were remarkably successful. In particular, Sir William Joynson-Hicks, the Home Secretary, who was a leading Low Churchman, attacked the Book as a surrender to the romanizing aims of the Anglo-Catholics. An even greater impression was made by a Scots M.P., named Rosslyn Mitchell, who did not know much about the subject but with rhetorical fervour beat the 'no popery' drum. The measure was defeated by 238 votes to 205. As G. K. A. Bell says in his *Life of Davidson*: 'In a single hectic night the House of Commons had apparently destroyed the work of more than twenty years.'

Clearly the matter could not be left there, but what was to be done? Some thought the Church should adopt the Book, despite the House of Commons, and leave the legislature to take what steps it liked, that is to disestablish the Church if it wanted to. But the bishops decided on a mediating course. They said that in the last resort they would have to take action 'in accordance with the Church's inherent spiritual authority', but they believed the House of Commons had misunderstood the proposals, and therefore they had resolved to reintroduce the measure with a few changes that would make quite clear what was intended. The changes consisted chiefly in drawing closer restrictions round the provision for reserving the sacrament. The changes were approved by the Church Assembly but by a smaller majority than in 1927. Some churchmen who had previously supported the measure were against making any concessions to parliament, and the new restrictions about reservation alienated more Anglo-Catholics.

When the measure came again before the House of Commons in June 1928 the debate was more even, but, so far from the opposition to the Book having been appeased, it was rejected by a slightly larger majority. Again, the question arose: what was to be done? and again the bishops decided on what seemed a temporizing policy. They issued a statement that the Church must retain its inalienable right to formulate its faith and arrange its form of worship, and they followed it up with a declaration that in administering their dioceses – during the present emergency – they would allow such deviations from the 1661 Prayer Book as were covered in the 1928 proposals. The present emergency lasted for about forty years; but then a new approach to Prayer Book revision was adopted, namely authorization of alternative services for use during an experimental period. The final outcome of this approach has yet to be determined. It will be deliberated upon by the National Synod which in 1970 became the Church's principal organ of self-government.

The rejection of the Revised Prayer Book by parliament in 1927–8 called in question the relations of Church and State. Since 1928 various commissions have been appointed by the Church to examine this question. They produce reports and recommendations, but so far nothing much has come of them, except that after the Second World War an immense amount of time and energy was devoted to revising the Church's canon law.

There are several reasons for the failure to carry the revision of the Prayer Book in 1927–8. Obviously the fear of Romanism, however irrational it may have been in this instance, was still more of a force than the church leaders had realized. Then the Church was not sufficiently agreed about what it wanted: if the proposals had had practically unanimous support, parliament would probably have approved without hesitation. Perhaps the whole idea of revising the Church's forms of worship as part of a plan to impose discipline on the clergy was perverse. The Revised Prayer Book was a compromise which the bishops hoped that they would be able to enforce. It has since been realized that there is a better way of revising forms of worship than by a deal between parties in the Church, namely the way of experiment in the parishes. Finally, Archbishop Davidson, who was responsible for leading the Church at this time, was not himself deeply interested in Prayer Book revision. He felt that there were more important things for the Church to be doing. While he was prepared to see the thing through if possible, he regarded it as a clerical pre-occupation to which the laity were more or less indifferent, and he sympathized with them. Who will say that he was wrong?

15

Stands Scotland Where It Did?

IT was inevitable that sooner or later the churches in Scotland would have to face the question that confronted all churches in the nineteenth century concerning the relation between traditional standards of orthodoxy and the critical study of the Bible. But there were circumstances in Scotland that deferred the impact of new learning and humanitarian sentiment longer even than in England. At the time of the Disruption in 1843 the authority not only of the Bible but of the Westminster Confession was regarded as unshakeable both in the Established Church and in the Free Church, by Moderates as well as by Evangelicals. It has been justly observed that 'a time of politico-ecclesiastical agitation is never favourable to theological advance, and any developments that might have grown out of the Irving and Macleod Campbell discussions were rudely arrested by the emergence of vital issues in Church and State'. Indeed, the evangelical fervour of the Free Church heightened its attachment to a rigid Calvinism and its determination to remain theologically immobile. The foundation of more than one college for the training of ministers was delayed because it was argued that in a plurality of theological institutions it would be more difficult to keep a careful watch over the teaching of professors and to guard against heresy. It was in the smaller bodies, which had not been involved in the crisis of the Disruption and which in 1847 came together to form the United Presbyterian Church, that a desire for a more flexible or liberal interpretation of Calvinistic dogma first made itself felt.

For thirty years or so after the Disruption no one arose in the Free Church to disturb the orthodoxy upon which it prided itself. Thus when at length the blow did fall, it fell upon a church entirely unprepared for it. The climate of opinion was quite different from that in Germany or Holland where the Bible had for long been studied in an atmosphere of theological rationalism and where the higher criticism had been readily assimilated. It was not until the beginning of the third quarter of the century that the issue came to a head in Scotland chiefly through the case of William Robertson Smith (1846–94), which occupied the courts and the leaders and the rank and file of the Free Church from 1876 to 1881.

Smith was the son of a minister who had sacrificed the prospect of a prosperous academic career at the time of the Disruption, and who spent the rest of his life in a country parish near Aberdeen. After receiving his schooling at home, William went at the age of fourteen to Aberdeen University where he carried all before him. From there he went to New College, Edinburgh, and studied under the Old Testament scholar, Andrew Bruce Davidson (1831–1902), whose Hebrew Grammar is still well-known. He also went to Germany where he attended the lectures of Ritschl among others. Both at Aberdeen and at Edinburgh professors had pressed Smith to go to Cambridge and devote his life to mathematical and scientific scholarship, but he had a strong sense of vocation to the ministry and nothing would induce him to turn his back on it.

In 1870, when he had only just completed his theological course, the Assembly of the Free Church appointed him to the chair of Hebrew and Old Testament Criticism in its College at Aberdeen. In his inaugural lecture he used words which caused no particular remark at the time but were significant of what was to come:

The higher criticism does not mean negative criticism. It means the fair and honest looking at the Bible as a historical record, and the effort everywhere to reach the real meaning and historical setting. ... This process can be dangerous to faith only if it is begun without faith – when we forget that the Bible history is no profane history, but the story of God's saving self-manifestation.

During the ensuing years, Smith built up an unsensational reputation as an able and devout teacher and scholar. He was an earnest evangelical who accepted the Calvinist doctrines of the Westminster Confession. He also continued to visit Germany and became closely acquainted with Julius Wellhausen (1844–1918), who was elaborating a theory about the documentary sources of the Pentateuch.

In 1875 a new edition of the *Encyclopaedia Britannica* began to be published, and the articles on biblical subjects had been entrusted to Smith. It was his first considerable opportunity of giving expression to his opinions. His first article was entitled 'Angel': its frankness about the personality, or rather the non-personality, of angels gave rise to some comment, but it was not a vital subject and by itself would not have caused much trouble. It was otherwise with his next article which was on the 'Bible': this was not only written from the point of view of the higher criticism but appeared to go a long way towards accepting what were then regarded as advanced conclusions, with regard, for instance, to the origin of the Pentateuch, the authorship of the Psalms, the non-predictive character of Old Testament prophecy, and the composition of the Gospels.

Since traditional views about the history, authorship, and verbal inerrancy of the Bible were at this time unchallenged in the Church, Robertson Smith's article seemed not only to be revolutionary, but to strike at the heart of the Christian faith, dependent as it was on the infallible authority of the Bible. He himself was now so accustomed to the new views, which were widely accepted in Germany, that he was amazed at the storm he started. When a friend had remarked to him that there would be trouble over his articles, he had answered: 'You don't say so.' He had not found his own faith as a Christian upset by his conclusions, and he did not see why they should upset other people. He held that they were quite consistent with the Westminster Confession, which he claimed to accept *ex animo*. Naturally the Westminster Confession did not explicitly exclude views about the composite nature of the Pentateuch, which had not been heard of when it was drawn up! But the guardians of evangelical orthodoxy perceived that the whole traditional attitude to the Bible was in effect being called in question.

The attack was opened by a Professor of the Established Church who was not averse to calling attention to so glaring an instance of heterodoxy in the Free Church. Very soon an agitation blew up for the removal of Robertson Smith from his chair. The case, as has been said, went on for five years, and became involved in extraordinary and dramatic complications. To follow it in detail is to get a fascinating insight into the operation of the Presbyterian system of church discipline. The whole chain of events is narrated, from different points of view, in the biographies of the two chief participants, Smith himself and Rainy.[1]

Robert Rainy (1826–1906), Principal of New College, Edinburgh, was the acknowledged leader of the Free Church and an ecclesiastical statesman of no mean order. He stood somewhere between Smith and his extreme opponents. He pursued a tortuous course in this case: he was bent on achieving a compromise which would keep open the possibility of 'reasonable' or 'reverent' criticism in the Church, while he was prepared, if necessary, to sacrifice Smith himself whose confident and unyielding pugnacity riled him. In the end Smith was deprived of his chair at Aberdeen, but throughout the proceedings he had stated his case with such superb eloquence and persuasive skill that the churchpeople of Scotland, however little they wished for it, had received an unforgettable education in the need to combine a critical approach to the Bible with evángelical faith.

The proceedings at each stage were reported at length in the daily newspapers, and excited immense interest all over Scotland. The debates were followed and reproduced in railway carriages, workshops, and country smithies. Not even Mr Gladstone's Midlothian campaign, which greatly moved the Scottish people at this time, was able to overshadow their absorption in the theological controversy that was raging. The Robertson Smith case was a turning-point since, although he was condemned, the cause of critical freedom and the new attitude to the Bible was really won. A few days after the decisive vote in 1881, three hundred of his friends and supporters, who included most of the future leaders of the Church, met and passed this resolution:

We declare that the decision of the Assembly leaves all Free-Church ministers and office-bearers free to pursue the critical questions raised by Professor W. R. Smith, and we pledge ourselves to do our best to protect any man who pursues these studies legitimately.

One of them, Professor T. M. Lindsay (1843–1914), father of Lord Lindsay of Birker, went further and publicly committed himself to the main positions Smith had advanced: he challenged the conservatives to take action against him, but the challenge was never taken up.

Within a generation dynamic conceptions of divine revelation and non-infallibilist conceptions of biblical inspiration became familiar and acceptable in all the principal Scottish churches, and the terms of subscription to the Westminster Confession were so modified as to allow for relaxed opinions about such matters as a limited atonement, absolute predestination, total depravity, and the non-salvability of the heathen. There were for a time some further heresy hunts, but in the end diehard traditionalism was to be found only in the minor sects and secessions.[1]

*

There is another important respect in which Scotland no longer stands where it did: church unity and the relations of Church and State. In the second half of the nineteenth

1. For a survey of Scottish theology after 1890, see Chapter VI of J. K. Mozley's *Some Tendencies in British Theology* (1951).

century there were three major Presbyterian churches in Scotland as well as several minor ones. The three major churches were the Established Church (the Auld Kirk), the Free Church, and the United Presbyterian Church (the U.P.s). The main point of difference between the Free Church and the U.P.s had to do with the relations of Church and State. The U.P.s were 'Voluntaries', that is they believed in the separation of Church and State; the Church should be a voluntary society dependent on the support of its members and looking for no establishment or endowment from the civil government. The Free Church, on the other hand, although since the Disruption it had in fact been disestablished, did not believe in disestablishment on principle. It advocated a national recognition and support of religion, provided that the liberty of the Church was not impaired thereby.

Although this principle was not actually written into the formularies of its Faith, there were many in the Free Church who continued to regard it as a vital theological principle. Apart from this question, there was little to divide the Free Church and the U.P.s, and the possibility of a union between them had always been before the minds of the more far-sighted members of both communions. In the 1860s and early 1870s there were prolonged negotiations to this end, and a plan of agreement was worked out that would allow for difference of opinion about the ideal relations of Church and State. The U.P.s were altogether ready for union on this basis, but the project was wrecked on the side of the Free Church by the emergence within it of a die-hard party that would hear of no compromise of what it regarded as the Disruption principle about establishment. It became clear that, if the union negotiations were proceeded with, this party, which was ably led by James Begg (1808–83), would carry its opposition to the extreme length of causing a new schism and, in order to avert that calamity, the project for union was abandoned in 1873.

Nevertheless, many in both churches looked forward to its

being revived in more favourable circumstances. It was in fact revived in the 1890s. Principal Rainy, who had been one of the earlier advocates of union, was now unchallenged in his leadership of the Free Church. Dr Begg, the leader of the ultra-conservatives, was dead and no one of his calibre had arisen to take his place. The U.P.s were again almost unanimous in their eagerness for union on practically the same basis as had been proposed before, and at first it looked as though the opposition in the Free Church would be insignificant. As a matter of fact, there were some in the Free Church who would have favoured a more comprehensive union which would have included the Established Church as well. But this idea was rebuffed by the Auld Kirk where language was used about 'finessing with dissenters' and Principal Rainy was described as 'this unprincipled Principal'. The way therefore seemed open for a union of the Free Church and the U.P.s.

Rainy had indeed some anxiety about the likelihood of opposition in the Highlands where most of the ultra-conservative elements in the Free Church were entrenched: the Highlanders still tended to be rigidly Calvinist in their theology and attached to the establishment principle. But they were able to rally only a trivial number of votes in the General Assembly when the question came up. Their threat to bring legal proceedings against the union, if it went through, was treated as bombastic and a matter for laughter. Eminent lawyers had advised the Free Church leaders that they need not be at all apprehensive on this score. The union negotiations therefore went ahead and were brought to what seemed a triumphant conclusion in October 1900, when the vote in favour of the union in the Free Church Assembly was 643 to 27: the U.P.s accepted it with acclamation.

The tiny minority in the Free Church (henceforth known as the 'Wee Frees') stood, however, to their warning that they intended to go on as a continuing and protesting body on the basis of 'the maintenance inviolate of the whole superior and secondary standards of the Church in their entirety (i.e. of strict Calvinism), and of the special testimony of the Church in regard to the right and duty of the civil magistrate to maintain and support an establishment of religion'. Hardly had the union of the United Free Church (U.F.s) been consummated than the Wee Frees took legal steps to assert their claim that they were the real Free Church, from the standards of which the great bulk of the Church was departing and so forfeiting its rights to the Church's property. They started proceedings in the Scottish civil courts, claiming that the entire property of the Free Church – funds, churches, manses, colleges, and assembly hall – should be handed over to them.

When their case had been rejected in two Scottish courts, they appealed, as they were entitled to do, to the House of Lords. Distinguished judges were appointed to hear the case, and the judgement was expected early in 1904. But one of the judges died on 6 March, which necessitated a complete rehearing. The proceedings were also spun out by the tremendous length and sophistication of the arguments that were used on both sides. One of the counsel for the U.F. Church was R. B. Haldane, who was a Hegelian philosopher as well as a lawyer. He did not hesitate to embark on the most recondite mysteries of the doctrine of predestination, and the judges were treated to such a feast of metaphysics as they could hardly be expected to digest. Haldane argued, for instance, that from the higher Hegelian standpoint Calvinism and Arminianism were really the same thing.

The judgement was given at last in August 1904, and by a majority of five to two the appeal of the Wee Frees was allowed. Consequently they were given legal possession of the entire property of the Free Church. The situation was ridiculous, since it meant that a mere pocket of dissident ministers and lay people, chiefly located in the Highlands, had the buildings and funds of a nation-wide church assigned to them. But they were in no mood for compromise, and declared that they were going to rise to their responsibilities. The only possible course was for the British government to intervene so as to see that real, as distinct from legal, justice was done. After a Royal Commission had reported on the matter, a measure was passed through parliament that made an appropriate division of the property of the Free Church. The Wee Frees were treated generously, and they have ever since claimed and used the title 'the Free Church of Scotland': their General Assembly from time to time receives publicity when it protests against royal infringements of the Sabbath. They have a total membership of about 25,000.

What was at stake in the Scottish Free Church case, and made it of great interest to political theorists like H. J. Laski as well as to theologians, was the question whether a Church is a legal corporation, fixed and static, tied down by its trust deeds, or a living, growing organism with an inherent right to adapt the formulation of its doctrines and the definition of its principles to new conditions. The British government's virtual reversal of the House of Lords judgement was hailed as a recognition of the principle that churches are not mere creatures of the State or of the law of the land but have an intrinsic title to a life of their own.[1]

It was now possible to envisage a more comprehensive union of the Presbyterian churches in Scotland. A new generation of church leaders was coming up who were no longer under the spell of the battles of the previous century. There was a readiness in the Established Church to consider a modification of its relation to the State which would make the Church's assertion of its spiritual independence unequivocal. On the other hand, in the U.F. Church the straitest sect of the Voluntaries was dying out, and there was an increasing disposition to welcome a union that would combine a national recognition of the Church with its freedom from any kind of State control.

Negotiations were therefore set on foot, and had made a promising start before the First World War. They went

1. See J. N. Figgis. *Churches in the Modern State.* 1913, Chapter 1.

steadily ahead afterwards. In 1921 an Enabling Act was passed through parliament which acknowledged the spiritual autonomy of the Church of Scotland in these terms:

This Church, as part of the Universal Church wherein the Lord Jesus Christ has appointed a government in the hands of Church officers, receives from Him, its Divine Head and King, and from Him alone, the right and power, subject to no civil authority, to legislate and adjudicate finally in all matters of doctrine, worship, government, and discipline.

There were still a good many financial and other difficulties to be overcome, but the union was completed in 1929, and since then there has been in existence the Church of Scotland as it is known today.

The new relationship of the Church to the State – which was new in the sense that it was now written into the British constitution – was symbolized in a change in the role of the Lord High Commissioner who, since the Reformation, has always attended the General Assembly as the representative of the Crown. The Stuart kings in particular regarded his presence as a useful way of keeping a check and control on the proceedings of the Assembly. The ceremonial expressive of this relation had continued till this century. It was the practice that the Lord High Commissioner should at the end of each Assembly dissolve it 'in the King's name' and appoint the day in the following year when it was next to meet. In 1927 a new formula was adopted. The Lord High Commissioner now says: 'I shall inform Her Majesty that having concluded your business for which you assembled, you have passed an Act appointing your next meeting (to be on such and such a date), and now in the Queen's name I bid you farewell.' In other words, this ancient office which symbolizes the national recognition of, and interest in, the Church has been retained, but any suggestion that it compromises Christ's sole and exclusive Headship of the Church has been eliminated. To this point Scottish churchmen have been as sensitive as English churchmen have appeared to be indifferent.

16

Catholic Modernism

A FEW years ago the *News Chronicle* described an episode in Islington where two gangs of youths had been knifing one another: the report concluded with a remark made by one youth to a bystander: 'Don't call them Teddy boys, guv. They was Modernists.' This is an extreme instance of the variety of meanings that the word 'modernist' has acquired. Even in theological or ecclesiastical contexts it is vulgarly used to indicate, if not to abuse, any position, line of thought, or tendency that represents a further departure from a traditional orthodoxy than this or that speaker happens to regard as acceptable. But here we will use the terms 'modernist' and 'modernism' solely with reference to the movement and persons to which they were originally applied, that is to the movement in the Roman Catholic Church which began about 1890, which was condemned by the papacy in 1907, and which virtually came to an end about 1910.

If we consulted the papal encyclical *Pascendi gregis*, by which Pius X condemned the movement, we should get the impression that the modernists were a more or less organized group of persons in the Roman Church who were plotting a complete overthrow of traditional Christianity. We should be led to suppose that they formed a definite party or school of thought, and that they advocated, implicitly if not explicitly, a doctrinal system which entirely contradicted the scholastic system of orthodoxy. In particular, the encyclical affirms that the biblical criticism of the modernists was the outcome of the acceptance of *a priori* principles, indeed that their whole attitude to Catholic teaching was vitiated by their adoption of false philosophical presuppositions. Finally, the pope alleged that the errors of modernism were the result of the pride of the modernists, and this easy explanation of the movement was naturally taken up. In the 1930s a writer in the *Catholic Times* summed the matter up thus: 'About thirty years ago there ended a movement within the Church which would never have started had the chief participators not succumbed to the temptation of intellectual pride.'

The modernists themselves – both at the time and subsequently, in so far as they had opportunity – declared that the pope had misrepresented the movement from beginning to end. They denied that they ever formed a party or organized school of thought, or that their writings implied any such logical system as the encyclical attributed to them. They denied that they started with philosophical presuppositions. They had first been struck by the incompatibility between many traditional tenets of Catholicism and the findings of modern scholarship, and they had felt bound to use scientific and historico-critical methods of study and to follow the argument wherever it led. They had thereby been driven to recognize the need for a reinterpretation of much traditional teaching, and finally to question the presuppositions of the scholastic system. Although they did not claim to be saints, they said that their movement was not the result of undue pride: it had been occasioned and necessitated by the situation of Roman Catholic theology and the condition of the Church at the end of the nineteenth century. What they had attempted to do was, while remaining sincere and loyal Roman Catholics, to forward such a revision and fresh presentation of the Church's teaching as would acclimatize it in the modern world.

The best way to judge between these contradictory claims is to survey the course of the movement. It should however be said at the outset that the modernists were never agreed on any single programme of reform or on anything like a party line. Some of them, for example, were more interested in social reform than in doctrinal revision. They were a number of individuals or groups of friends and collaborators who in one way or another desired and worked for a new orientation of Catholicism towards the modern world and modern culture.

The movement must be seen in its historical context. We have seen[1] that earlier in the nineteenth century there had been various attempts to give Roman Catholicism a liberal orientation but they had all come to grief because of the ascendancy of ultramontanism in the Church and especially because of the policy of Pius IX. If he had been succeeded by a pope of similar outlook, it is unlikely that there would have been any modernist movement at the end of the century, since it would have seemed futile to try to secure any modification of traditional orthodoxy under the conditions that prevailed in the Church. Leo XIII, who became pope in 1878 and had an unexpectedly long reign – he was over ninety when he died in 1903 – could hardly be described as a liberal by conviction, but he was a great diplomat.

He realized that the only way to restore the prestige of the papacy and the influence of the Church in the eyes of the world was to pursue a policy of conciliation with modern society and to some extent with modern learning. So one of his earliest acts was to confer a cardinal's hat on Newman who had hitherto been under a cloud because of his supposed liberalism. Newman had not really been a Liberal Catholic like Acton, but the papal theologians had rightly discerned that his essay on *Development* and his *Grammar of Assent* contained suggestions that were subversive of traditional scholastic orthodoxy, and also that he was entirely out of sympathy with the attitude of the ultramontanes. Leo saw that to honour Newman would assist the cause of the Roman Church in England: it is doubtful whether he had any particular sympathy with Newman's ideas or even understood them.

Leo wanted to be regarded as the friend of democracy as well as of sound learning. For example, he pressed

1. See Chapters 6 and 13.

the Church in France to abandon its attachment to the royalist cause and to rally to the Republic. He purported to encourage historical research, and opened the Vatican Archives. But it would be a mistake to suppose that he ever intended to allow any substantial modification of traditional teaching with regard, for instance, to the Bible or to Christology. Nevertheless – and this is the important point – his apparently liberal policy encouraged a new and younger generation of Catholic scholars to hope that a synthesis of Catholic theology with biblical criticism and with the advancing tide of human knowledge was worth attempting. It seemed possible after all that Rome was not irretrievably committed to an unbending traditionalism and might at least be willing to allow its scholars to deal frankly with embarrassing subjects.

The modernist movement arose in the atmosphere which Leo's policy produced. The movement began in France, where also it probably attained the largest proportions. The well-known ecclesiastical historian, Louis Duchesne (1843–1922), had a good deal to do with its initiation, though he did not himself become a modernist. From 1877 he was a professor at the Institut Catholique in Paris, and he was an apostle of the application of critical methods to church history. But after a few early indiscretions he resolutely avoided all biblical questions and steered clear, so far as possible, of the issues which modern knowledge raised for dogmatic orthodoxy. He soon realized that in those fields the Roman Church would not allow any modification of its traditional teaching if it could possibly avoid doing so, and therefore he did not share the hopes of the modernists.

But Duchesne's pupil, Alfred Loisy (1857–1940), also a priest, was by no means disposed to evade the issues, and he felt called to inaugurate a renovation of the Church's attitude to the Bible. When, however, in 1890 and the following years – himself now a professor at Paris – he began to give teaching from the point of view of modern criticism, he quickly got into trouble, and in 1893 was deprived of his

professorship. In the same year Leo XIII issued the encyclical *Providentissimus Deus* which affirmed the complete
inerrancy of the Bible. But Loisy did not give up his belief
in the possibility of a synthesis between Catholicism and
criticism at the first blow, and he was henceforth encouraged in his work by the close friendship of Baron Friedrich
von Hügel (1852–1925) and the French Archbishop Mignot
(1842–1918), two of the most highly cultured and respected
Catholics of their generation.

In 1897 Loisy wrote an apology for Catholicism as a reply
to Harnack's *History of Dogma* and Auguste Sabatier's *Out-
lines of a Philosophy of Religion*. (Sabatier was the leading
French Liberal Protestant.) It has never been published as
a whole though he quotes much of it in his *Mémoires*, but it
provided the material for *L'Évangile et l'Église* (1902), which
took the form of a refutation of Harnack's more popular
work, *What is Christianity?* Harnack had succeeded Ritschl as
the principal exponent of Liberal Protestantism.

According to Harnack, the essence of Christianity was
what he regarded as the essence of Christ's teaching: the
fatherhood of God and the brotherhood of man. It was the
religion *of* Jesus, rather than the religion *about* Jesus.
Traditional Christianity, with the institutional Church, the
christological and other dogmas, and the Catholic cultus,
was a perversion of the simple, original gospel. The Reformation had been an attempt to recover it, but only a par-
tially successful one. It had not made a clean sweep of
ecclesiasticism. The time had now come to reduce Christianity to its true essence, filial and individual trust in the
divine fatherhood.

Such in barest outline was the Liberal Protestant view of
Christianity which Loisy set out to refute, and in doing so
he offered a quite fresh line of apologetic for Catholicism.
Harnack and Sabatier had appealed to history; to history
they should go. Loisy pointed out that to identify Christianity with trust in the divine fatherhood was the result of an
arbitrary prejudice. If a historical religion is to be rightly

appreciated, it must be considered as a whole in its organic development. It should be judged by its permanent characteristics, not just by one or two elements in the teaching of its founder or its sacred books that were still felt to be tenable.

At all events, if Christian origins were objectively examined, it would appear that the original Gospel was by no means exclusively concerned to inculcate individual trust in the divine fatherhood. It was concerned primarily with the proclamation of the eschatological kingdom of God, and the messianic claims of Jesus were an integral part of that proclamation. To divorce Christology from Christianity was therefore unhistorical. In any case, he said, every religion must be embodied in social and symbolic forms – must be both institutional and dogmatic. The conception of the eschatological kingdom of God and of the Messiah was the mould in which Christianity had to be born before it spread out into the world. Jesus foretold the Kingdom and it was the Church that came. The Church, with its hierarchy, its dogma, and its cultus, was the necessary form in which the Gospel had to be preserved, expressed, and developed, if it was to survive and to do its salutary work for mankind. Catholicism should thus be regarded as the vital and organic continuation of the original Gospel.

Even so inadequate a summary of the argument of *L'Évangile et l'Église* may suggest that it opened up a singularly arresting line of apologetic for Catholicism. As such it was enthusiastically welcomed not only by von Hügel and Mignot, but by many others, including Wilfrid Ward (1856–1916), a leading Newmanite, who said that 'it showed a consummate knowledge of what Newman wanted and aimed at'. Loisy had in effect turned the tables on the Liberal Protestants, and shown that an objective and even radical historical criticism of Christian origins could be held to justify, not a reduced and attenuated version of Protestant piety, but the full and rich corporate life of the Catholic Church. But, in doing so, he had of course given up the traditional view of biblical inerrancy and the scholastic system of christological and ecclesiastical orthodoxy. No one expected the Roman authorities officially to endorse the new apologetic forthwith, but there were many who hoped that they would allow its further exploration. What Rome did in fact was to condemn it out of hand, simply because it was sacrilegious to suggest that traditional teaching required any modification or revision whatever. After all, had not the Holy Office recently decreed that the authenticity even of the *Comma Johanneum* (the Trinitarian verse in St John's First Epistle which appears in no Greek manuscript whatever) could not safely be called in question?

Loisy now was not slow to perceive – like Lamennais seventy years before – that his dreams of a reorientated Catholicism, about which anyhow he had been less confident than many of his admirers, were incapable of realization. He was not prepared to remain a Catholic indefinitely, unless he could retain his sincerity as a critic. In the circumstances of the time this made his excommunication inevitable. It was only by a compromise that it was deferred till 1908.

Meanwhile, however, Loisy's work and that of other less prominent modernists had enlisted the enthusiasm of a certain proportion of the younger priests and seminarists in France, and to some extent in other countries too. All these modernists or sympathizers with the movement differed indefinitely in their standpoint and in the degree to which they desired a reform of the Church's official teaching, but they were of one mind in recognizing the need of some measure of doctrinal reform or reinterpretation and in wishing for some fresh air to circulate in the ecclesiastical system.

We can notice here only the case of Father George Tyrrell (1861–1909), who came into the movement later than Loisy and whose story illustrates different aspects of it. Tyrrell was an Irishman, brought up in the Church of Ireland, who had been converted to the Roman Church in his youth. He had become a zealous member of the Society of Jesus, and in the first phase of his career was a scholastic of the scholastics and trenchantly orthodox. Between 1897 and 1900 various factors, most of all the friendship of von Hügel, brought home to him the limitations of the scholastic theology, and he became increasingly dissatisfied with the logical and rationalistic conception of revelation and dogma as a body of propositions guaranteed to be infallible. For a time he rested in the position of Newman, and of Newman's disciple, Wilfrid Ward, but he soon pressed on to a more radical position.

He was convinced that the life of the Catholic Church mediated the fullest experience of God and of Christ and of the spiritual life. But he held that the Church's theological system need not, and should not, be treated as an adequate or immutable statement of absolute truth. Theology is the inevitably inadequate expression or formulation of the continuous living experience of the Church. Revelation consisted in the living experience, not in its intellectual formulation. This dynamic view of revelation and dogma appeared to many Catholics to have much to commend it when compared with the deductive and static rationalism of the official theologians. It obviated the discord between dogma and scientific and historical knowledge. Dogma is a direct and unsophisticated guide to revelation and the classical religious experience, which theology attempts to rationalize, but in a manner that is always susceptible of improvement and development.

Here again, as in the case of Loisy, was a fresh type of apologetic for Catholicism which seemed to open up an approach to dogma that was worthy of further investigation. But that was not the view of the scholastic theologians who dominated the Society of Jesus and the papacy. They saw to it that Tyrrell was condemned, and in Pius X who had succeeded Leo XIII in 1903, and who did not even wish to pose as a liberal or to manifest any sympathy with modernity, they had a willing instrument for a policy of rigorous suppression.

Even so, the condemnation of the modernist movement

was remarkably severe in its method and manner. First, in the decree *Lamentabili* the pope condemned a number of propositions which made even a moderately conservative use of biblical criticism well-nigh impossible for Catholic scholars. Then, in the encyclical *Pascendi* the supposed teaching of the modernists was constructed into an ingeniously imagined system which was condemned *in toto* as heretical. Finally, the condemnation was enforced by practical measures such as the appointment of councils of vigilance in every diocese, and in 1910 by the imposition of an anti-modernist oath on all clerics.

As a matter of fact, by 1910 the modernist movement was pretty well extinct. Loisy had broken with the Church, Tyrrell was dead, and the other leading modernists had either been excommunicated or decided to submit and remain in the Church. Attempts that were made to organize groups of modernists all proved abortive. The movement had had no organization and very little coherence, and it had not been allowed to approach a degree of development in which it could seriously challenge the power of the papacy.

Not only were the modernists themselves routed, but Roman Catholic scholars who had deliberately and prudently dissociated themselves from the movement, but who wanted to make a moderate use of critical methods in the cause of orthodoxy, were victimized. Thus the work of men like Pierre Batiffol (1861–1929) and Marie-Joseph Lagrange (1855–1938) had to conform to the ultra-conservative pronouncements of the pope and of the Pontifical Biblical Commission. The Biblical Commission had been appointed by Leo XIII and its original membership was comparatively liberal, but later it was packed with conservative theologians, and it proceeded to oblige Roman Catholics to maintain, or at least not to call in question, such opinions as the Mosaic authorship of the Pentateuch, the unity of the Book of Isaiah, the priority of St Matthew's Gospel, and the Pauline authorship of the Epistle to the Hebrews – opinions which had been abandoned by nearly all independent scholars.

The outcome of the modernist movement was then at the time exactly the opposite of what was intended by its promoters. They had designed to make the Church more habitable for men of contemporary culture. In the event they provoked the Church to a condemnation of all the new knowledge that they had hoped to acclimatize. The Church of Rome simply reiterated its claim to be the one infallible repository of an unchanging Christian tradition. It was rather like the claim of the old firm to be carrying on the old business in the old way.

In reality, of course, the Roman Church has never been as stationary or unchanging as it liked to appear to be. The anti-modernist measures, even if they were not repealed, were gradually relaxed after the death of Pius X in 1914, so far as their application went. The reign of terror, which he had countenanced, was eased by his successor, Benedict XV. Later there was a renascence of biblical studies in the Church, and Roman Catholic scholars were permitted to use critical methods with a freedom that had been peremptorily denied to the modernists. Moreover, it became possible to publish books with the *imprimatur* that acknowledged the dynamic character of dogma and the necessity of development and reinterpretation. Since the definition of the Assumption of the Blessed Virgin in 1950 by Pius XII Roman Catholic theologians have found themselves impelled to assign a vital, even a creative, role to tradition in the development of doctrine, since there is by general consent no strictly historical evidence for that dogma: and this is an idea that would have been thoroughly congenial to many of the modernists.

It is now commonly allowed that the indiscriminate condemnation of the modernist movement and its drastic suppression were due to a panic-stricken reaction and to the grip that the so-called integrists had on the Roman Church at that time. It is no doubt the case that some of the modernists were too much under the spell of current (evolutionary, immanentist, or pragmatic) fashions of thought and, when driven to extremes by oppressive measures, advocated ideas that it would be difficult, if not impossible, to reconcile with historic Christianity, but this was after they had been made more or less desperate by the Church's refusal to look in the face the questions that they had raised. It is an unwarranted assumption that they would have gone to such lengths if they had been treated by the authorities with respect and understanding.

On behalf of the Roman authorities it may be said that they were responsible for the government of a Church the vast majority of whose members were peasants, so that pastoral solicitude inclined them to protect the faith of simple believers, however much they might scandalize the educated in the process. Nonetheless, it may seem in retrospect that a Church which made such august claims for itself as did the Church of Rome, ought to have been able to handle the modernist crisis without resorting to panic measures, and to have been able to discriminate between what was important and what was not, and also to have availed itself of the services of honest, intelligent and devoted men who were doing their best to face genuine problems that would certainly have to be faced sooner or later.

17

Ebb and Flow in English Theology

IN the 1880s English theology was still at a low ebb. It had not really recovered from its negative and frightened reaction to Darwinism and to *Essays and Reviews*. But, as we have seen,[1] in the work of the Cambridge Triumvirate, Light-foot, Westcott, and Hort, foundations were already being laid for a new period of construction, and there were other signs of promise. In the Church of England the strictly conservative tradition of Tractarianism, which had been maintained by Pusey and Liddon, was being questioned or disturbed by free-lances like Stewart Headlam and his associates in the Guild of St Matthew,[2] and there was J. H. Shorthouse (1834–1903) whose best-selling novel *John Inglesant* (1881) was evidence that thoughtful High Anglicans were looking for a way of combining Catholic faith and practice with an open and liberal theology. In the Free Churches Spurgeon, who stood out as the principal apostle of biblical inerrancy, the penal-substitutionary theory of the atonement, and Calvinism, was moved to launch an attack on heretics within the fold in what was known as the 'Down Grade' controversy, which was a sure sign that broader views were gaining ground among evangelicals. But what more than anything else signified the turn of the tide in English theology was the publication in 1889 of *Lux Mundi*, of which it has been said that 'few books in modern times have so clearly marked the presence of a new era and so deeply influenced its character'.

The genesis of this volume goes back to 1875 when a group of young High Church theologians at Oxford, who had been influenced by F. D. Maurice and the idealist philosopher T. H. Green, started going away together from time to time

1. See pp. 130–33.   2. See p. 119.

for the purpose of sustained discussion. Edward Stuart Talbot (1844–1934), the first Warden of Keble College, who was one of the group, said of the Tractarians:

> We feel ourselves their children and disciples, yet we cannot be called merely to repeat, or even to continue their work. . . . Theirs was a time for relaying the foundations, for planting roots firm and deep. For them it was a duty, as well as a policy, to concentrate, to bring out the old theology, the lines of the old tradition, the old Church system, with all its many-sidedness, the courage of its appeal to supernatural premises and forces, and yet the wisdom of its balance. . . . We do not know half of what we owe to them.

But, for himself and his friends, he said he was wanting

> A Catholic theology utterly fixed in its great central principles and in many of their corollaries, yet ever yielding up new meanings, even from its central depths in the light of other knowledge and human development. Such a theology, and at the same time a Church system, unchanging in one sense, yet elastic in another – and these two together capable of laying hold upon the future, its movements, questions, temptations, advantages, discoveries: this is what we want.

It was only after the members of what eventually came to be known as the *Lux Mundi* group had been meeting and thrashing out their problems together for about twelve years that they decided to produce a volume of essays which would embody the common view of Christian doctrine that they had come to hold. The sub-title of the volume was 'a series of studies in the Religion of the Incarnation': that was its governing theme in the light of which the whole range of the Christian faith was considered. There were essays on Faith, the Doctrine of God, the Problem of Pain, the Preparation in History for Christ, the Incarnation in relation to development and as the basis for dogma, the Atonement, the Holy Spirit and Inspiration, the Church, the Sacraments, Christianity and Politics, and Christian Ethics.

The standpoint of the authors was indicated in the preface by the editor, Charles Gore (1853–1932):

We have written . . . not 'as guessers at truth' but as servants of the Catholic Creed and Church, aiming only at interpreting the faith we have received. On the other hand, we have written with the conviction that the epoch in which we live is one of profound transformation, intellectual and social, abounding in new needs, new points of view, new questions; and certain therefore to involve great changes in the outlying departments of theology, where it is linked to other sciences, and to necessitate some general restatement of its claim and meaning.

The essayists, who in addition to Gore and Talbot included Henry Scott Holland (1847–1918), J. R. Illingworth (1848–1915), and R. C. Moberly (1845–1903), wrote with great confidence; they evidently believed that the historic Christian faith, when reasonably interpreted, would commend itself to reasonable men. At the same time, they tried to meet frankly the difficulties which they had themselves had to face. They saw God's revelation of himself as progressive, and this enabled them to accept not only the methods of biblical criticism but its assured results as they seemed then to stand. They were thus able to bring enormous relief to educated Christians, especially with regard to the Old Testament which had been the chief battleground in the conflict between religion and science.

The early chapters of Genesis were accepted as folk-lore and poetry. The history of Israel was seen as a slow ascent from savage beginnings to the ethical monotheism of the prophets which was to culminate in the faith of the incarnation, with its sequel in the sacramental life of the Church. The essay that received most attention was Gore's on Inspiration – 'the first and the crucial instance', it has been said, 'of the acceptance by a whole-hearted adherent of Catholic Christianity of the principle of criticism'. He faced the fact that in the Gospels Christ is represented as ascribing the authorshop of the Pentateuch to Moses and of Psalm 110 to David. For the older Tractarians that settled the matter, whatever the higher critics might say. Gore tackled the question by considering the nature of Christ's consciousness as man; he maintained that it was consistent with the Catholic faith to confess that the knowledge of the Incarnate Lord was limited by the conditions of the time. Gore was to develop this line of thought further in his Bampton Lectures on the Incarnation, in which he worked out a 'kenotic' Christology, based on the idea that the Eternal Logos in becoming man 'emptied himself' of his divine attributes and prerogatives, in so far as they were not compatible with a genuine incarnation.

Liddon was particularly distressed by Gore's contribution to *Lux Mundi*. He was deeply attached to Gore and had been largely responsible for his appointment to the Principalship of Pusey House in Oxford. It seemed treachery to Pusey that such views should come out of an institution founded in his memory. Liddon's distress is said to have hastened his death in the following year. The leadership of the Tractarian old guard then devolved upon George Anthony Denison (1805–96), Archdeacon of Taunton, who had led the attack on *Essays and Reviews* a quarter of a century before. He described *Lux Mundi* as 'this negation issued from what was the Pusey House'. Its rationalism was another symptom of the decadence of England under Mr Gladstone, to be classed with universal suffrage, Welsh disestablishment, secular education, and schemes for a Channel tunnel.

However, this was a voice from the past. To the majority of Anglo-Catholics, and to thoughtful churchmen generally, *Lux Mundi* was a bearer of good news. It went through ten editions in a year, and together with the subsequent works of the members of the group, marked the definite emergence in the Church of England of what Gore was fond of calling 'a liberal Catholicism'. Gore himself, who became the most prominent and influential Anglican theologian of the first quarter of the twentieth century, never retreated from the *Lux Mundi* position which he continued to maintain till the end of his life, but neither did he ever move forward from it. Thus far and no farther, he seemed to say. The consequence was that, while in the 1890s he was looked upon as the pioneer of a liberal and advancing theology, thereafter he appeared more in the role of a resolute defender of orthodoxy. Theologians, even High Church theologians, who found they had to go further than he did in restating the grounds of belief or in modifying traditional tenets incurred his strong disapprobation and, as a bishop, he sought to discipline them.

But the tide that had turned with *Lux Mundi* could not be halted, though there was of course every justification for examining the character and effects of the incoming waters. Certainly, during the twenty years that followed the publication of *Lux Mundi* the tides of research and speculation in biblical history and religious philosophy did not stand still. During this period, for instance, Harnack's Liberal Protestant manifesto and the striking counter-phenomenon of Catholic Modernism made their appearance; the thoroughgoing eschatological view of the Gospel of Jesus (namely, that he had expected the world to come to an end almost immediately), which was propounded by J. Weiss and A. Schweitzer[1] as well as by Loisy, caused a turmoil in the minds of students of the New Testament; attention was powerfully directed to the importance for Christian theology of religious and mystical experience by William James, W. R. Inge, Baron von Hügel and others; and in philosophy the intuitionism of Bergson and the pragmatism of William James and F. C. S. Schiller were making a considerable impact on the Christian mind.

These developments had not been foreseen by, and were by no means congenial to, Gore and the *Lux Mundi* school, though they were of course already familiar and dissatisfied with the kind of Liberal Protestantism that had been canvassed in England under the aegis of Broad Churchmanship, for example by E. Hatch (1835–89) who, as Harnack himself acknowledged, had anticipated his theory that the original Gospel had been perverted by Hellenism. An extreme and superficial form of Liberal Protestantism with

1. See p. 214.

the caption 'The New Theology' was widely publicized in
England in the first decade of the new century by the eloquent preacher R. J. Campbell (1867–1956) at the City
Temple in London. Gore attacked this so effectively in his
book *The New Theology and the Old Religion* (1907) that
Campbell subsequently recanted and was received into the
ministry of the Church of England. In this matter Gore had
with him Anglicans as a whole, and indeed the New Theology was no less severely dealt with by the outstanding
Congregationalist theologian, P. T. Forsyth (1848–1921).[1]

The work of the *Lux Mundi* group – their ideal of an
English Liberal Catholicism – had then a decisive and
enduring influence, not only on professed Anglo-Catholics.
G. L. Prestige (1889–1955), who went up to Oxford in 1908,
bore this testimony in 1941 to the *Lux Mundi* school: 'The
whole foundation of my own theological position, and that
of *all my Oxford contemporaries*, was based on the teaching of
its authors', though he went on to say that many of his
contemporaries 'were apt to raise local rebellions and to do
a bit of sharp-shooting from behind convenient rocks'.[2] The
expressions 'local rebellions' and 'sharp-shooting from
behind convenient rocks' perhaps did not do justice to the
disposition, by the time of which he was writing, of younger
theologians to go further along the paths of criticism and
reconstruction than Gore himself would allow.

The fact is that when *Lux Mundi* took shape, the critical
approach to the Bible meant primarily the critical approach
to the Old Testament. New Testament criticism at that
time in England was still in its infancy. Gore and his friends
were quite willing to grant that much in the Old Testament
that had traditionally been regarded as historical, consisted
of stories related for a moral purpose or of popular legends,
but they assumed that the New Testament was fully historical and they considered that it was vital to Christian
faith to hold that it was so. While Gore maintained that

1. Cf. p. 219.
2. See *Theology*, March 1941, p. 166. Italics mine.

critical methods of study must be applied to the New Testament as well as to the Old, he succeeded in persuading himself that, if they were rightly applied, the full historicity of the Gospels in particular stood up to the test.

But as critical work on the New Testament developed and its instruments were sharpened, it was borne in upon many Christian scholars that the relation between fact and interpretation, and between history and theology, in the records of Christian origins was much more complex than the *Lux Mundi* school had perceived. At the same time, they were increasingly inclined to urge that the authority of the Catholic faith did not rest simply on historical evidences, as ordinarily understood, or on the testimony of the apostles, but on the whole continuum of Christian experience. Gore did not entirely discount the appeal to Christian experience, but he took his stand on the historical dependability of the New Testament.

That a new generation of theologians was not content to stop where *Lux Mundi* stopped became evident when another volume of essays by a younger group of Oxford scholars appeared in 1912. It was entitled *Foundations: a Statement of Christian Belief in Terms of Modern Thought*. The essay that attracted most attention was one by the editor, B. H. Streeter (1874–1937), on 'The Historic Christ', and that by reason of a passage on the resurrection in which he affirmed the reality of the Risen Lord's appearances as 'objective visions' but, while accepting as conclusive the evidence that the tomb was found empty on the third day, refused to believe that the body of Jesus had been resuscitated and offered instead a highly conjectural explanation of what might actually have happened. But the real interest of Streeter's essay lay in its being the first notable attempt by an Anglican theologian to interpret the life of Jesus in the light of current advances in critical work and the new emphasis on eschatology, associated with the name of Schweitzer. It was not to be supposed, he said, that the Gospels gave a correct chronological account of the ministry of Jesus. They were written for practical and devotional purposes, not to serve the interests of the modern scientific historian. And with reference to the work of Schweitzer, he wrote:

Modern lives of Christ, whether written from a radical or from a conservative standpoint, have been too modern. The pseudo-Romantic Christ of Renan, and the 'bourgeois Christ' of Rationalistic liberalism are quite as far removed from the actual historical figure as the personified abstraction of scholastic logic or the sentimental effeminacy dear to Christian Art. But if we agree with Schweitzer here, yet it is not without a feeling that he himself cannot quite escape the charge of modernizing, and that his own boldly-outlined portrait is a little like the Superman of Nietzsche in Galilean robes.

If Streeter's essay, compared with *Lux Mundi*, revealed a more realistic understanding of how matters stood with regard to the historical foundations of the Christian faith, an essay by A. E. J. Rawlinson (1884–1960) on 'The Principle of Authority' clearly showed a desire for a more free and empirical attitude to the credal definitions which Gore treated as practically infallible. Rawlinson had felt much more sympathy than most Anglicans with the Roman Catholic modernists. He argued that, while authority is necessary in religion as in other fields of belief, it should not be confused with infallibility or a legal despotism. Authority attaches to the testimony of those who speak from experience of spiritual realities, especially the experts, that is the saints. Christian theology may be defined as 'the process of drawing out and formulating in intellectual terms the inferences, historical and metaphysical, which are legitimately involved in the present and past experience of spiritual persons; and more especially, no doubt, in the experiences – "classical and normative" for Christianity – of the apostolic age'. The promise of divine guidance to the Church gives no more warrant for looking for infallibility in the sphere of intellect than for impeccability in the sphere of conduct. There had been a regrettable tendency in the course of church history to treat ecclesiastical authority as if it were mechanically

infallible in its utterances and qualified to impose dicta-
torially on the faithful what they must believe, instead of as
'a guiding-line, a preliminary orientation of the mind as it
embarks upon its voyage of individual discovery and construction'. This tendency had reached its logical culmin-
nation in modern Romanism of the ultramontane type.

This empirical approach to Christian doctrine was further
worked out in later books by Rawlinson himself and by other
liberal Anglo-Catholics – such as Will Spens (1882–1962),
E. G. Selwyn (1885–1959), and W. L. Knox (1886–1950) –
who realized that they were going considerably beyond what
the *Lux Mundi* school had intended. It would be true to say
that they were following up lines of thought that had been
adumbrated by some of the Catholic modernists. The theology of this group eventually found expression in a further
symposium, entitled *Essays Catholic and Critical* (1926).

We have traced the liberalizing of theology among the
High Anglicans because it was most conspicuous there. But
there was a parallel process at work among Evangelicals
both in the Church of England and in the Free Churches. In
addition, a new association of liberal Anglicans, known as the
Churchmen's Union, had been formed in 1898, which was in
the succession of the nineteenth-century Broad Churchmen:
later its members became known as 'Modern Churchmen'
or as 'Modernists', but their affinities were much more with
Liberal Protestantism than with Catholic Modernism.

These developments did not take place without challenge
or disturbance. In fact, during the second decade of the
century there was a pretty violent conservative reaction in
the Church of England as a result of alarm about Streeter's
essay in *Foundations* and a number of other even more provocative publications. R. A. Knox (1888–1957), at this time
the *enfant terrible* of Anglo-Catholicism, published a clever
but superficial attack on the whole liberal movement in
theology, wittily entitled *Some Loose Stones*. More serious
was the outcry of Frank Weston (1871–1924), the learned
and courageous Bishop of Zanzibar, who was faced in his

diocese by Mohammedan propagandists who did not scruple to exploit for their own ends the liberal teaching of theologians in England. It was as difficult for dons at Oxford to accommodate their investigations to the situation in Zanzibar, as it was for the Bishop to feel much sympathy or patience with the atmosphere of academic research that prevailed in an English university.

Not indeed that the atmosphere in the English universities was exactly pacific. For several years a continuous war of pamphlets raged between professors, prelates, and other divines. Gore, now Bishop of Oxford, focused attention on the question whether clergymen were at liberty to doubt or deny the clauses in the creed about the virgin birth and the physical resurrection of Jesus. It looked as though the tide of liberal theology was going to ebb, or at least that essays in theological restatement would be subject to repression by the Convocations. However, the sagacious leadership of Archbishop Davidson of Canterbury more than once averted a crisis. In 1914, for instance, Resolutions were passed affirming that the historic facts stated in the Creeds were an essential part of the Faith of the Church, with this qualifying rider:

At the same time, recognizing that our generation is called to face new problems raised by historical criticism, we are anxious not to lay unnecessary burdens upon consciences, nor unduly to limit freedom of thought and inquiry, whether among clergy or among laity. We desire, therefore, to lay stress on the need of considerateness in dealing with that which is tentative and provisional in the thought and work of earnest and reverent students.

There were further bouts of controversy when, in 1917, Hensley Henson (1863–1947) was nominated to a bishopric and after the war when the Modern Churchmen held an outspoken conference at Girton College, Cambridge, in 1921. Shortly after this, the Archbishop yielded to a suggestion that a Commission should be appointed with members representing Anglo-Catholicism, Modern Churchmanship, and Evangelicalism, which over a period of years should 'consider the nature and grounds of Christian Doctrine with a view to demonstrating the extent of existing agreement within the Church of England and with a view to investigating how far it is possible to remove or diminish existing differences'.

It was a weighty as well as a representative commission and it wisely took its time and did its work thoroughly. Though appointed in 1922, it did not produce its report till 1938. The first chairman of the Commission having died in 1925, he was succeeded by William Temple who continued to preside over its deliberations when he became Archbishop of York in 1929. The Report of the Commission, which was published under the title *Doctrine in the Church of England*, was a substantial volume. It covered with considerable precision the following main topics: The Sources and Authority of Christian Doctrine; The Doctrines of God and of Redemption; The Church and Sacraments; and Eschatology. The Report was unanimous, but the ardent hope of at least one of the members of the Commission (W. R. Matthews) that it would result in the displacement of the XXXIX Articles by a new statement of Anglican belief was disappointed.

Doctrine in the Church of England is the best register that exists of the state of doctrinal belief among Anglican theologians between the World Wars, and it still repays careful study. Discerning readers will see that the contributors to *Foundations* and *Essays Catholic and Critical*, who were strongly represented on the Commission, must have exercised a good deal of influence on its findings, which were however equally acceptable to Liberal Evangelicals. This was indeed the high tide of liberal theology in England. Before the Commission reported, the continental reversion from theological liberalism was already beginning to have its repercussions on this side of the Channel, and Archbishop Temple in his introduction to the Report said that, if it were beginning its work again, 'its perspectives would be different'. The next two chapters will perhaps explain what he had in mind when he said that.

18

Kierkegaard

IT may seem odd that Søren Kierkegaard, who lived from
1813 to 1855, should make his appearance in a history of the
modern church only at this stage. But that is because, in a
real sense, he belongs to the twentieth rather than to the
nineteenth century. In his own time he did indeed make a
great, if baffling, impact on his own country, Denmark, and,
although he had some followers in Germany in the latter
part of the nineteenth century, he made no general impact
on European thought until after the First World War. Since
then, his life and character and writings have been more
studied and discussed than perhaps those of any nineteenth-
century thinker. He has been credited with responsibility for
what is called 'existentialism' and with having given a
decisive impetus to the theology of crisis with which we shall
be concerned in the next chapter. His voluminous works,
which were written in Danish and so were inaccessible to
most of his contemporaries, have now been translated into
other languages, including English, and a vast literature has
grown up around and about him.

He is one of those thinkers whose thought was the product
of his own experience, his own very peculiar experience.
Even his greatest admirers are inclined to allow that his
experience was not only abnormal, but more or less patho-
logical. His detractors go further; they deplore the cult of
which he has been made the subject in our time, seeing in it
an illustration of the morbid irrationalism of many contemporary intellectuals. But whether it be approved or
deplored, there is no doubt that he has had an extraordinary
influence, and an attempt must be made to account for it.
Because his thought was wrung out of his own experience,
it is necessary to know something about his life story, and

also about his father with whom his character was mysteriously bound up.

The father, Michael Pedersen Kierkegaard, was one of a large and poor family: he was brought up on the desolate heaths of Jutland, and worked as a shepherd boy. One day he stood on a height in the heath, and cursed God. This action preyed on his soul for the rest of his long life, for he was an extremely religious man of the austere and gloomy type that in France would be called Jansenist. But material prosperity awaited him. An uncle in Copenhagen took him into his business, and at the age of forty he had done so well that he was able to retire and live in comfort. His first wife died childless in 1796 and he then married his housekeeper by whom he had seven children of whom Søren was the youngest. The boy's life was from the first dominated by his father, who was a man of cultivated intelligence. Michael Kierkegaard had gathered round him a circle of intellectual friends. From an early age Søren listened to their conversations, and his mind was precociously stimulated. In afterlife he complained that he had never been a real child or played games or made friends with his school-fellows. They made him the butt of their jests, and he retaliated by using his sharp, caustic wit. His religious upbringing was strict and serious, but it was in the melancholy, puritanical religion of his father, who wanted him to prepare for the ministry of the Church.

As a university student he began to rebel against the strait-jacket in which he found himself. Ten years elapsed before he took his final examination in theology. He spent the intervening period for the most part in dilettante reading in literature and philosophy, and in exercising his dialectical powers in discussion and debate. He also fell into a spendthrift manner of life. Although his father paid his debts, he regarded his favourite son's aimless frivolity as a punishment for his own sins, especially for his having cursed God as a child, and also apparently for something to do with the circumstances of his second marriage. It is not possible, however, to be sure of the precise facts about the father's sense of guilt nor indeed of Søren's own sense of guilt which he felt he had inherited from his father, since he wrapped up his references to these matters in fictitious and parabolic forms. There is, for instance, this disconcerting entry in his journal:

> After my death, no one shall find in my papers ... a single explanation of what, properly speaking, has filled my life. No one shall find the writing in my inmost soul which explains everything.

The other determining experience in his life was his engagement to Regina Olsen. He knew that he had a dark, unhappy, brooding temperament, and he seems to have hoped that the spontaneous simplicity of Regina would somehow reconcile him to life and give him security. But within a few days of his proposing and being accepted, he began to wonder whether he had not made a mistake, and after little more than a year he broke off the engagement in an apparently cruel manner which caused public scandal and increased his sense of isolation and of being out of joint with his times and the accepted conventions of society. His reflections on this affair are also cast in fictitious form and are difficult to unravel. It would seem that his deeply ingrained sense of guilt, inherited and personal, made him doubt whether he was fitted for the marriage relationship. Was he not destined for a solitary life in which he would have to wrestle with his fate alone? And would not his melancholy, tormented nature be quite unintelligible to Regina, so that their union could not be a true marriage of minds? Still, it is clear that his love for her never abated, and to the end of his life he was perplexed by the question whether he had acted rightly.

Kierkegaard was now (1841) twenty-eight years of age. His father had died, and bequeathed to him his house in Copenhagen and enough to live on. Sometimes he dallied with the idea of becoming a country pastor, but he was never ordained. He believed his vocation was to be an independent author, and during the fourteen years that remained to him he threw himself into literary activity. His collected works fill fourteen large volumes, and after his death his diaries and other papers produced a further six volumes. Though always a solitary figure, he was not a recluse. He constantly walked about Copenhagen, entering into conversation with all sorts and conditions of people. It was said of him that 'his smile could express everything, and its effect was as when the sun bursts through a cloud', and of his conversation that 'there was always something unexpected in his speech . . . he could create a feeling, purely by means of words, that one was standing in the midst of a drama or story'.

What was it then at bottom that he had to say? He had no system of doctrine. He threw out, or rather flashed out, ideas, as he reflected on his own tortuous experience, like an artist or poet or prophet. But we can dwell a little on certain characteristic features of his thought.

First, his anti-Hegelianism. Hegelianism[1] was the reigning philosophy in Denmark at the time, and the leading Danish theologian, Hans Martensen (1808–84), was in the fashion. Nature, history, and God were embraced in a rational system, and the whole was seen as an evolving process. Everything was given its appropriate place in the system: law, culture, literature, and art. It was the office of the State to embody and organize all these elements, and the Christian State was a realization of the Kingdom of God. To Kierkegaard this seemed to be an emasculated theology, a 'ballet of bloodless categories'. God was no longer on the throne of the universe, but human reason, and God was assigned his place by grace of human reason. The world was regarded as an aesthetic harmony, not as a battleground for moral struggle. Sin was but a necessary stage in the self-revelation of Absolute Spirit. Everything was explained in terms of gradual transition. There were no sharp edges in this Hegelian world, and above all no precipices.

1. See pp. 28–31.

The effect of this way of thinking was, in Kierkegaard's view, the destruction of individual personality and responsibility. Everything was taken up into the whole, the collective. The radical difference between good and evil, and between God and man, was abolished. There was no ultimate difference between them, for they were to be reconciled in a higher unity. There was no place or need for a direct, personal divine intervention in human affairs to rescue man from sin, from his guilty estrangement from the source of his true being. But for Kierkegaard sin was the fundamental fact of man's spiritual and moral position.

It had cast its deep shadow over his own life and career, and he felt it to be his task to make individuals see its terrible power and to seek the only way of deliverance from it by a living faith in Jesus Christ. Sin was not to be overcome either by mere education or by substituting virtuous for vicious acts. What was required was the transformation of the whole life of a man, which could be accomplished only by a decisive act of faith, a leap or spring into a new relationship with God. This transformation or new creation could not be arrived at by speculation or by accepting a system on authority. It could be reached only subjectively, in the conflicts of personal experience. The truth could be apprehended, he said, only by someone who lay struggling for his life upon 70,000 fathoms of water. Here was a flat contradiction of the whole Hegelian system. For Kierkegaard life was a matter of 'either – or', which is the title of one of his books, whereas for the Hegelians it was always 'both – and'. Anti-Hegelianism is no doubt a negative way of looking at Kierkegaard's teaching, but it must be emphasized because he regarded it as his mission to destroy confidence in all philosophical systems, and to throw men back upon themselves, so that they had to make decisions for themselves in terms of their own individual experience.

A second feature of his teaching was his stress on Christianity as *paradox*. 'The thinker who is devoid of paradox', he said, 'is like the lover who is devoid of passion.' According to Kierkegaard, there is no intellectual proof of Christianity. Faith cannot be built upon such proofs or upon the authority of the Bible or the Church. Christian faith affirms an irreconcilable contradiction. There is an infinite, qualitative difference between eternity and time, and between God and man; yet Christianity affirms that they are united in the God-man. It is impossible for the intellect to accept the fact of the incarnation: it is a contradiction that can be accepted only by the leap of faith. Many have pointed out that Kierkegaard had much in common with Pascal.

God in human form is an absolute paradox, which can never be anything but a stumbling-block to the human mind. Therefore faith cannot be an act of the understanding. It is a venture of the will, which must be continually renewed because objections to it are continually arising. Kierkegaard seems often to glory in irrationality, but he did not deny that what strikes us as paradox is reasonable for God. So he wrote in his journal: 'The paradox in Christian truth is invariably due to the fact that it is truth as it exists for God. The standard of measure and the end is superhuman; and there is only one relationship possible: faith.' He was concerned to shatter men's trust in substitute securities, for example in philosophical, doctrinal, or ecclesiastical systems, and to bring them to the place where they do really have to trust in God alone, because every other object of trust has been knocked away from them.

We have yet to consider Kierkegaard's relations with the Church of his time, that is with the State Church of Denmark, which in its general ethos was much like established churches elsewhere, though in Scandinavia the Church was more closely bound up with the State than almost anywhere else. Although Kierkegaard had never proceeded to ordination, he had continued to be a conforming member of the Church. The bishop, Mynster by name, had been a close friend of his father, and Søren himself had owned that he had been much indebted to Mynster's teaching. Nevertheless, his interpretation of Christian faith obviously implied a profound questioning of the whole established set-up and of the official theology. But it was not till towards the end of his life that this became explicit. At the last, he was moved to make an all-out attack on the Church.

It happened thus. Bishop Mynster died in January 1854. Martensen, who was to be his successor, made the funeral oration, and spoke of Mynster as a 'true witness to the truth', as one in the chain of witnesses to the truth that reached back to the apostles. This was too much for Kierkegaard who had been waiting for an opportunity to say what he really thought about the official Christianity of the Church. He delayed for some months before opening his attack because, it is said, he did not want to prejudice Martensen's candidature for succession to the bishopric. But when he did attack, it was in violent terms.

He fastened on the fact that Martensen had described Mynster as a 'true witness to the truth'. 'A witness to the truth', he said, 'is a man whose life has brought him profound knowledge of inner conflicts, fear and trembling, temptations, spiritual distress, moral suffering. A witness to the truth is a man who bears witness to the truth in poverty, in humiliation, and contempt, misunderstood, hated, mocked at, despised, ridiculed. A witness to the truth is a martyr.' The idea that Mynster had been a witness to the truth was monstrous. He had been a time-server, a man of the world, a clever and successful ecclesiastical politician, who had 'had the pleasure of declaiming in "quiet hours" on Sundays, and then covering himself with worldly shrewdness on Mondays'. Who was he to be numbered with those who had sealed the truth with their blood?

This attack made a tremendous sensation in Copenhagen, not only because of Kierkegaard's long-standing friendship with Mynster, but because he had hitherto been regarded as politically conservative and a supporter of the Church. Many people thought he had gone mad, and they thought so all the more when he followed up his first article with a

whole series in which he attacked the very idea of respectable, official Christianity. The Christianity preached in the
State Church was an apostasy from the Christianity of the
New Testament. It was an attempt to make a fool of God.
The Church had ceased to be a real Church of Christ.
New Testament Christianity was no longer to be found anywhere in the world. The history of the Church was a history
of increasing degeneracy. It began on the day of Pentecost,
when the apostles admitted 3,000 persons on one day. How
could so many truly attach themselves to it at once?

Among the clergy of the Danish Church there was not an
honest man. They were all place-seekers, who had entered
the ministry merely as a profession in which they could earn
their daily bread in a secure position. A State Church could
not be a true Church: its clergy were only government
officials, bound to do what was pleasing to the government.
The whole idea of 'Christendom', of making Christianity
official and respectable and conventional, was criminal. It
concealed from the people what Christianity really was.

In the magnificent cathedral, the Honourable and Right
Reverend Geheime-General – Ober-Hof – Prädikant, the elect
favourite of the fashionable world, steps forth. He appears before a
chosen circle of the elect and preaches emotionally on a text
chosen by himself: 'God hath chosen the base things of the world,
and the things that are despised,' – and nobody laughs.

Or again:

We have what one might call a complete inventory of churches,
bells, organs, foot-warmers, alms-boxes, hearses, etc. But when
Christianity does not exist, the existence of this inventory, Chris-
tianly considered, is so far from being advantageous to Christianity
that it is actually a peril, because it so very easily gives rise to the
misunderstanding that, having such a complete Christian inventory, we naturally have Christianity too.

And with regard to the future:

Certainly things must be reformed, and it will be a frightful
reformation which will have for its watch-word, 'Will faith be
found upon earth?' and it will be characterized by the fact that

men will fall away from Christianity by the millions, a frightful reformation; for the fact is, Christianity does not exist, and it is horrible when a generation coddled by a childish Christianity, deluded into the vain notion that they are Christians, have to receive again the death-blow of learning what it is to become a Christian, to be a Christian.

So for months on end, Kierkegaard drove home his attack with biting irony and brilliant epigrams. He had hoped that the official Church would be spurred into taking some action against him, so that his witness could be the more effective. But the bishops and clergy decided to lie low and to ignore the challenge. On the other hand, many lay people, especially students, were deeply moved and perceived that he had raised a fundamental question about the nature of Christianity which could not be simply brushed aside as the jabbering of a madman. These were the first-fruits of all who were to be held and haunted by Kierkegaard's teaching long after his death. For the sands of his life were now fast running out. He fell ill while still at work, and, though unreconciled to the Church, he died in faith and sure and certain hope of the resurrection.

*

It is hardly surprising that Kierkegaard's voice fell on deaf or uncomprehending ears in his own time, but now he may appear to stand as a great question-mark over both the religious and secular thought and the church life of the nineteenth century. His being rediscovered after 1914 can be attributed to the breakdown of confidence in the idols of the Age of Reason and in the brave new world which democracy and science and moral idealism and liberal religion had promised to create. Had not Kierkegaard seen through the forces that were making for a collectivist culture and that were threatening the freedom of the human person? At least he had not been taken in by the progressive expectations that the Revolution had borne and nourished.

He had not been impressed, for instance, by democracy

with its confidence in majorities. 'One hundred thousand millions, of whom every one is "just like the others", equals One,' he said. 'Only when there appears some one who is different from these millions, or this One – only then is it Two.' And again: 'Truth is always in the minority, and the minority is always stronger than the majority, because the minority as a rule is formed of those who really have an opinion, while the strength of the majority is illusory, formèd by the gang who have no opinion.'

Nor had he been impressed by the advances of the natural sciences. They were represented as leading to a complete system of knowledge in which everything would be explained, including man. But in human personality there was something that was inexplicable in mechanical or evolutionary terms. 'Sciencemongery', he said, 'will be especially dangerous and corrupting when it wants to invade the territory of the spirit. Let them deal with plants and animals and stars like this, but to treat the spirit of man in such a way is blasphemy.'

In his attack on Hegelianism he had been withstanding the depersonalization of man. Hegelianism as such may have been on its last legs when Kierkegaard attacked it. But was not Marxism an inverted Hegelianism? Marx was a pupil of Hegel who, as it were, took the Master's concepts and brought them down to earth. As for Hegel thought was an expression of the world spirit, so for Marx human acts became part of a chain of cause and effect mechanically understood. What for Hegel was the necessity of world history became an economic determinism, and the processes of production took the place of speculation. There was just as little place for personal freedom in Marx's system as in Hegel's. Human consciousness was declared to be a reflection of material processes without a real existence of its own. Either way the individual is a mere cog in the machine, whether the machine is constituted by abstract thought or by economic production.

Thus Kierkegaard's protest against Hegelianism had by

no means lost its point. Men who felt themselves caught in the toils of collectivism, whether communist or fascist or of mass culture, turned eagerly to his vindication of the status of the individual human person. This too is why the existentialists looked back to Kierkegaard as their pioneer or herald. He had stood for the primacy of personal existence over against all ideal essences and abstract systems and collective authorities.

While for Kierkegaard it had been God, the Wholly Other, whom the individual person was above all to encounter concretely in the conflicts of experience as both his judge and his absolver, and it was in his decision *vis-à-vis* God that his personal existence was to be realized, yet we can see that there could also be an existentialism that left God out of the picture and saw the human person as ultimately alone in his freedom and in his obligation to decide what he was going to do with his freedom.

Thus the atheistic existentialism of Jean-Paul Sartre could also be said to stem from Kierkegaard, and it is interesting to observe that Sartre, like Kierkegaard, holding that the problems of life and morality do not lend themselves to abstract theorizing, finds that the best vehicles for conveying his message are not philosophical treatises, but the drama, the novel, and the diary. And if the question be asked: What *is* existentialism? perhaps there is no better answer than: Go and read Kierkegaard. But if a definition is demanded, what Karl Heim said of Kierkegaard's type of thought is as good as any: 'A proposition or truth is said to be *existential* when I cannot apprehend or assent to it from the standpoint of a mere spectator but only on the ground of my total existence.'[1]

1. See also Paul Roubiczek, *Existentialism For and Against*, 1964.

19

The Theology of Crisis

It would be foolish to suggest that 'the theology of crisis' or 'the dialectical theology', which began to come into prominence after the First World War and is associated preeminently with the name of Karl Barth (1886–1968), arose purely from a rediscovery of Kierkegaard. There is a whole complex of circumstances and factors that must be brought into the picture if its genesis and vogue are to be understood.

In the first place, there was the catastrophe of the First World War, which dealt a deadly blow to the idea of inevitable progress through intellectual enlightenment and moral endeavour. The tragic experience of being caught up in the irrationality and meaninglessness of war made men wonder whether life could really be explained in the easy, optimistic, and evolutionary way that had come to be generally accepted in the preceding period. Had not Christian theology and Christian preaching too readily accommodated themselves to the prevailing assumptions? Had the Church no message from beyond the reach of human reason, no revelation from on high which it must witness to and interpret, no goal to proclaim other than the refinements of bourgeois society? The Liberal Theology in its various forms, which, as we have seen, had been more and more in the ascendant, seemed to have little to say to the agonizing questions that the breakdown of civilization drove home.

Perhaps no better epitome of the Liberal Theology, as it appeared to those who were dissatisfied with it and were to react against it, has been given than that by Richard Niebuhr (1894–1962) in his description of what American Liberal Protestantism added up to in the end:

The romantic conception of the kingdom of God involved no discontinuities, no crises, no tragedies, or sacrifices, no loss of all things, no cross, and resurrection. In ethics it reconciled the interests of the individual with those of society by means of faith in a natural identity of interests or in the benevolent, altruistic character of man. In politics and economics it slurred over national and class divisions, seeing only the growth of unity and ignoring the increase of self-assertion and exploitation. In religion it reconciled God and man by deifying the latter and humanizing the former. . . . Christ the Redeemer became Jesus the teacher or the spiritual genius in whom the religious capacities of mankind were fully developed. . . . Evolution, growth, development, the culture of the religious life, the nurture of the kindly sentiments, the extension of humanitarian ideals, and the progress of civilization took the place of the Christian revolution. . . .

A God without wrath brought men without sin into a kingdom without judgement through the ministrations of a Christ without a cross.[1]

But, secondly, the Liberal Theology had been rudely shaken from within, well before the onset of the war. As early as 1893 Johannes Weiss (1863–1914), a New Testament scholar who had grown up in the Ritschlian tradition, had said that his study of the Gospels had convinced him that, for the Jesus of history, the Kingdom of God had meant something different from what Ritschl had taught. Ritschl had assumed that Jesus had consciously willed an enduring community in this world through which the Kingdom of God would be gradually extended and established. But the evidence of the Gospels showed that the Kingdom which Jesus had proclaimed was an eschatological reality to be revealed in the near future by the sovereign act of God. Ritschl's idea of it was the result of reading back into the New Testament notions of process, historical evolution, and progress, which were intelligible and congenial to men living in the nineteenth century, but altogether alien in the apocalyptic context of Palestine in the first century.

The point was later made by George Tyrrell when he said that Harnack looked at the Jesus of history down a deep well

1. H. Richard Niebuhr. *The Kingdom of God in America*. Harper Torchbook edn., pp. 191ff.; cf. my *Essays in Liberality*. 1957, p. 16.

and saw his own face reflected at the bottom. Early in this century Albert Schweitzer (1875–1965) administered the *coup de grâce* to the liberal lives of Jesus, which had been produced in profusion in the nineteenth century, in his *Quest of the Historical Jesus* (Eng. trans. 1910). He held that the whole attempt to portray Jesus and his message in terms that were acceptable to the modern mind had proved bankrupt. Schweitzer, who proceeded to become a medical missionary in Africa, subsequently worked out a philosophy of his own, of which the key concept was 'reverence for life'. Though he had prepared the way for the theology of crisis, he had no part in it. He once said to Karl Barth: 'You and I, Barth, started from the same problem, the disintegration of modern thought; but, whereas you went back to the Reformation, I went back to the Enlightenment.'

Liberal theology at its strongest had other weaknesses too. It had set itself to meet the intellectual challenge to Christianity from modern science, philosophy, and historical criticism, and it had done so with such success that students from other lands flocked to the German and Swiss universities to sit at the feet of the theological professors who were men of vast learning and prestige. But, so far as the ordinary pastors and preachers and the laity were concerned, the teaching of the professors was either over their heads or left them with little more than a vague moral idealism which was scarcely distinguishable from that of non-Christian humanitarians. When the war led to a general loosening of moral standards and placed a moratorium on the ethical values, a gospel was called for with more of a cutting edge. The situation was intensified tenfold in Germany where on top of the strain of war came the calamity of defeat, the paralysing provisions of the Treaty of Versailles, and the frustrations of the Weimar Republic.

Barth himself was originally a theological liberal of the Ritschlian school. He was also what in Germany was called a 'religious socialist', that is a Christian socialist, and he remained a socialist when he ceased to identify the objectives of socialism with the Kingdom of God. During the First World War he was pastor of a little parish on the borders of Switzerland. His sermons were preached within sound of the gunfire in Alsace. He became convinced of the hopeless inadequacy of the liberal social gospel which was then his pulpit matter. Here were people waiting pathetically to be assured of the reality of God in a world that had gone mad. Here was the Bible, whose every page spoke of the reality of God, and here was he, supposed to be preaching the Word of God, and unable to do so to any effect.

It was then that Kierkegaard opened his mind, and made him doubt the idealistic world-view of history as a process of thesis and antithesis, leading up to a grand synthesis in which all contradictions would be resolved. Human life seemed rather to be an insoluble paradox, a question without an answer. As Barth read not only Kierkegaard, but the Bible and Luther and Calvin and Dostoyevsky, it was borne in upon him that the true God, the living God, was wholly different from any God that could be discovered on the human plane, from the so-called God who had been argued into existence by the philosophers. Men would never come to hear the authentic Word of the true God till they had acknowledged their own plight; till they had discovered that all their last questions were unanswerable questions, and that all the alleys they went down in their enlightenment, including the alley of religion, proved to be blind alleys. It was only the blind, and those who knew themselves to be blind, who could receive their sight.

It was in this frame of mind that in 1918 Barth published his *Commentary on the Epistle to the Romans*.[1] It was in the form of an exegetical commentary on the text of the Epistle, and Barth wished it to be judged as such. But it was unlike any commentary that had been seen before. It abounds in passages like the following:

We know that human language can never break through to the absolute: for that would be the end of all things, and to that we

1. Admirably translated into English by Sir Edwyn Hoskyns (1933).

can never be so bold as to set our hands . . . there exists the abnormal, irregular, revolutionary – in the most significant sense of the word, 'Revolutionary' – possibility of venturing, half seriously, half jocularly, upon an advance into the absolute. The Epistle to the Romans is such an advance. It is theology, a conversation about God, undertaken with penetrating understanding of the One in all.

There are no human avenues of approach, no 'way of salvation'; to faith there is no ladder which must first be scaled. Faith is its own initiative, its own presupposition. . . . For all faith is both simple and difficult . . . for all it is a leap into the void. And it is possible for all, only because it is equally impossible for all.

It has been said that the publication of Barth's *Romans* 'coming after a generation of cool, objective Biblical scholarship, gave the theological world a sudden shock, for it dared to translate Paul's epistle to the Romans into a special-delivery letter to the twentieth century'. It was as though Barth had opened a door and let the Transcendent God, the Unknown God, the God who is Wholly Other, back into the world. He found himself hailed as a prophet, or as the founder of a school – which he has always disowned. Others regarded his incomprehensible paradoxes, his disparagement of all human capacities, and his revival of the doctrine of total corruption, as a sad manifestation of wartime mentality, a rocket that might dazzle for a moment but would disappear and leave things as they were.

But that at least was not to happen. Barth himself realized that he could not leave matters there. So he set himself to work out the implications of what had come to him as a revelation, and he went on doing so for the rest of his life with the utmost theological seriousness. His immense work on *Dogmatics* was never completed. One thing that has been greatly to his credit, though very embarrassing for those who seek to be his disciples, is that he has never scrupled to change his mind or to modify opinions that he had previously expressed. On all hands he has been recognized as the greatest theologian of his time, and it is striking that many Roman Catholics have regarded him as such and have sought to engage with his thought. It was a German Catholic who said that Barth's *Romans* 'fell like a bomb on the playground of the theologians'. It is too early yet to say what the long-term effects of the dropping of that bomb may be, or to attempt a definitive appraisal of Barth's theology and its influence. Only some provisional remarks can be made.

First, it is likely that what he has had to say about God will be seen to be more important than what he has had to say about man. Like John the Baptist in Grünewald's painting of the Crucifixion Barth pointed a long, bony finger to God the Transcendent in his inscrutable and ineffable majesty. He made the point, to use his own words, that 'one can *not* speak about God simply by speaking of man in a loud voice'. On the other hand, it often seemed as though Barth imagined that the more he denigrated man, the more he was glorifying God. His attacks on 'natural theology' and human reason may have been justified as a corrective, but he appeared to leave no possible point of contact between God and man. However, this is one of the respects in which he modified his earlier statements.

Secondly, the first impression many people had was that Barth's teaching must cut the nerve of human endeavour and responsibility. If man, apart from the miraculous gift of faith, could do nothing but evil, if it was sheer blasphemy to suppose he could do anything whatever about building the Kingdom of God, and if all he ought to do was to wait for it to be given as an eschatological reality, then there was nothing to be done but to adopt an attitude of passive expectancy. But the effect of Barth's teaching and example were entirely different from that. It was he who nerved the Confessing Church in Germany to resist the attempts of the Nazis to corrupt the Christian witness, and who was driven into exile for doing so. He was far from being a pacifist. During the Second World War he addressed a 'Letter to Great Britain' in which he said that 'the Christians who do not realize that they must take part unreservedly in this war must have slept over their Bibles as well as over their newspapers'. He has always been definite and outspoken about the political obligations of Christian men.

Thirdly, although some who have disliked his teaching have spoken of him as a theological reactionary or obscurantist, he has never been that. For instance, he has never gone back on the critical study of the Bible, but would claim to have gone on from it. His attitude to the historical Jesus and to miracles has been more radical, and even sceptical, than that of most English theologians. He did not claim that the resurrection of Christ, which was basic to his whole theology, was empirically verifiable as a historical event.

Much the same applies to his reputed Calvinism. Certainly he called to life again Calvin's teaching about the glory and majesty of God, but in the matter of predestination, though Barth has had much to say about it, he has said something different from Calvin. According to Calvin, God by an arbitrary decree predestined some men to salvation, leaving the rest to inevitable damnation. According to Barth, who sees in Christ the elect and predestined Head of the new and redeemed humanity, all men are predestined to damnation in so far as they are sinners, and all men are predestined to salvation in so far as they have been redeemed in Christ. In fact, Barth appears to be a universalist, though in no easy-going or optimistic way, as was pointed out by Dr N. W. Porteous in *The Criterion* in 1934. A dozen years later, Dr C. van Til, an orthodox Calvinist of the traditional kind, in a book entitled *The New Modernism*, was charging Barth with being a dangerously liberal theologian!

We have been speaking as though Barth stood on a solitary eminence with the theology of crisis in his hands, or like Moses went up on to the mountain of the Lord alone. It would not be a wild exaggeration to say so, but in fact there is a large company of theologians that has more or less followed where Barth led. Many no doubt followed him too blindly, as is ever the case with men of genius; but he has had distinguished collaborators, like Emil Brunner (1889–1966), who have not hesitated to differ from him. Brunner, it may be noted, was found to be more digestible in the Anglo-Saxon world, partly because his works were less voluminous, but also because his theology was less blatantly paradoxical. It is also worth while pointing out to English readers that Karl Barth's son, Markus, after he had been studying theology in Britain before the Second World War, wrote an article for *The Congregational Quarterly* (October 1939), in which he said in effect that the British could best get the message his father had to deliver from a theologian of their own, P. T. Forsyth,[1] 'the theologian for the practical man'. And it is true that Forsyth in a succession of books had made the same points as Barth, and made them in an English, if highly rhetorical, idiom and against the English background. It is significant that Forsyth is one of the few British theologians who before 1914 showed any acquaintance with Kierkegaard: James Denney (1856–1917) was another.

The reader may by now wish to have some explanation of the expressions 'theology of crisis' and 'dialectical theology'. The term *crisis* refers here not so much to the fact that both civilization and theology were felt to have come to a crisis in the ordinary sense of a grave turning-point, as to the perpetual *Krisis*, that is, the Judgement, under which man always falls when he tries to solve the problem of his destiny by his own powers. Over every man, every institution, every culture, yes and over every church, God's judgement and condemnation lowers like a thunder-cloud, and only when this is admitted can man find the divine mercy and forgiveness. In other words, according to the theology of crisis, the divine judgement is operative always, not only at the termination of history, and it is the task of the preacher and the theologian to read the signs of its presence.

The expression 'dialectical theology' is not of course used here in the Hegelian sense of an immanent dialectical process which works through thesis and antithesis to synthesis, for this theology looks for no synthesis on the horizontal

1. Cf. p. 195.

plane of development. The horizontal line of man's existence is at every moment intersected by the vertical line of God's transcendence, which reveals the paradoxical character of all that men think or say or do. There is a No as well as a Yes to be said even to the highest human ideas and doctrines and achievements. If it be said that God was revealed in Jesus Christ, it must also be said that he was hidden and incognito. If it be said that the Church is the body of Christ, it must also be said that it is a wretched company of sinful men. This ambiguity will be the character of all things human, including the redeemed humanity, as long as history lasts. A dialectical theology is persistently critical. A church whose theology is dialectical will realize that it always stands in need of reformation, and will never claim that its Reformation was accomplished once and for all in the past. In its moments of most confident proclamation it will be kept humble by the consciousness of its frailty. He who glories must glory only in the Lord.

*

There have been other influential theologians who have moved within this post-Kierkegaardian circle of ideas, though it would be misleading to put them in a class with Karl Barth. The American Reinhold Niebuhr (1892-1971) reacted almost as violently as Barth against the moral idealism of Liberal Protestant theology. Ever since the 1930s when he published his book *Moral Man and Immoral Society*, he has been applying the methods of dialectical theology in the sphere of Christian ethics and of national and international politics, and has kept up what many would call a prophetic commentary on current events. His interest in Christian dogma has been less direct and less precise than Barth's, but he did as much as anyone to reinstate and to reinterpret the ideas of 'original sin' and 'justification by faith' as categories that bring illumination to social and political issues.

His influence extended far beyond the U.S.A. and was

particularly powerful in Britain before and during the Second World War. On his visits to Britain he was one of the rare theologians to be invited to write for the *New Statesman* and other secular periodicals. In so far as Christian thought has become realistic and ceased to be idealistic, it is largely the result of his demonstration of the complexity of all apparently simple ethical decisions. 'An adequate politics is possible', he said in 1934, 'only if the task of achieving some kind of decent harmony in social relations is essayed with a clear understanding of the stubborn inertia which every social purpose meets in the egoism of individuals and groups.' And again: 'The genius of classical religion is that it finds a basis for optimism after it has entertained the most thoroughgoing pessimism.' And again in his Gifford Lectures (1943): 'The truth, as it is contained in the Christian revelation, includes the recognition that it is neither possible for man to know the truth fully, nor to avoid the error of pretending that he does.' By 1960 Reinhold Niebuhr, like Karl Barth, was acknowledging that some of his earlier statements had been too extreme. 'When I find neo-orthodoxy turning into sterile orthodoxy or a new Scholasticism, I find that I am a liberal at heart, and that many of my broadsides at liberalism were indiscriminate.'

Paul Tillich (1886–1965), since 1933 an exile from Germany settled in the U.S.A., was also in a class by himself. Whereas Barth's theology was, in intention at least, entirely biblical and he would not allow that philosophy offered even a subsidiary way to the knowledge of God, Tillich's was highly metaphysical and he denied that there was any one biblical norm of divine truth which theologians must go on expounding in age after age. In his view, theologians must attend closely to the philosophical quest in every generation and to the questions it poses, and the meaning of Jesus Christ must be stated in answer to the questions which philosophy formulates. In Tillich's work there was a correlation of metaphysics – a philosophy of what he called 'The New Being' – with a terminology derived from the

Bible. This may have made his thought more complex, but it also meant that he could get on to speaking terms with lay minds in a way that Barth was hardly able to do. He made a determined attempt to bridge the gulf between religious and secular thought.

Rudolf Bultmann (b. 1884) also believes that the forms in which the Gospel is presented must take account of contemporary man's understanding of his own existence. That is why he has insisted on the need to 'demythologize' the Gospel. The Bible, he says, is written within the framework of an ancient and now incredible world-view: the three-storey universe, supernatural beings coming to the earth from above and below, etc. He wants to separate the positive content of the Gospel from this mythical world-view, which is now an obstacle to grasping its real substance. Demythologizing, he maintains, will not involve a rejection of the authority of the Bible as the medium of the Word of God; it is the only way in which it can be set free from outworn beliefs and so get across to men who regard the scientific world-view as axiomatic. Bultmann's own way of representing the Gospel is in terms of an existentialist philosophy, but his main point would hold good even if some other philosophy were regarded as more satisfactory.

20

Eastern Orthodoxy

FOR the Orthodox Churches of the East, the nineteenth and twentieth centuries have also been 'an age of revolution', but the changes that have taken place in their condition have been primarily determined by their own history and circumstances. Nevertheless, although the French Revolution and the forces that flowed from it did not have a direct and immediate effect on the Eastern Churches, the East was not altogether impervious to them. In particular, there are obviously similarities as well as differences between the French and Russian Revolutions.

At the end of the eighteenth century, the Eastern Churches were almost as bewildering in their variety as the Churches of the West, but three broad distinctions can be drawn between them.

First, there were the Churches which in antiquity (that is from the fifth century) had been organized under the four patriarchates of Constantinople, Alexandria, Antioch, and Jerusalem. Their patriarchal status meant that the bishops of those sees were considered to have jurisdiction over the surrounding territories and the right of appointing metropolitans. The Patriarch of Constantinople, the New Rome, was known as 'the Oecumenical Patriarch'. There was a long struggle for pre-eminence between him and the Pope of Rome, the Patriarch of the West, until the Great Schism of the eleventh century. But, though the Oecumenical Patriarch failed to win this struggle, he remained pre-eminent in the East.

When Asia Minor, the Balkans, and the countries around the Eastern Mediterranean fell under the Moslem dominion of the Ottoman Empire, the lot of the Church in those territories became a melancholy one. They lived a miserable existence as tolerated aliens and were confined within a sort of ghetto. The power of the Oecumenical Patriarch, however, increased with regard both to the other patriarchates and to these territories as a whole, because the Turks found it advantageous to use him as the representative of all his co-religionists and to make him their civil as well as their ecclesiastical head. He became in fact a servant of the Ottoman Empire, and had under him an order of Greek officials, known as the Phanariots (from the Phanar, the Greek quarter of Constantinople), who were charged with the collection of taxes and were as unpopular as the 'publicans' in the time of Jesus. By a shameless system of corruption the Sultan controlled the elections to the patriarchate. During the eighteenth century forty-eight patriarchs had succeeded one another within sixty-three years.

Secondly, there was the Russian Church which, after a long struggle for autonomy, had had its independence recognized by the creation of the Patriarchate of Moscow in 1589. By that time it had become the largest and most influential of the Eastern Churches, and the mystique of 'the Third Rome'[1] had been developed, according to which the Tsars were the legitimate successors of the Byzantine Emperors and 'Holy Russia' was the residuary legatee of the ideal of a universal Christian Empire. The Russian Church had however been beset by schism in the seventeenth century when 'the Old Believers' broke away in protest against the introduction of graecizing liturgical reforms, and its freedom as a self-governing Church had been gravely impaired when Peter the Great (1672–1725), as part of his westernizing policy, suppressed the Moscow patriarchate and substituted for it the so-called 'Holy Synod', a committee administered by a lay 'Procurator' who was appointed by the Tsar. The Russian Church was governed in this way until the Bolshevik Revolution.

Thirdly, there were a considerable number of other

1. Cf. G. R. Cragg. *The Church and the Age of Reason*. Penguin Books, 1960, pp. 107ff.

Eastern Churches of various origin. Some derived from schisms that had arisen in the early Church, Nestorians and Monophysites, for example, others from the missionary activity of the Byzantine Church, and there were also 'Uniate' Churches, that is communities which were in communion with the See of Rome but allowed to retain their own rites and customs. The story of many of these Churches is full of interest, not because of any revolutionary changes that they have undergone, but on the contrary because of the dogged persistence with which they have preserved, in what might almost be called a fossilized form, ancient patterns of Christian life and worship. But we must limit our attention here to the Churches of the Oecumenical Patriarchate and to the Russian Church.

During the nineteenth century, the Balkan countries gradually succeeded in gaining their independence from the decadent Sublime Porte, and their Churches in asserting their claim to be autocephalous, that is their right to elect their own primates and to be self-governing. The struggle for independence, which was stimulated by the revolutionary and nationalist movements in Western Europe, was no doubt heroic, but it was not altogether edifying. For instance, the Greek insurgents, who in 1821 freed the Morea (the Peloponnesus) from Turkish rule, massacred the whole Moslem population of ten to fifteen thousand. The Sultan took his revenge by executing the Oecumenical Patriarch, a Phanariot Greek, and exposing his body for three days before it was given to the mob, dragged through the streets, and thrown into the sea. The Greeks finally secured their political emancipation as a result of the naval battle of Navarino (1827) when the British, French, and Russian fleets defeated the Turks and the Egyptians. In 1829 Greece was recognized as an independent monarchy. The Greek Church, on account of doubts about the character and intentions of the insurgents, had not been unreservedly behind the War of Independence, but parliament in 1833 declared the Church to be autocephalous and set up a

Holy Synod, after the Russian example, to govern it. This was not at all agreeable to the Oecumenical Patriarchate, which did not accept the situation till 1850.

The struggle of the Serbs for independence from Turkish rule was more protracted. While they secured partial political autonomy early in the century and the Archbishop of Belgrade was recognized by the Oecumenical Patriarchate as Metropolitan of Serbia in 1832, it was not until 1878 that full independence was achieved and in the following year the Church too became self-governing.

The Church in Bulgaria had maintained its independence till 1767 when the Sultan had placed it under the control of the Oecumenical Patriarch, who proceeded to appoint Greek bishops to the Bulgarian sees. This led to bitter and prolonged strife which continued throughout the nineteenth century, and the Turkish government skilfully exploited the feuds between the Christians. The 'Bulgarian Atrocities' of 1876, which roused the indignation of Mr Gladstone, were a by-product of this strife. Although the Bulgarians won partial political independence shortly afterwards and complete independence in 1908, the independence of the Bulgarian Church was not finally recognized by the Oecumenical Patriarchate till 1945.

Rumania won its political independence in 1880 and its ecclesiastical independence in 1885. In 1925 the Archbishop of Bucharest adopted the title 'Patriarch of the Rumanian Church'. Other Churches, which had been subject to the Oecumenical Patriarchate, for example Montenegro and Albania, likewise sooner or later became self-governing. Thus the power of the Oecumenical Patriarchate (which the Turks had extended and buttressed for reasons of administrative convenience), and the number of the faithful directly subject to it, were vastly diminished; they were diminshed still further when the Greco-Turkish War of 1922 led to the evacuation of the Greek population from Asia Minor. The Oecumenical Patriarch now exercises direct jurisdiction only over four metropolitans in Turkey and over some dioceses of the Orthodox Church of the dispersion, as in Western Europe and America, but he still clings to his traditional prerogatives and is accorded a primacy of honour by the autocephalous Churches.

What was the effect of these developments on the inner life of this group of Churches?

Take the Church of Greece for example. The parliament, as soon as it had declared the Church to be autocephalous, suppressed about four hundred monasteries which had less than six monks each, but this measure probably served the true interests of monasticism. The parish priests continued for the most part to be peasant farmers like their parishioners and their religious work to consist chiefly in administering the sacraments, but steps were taken to improve their status and their education. There was a striking revival of home missions in the nineteenth century through itinerant preachers, though they were often in trouble with the ecclesiastical authorities, as the Methodists had been in eighteenth-century England. Early in the present century an important society of theologians, mostly laymen, known as 'Zoë', was founded: the members live in community for a month of each year, and for the rest of the time are dispersed through the country, preaching, teaching, and promoting Bible-reading. Their Journal, also called *Zoë*, has 170,000 subscribers, and the movement has given birth to a number of other organizations for intellectuals as well as for peasants. Much has been done in this way to deepen appreciation of the liturgy, to encourage frequent communion, and to awaken interest in the message and life of the Church. There are theological faculties in the Universities of Athens and Salonika. Most of the students remain laymen and teach religion in secondary schools, but some, who are destined for the higher ranks of the ministry, have studied also in Western Europe. Critical work on the Bible was assimilated by Greek theologians, though not without controversy. Greek theologians have already made valuable contributions to the thought of the ecumenical movement.

Conditions have been more favourable in Greece than in the other Balkan countries for such a renewal in the vitality of the Church, but there has been some measure of revival in all of them. But they had been on the defensive so long under Moslem domination, their religion has always been so closely bound up with national aspirations and national rivalries, and again they have been so constantly distraught by political upheavals, that church reformers have had great handicaps to overcome. These Churches have welcomed contacts with the West. The Œcumenical Patriarch Athenagoras (1886–1972) had meetings with Pope Paul VI and with Archbishops Fisher and Ramsey of Canterbury. Western Christians realize that they have much to learn from the liturgical traditions of the East and from the treasures of spirituality that have been preserved in the monasteries.

The history of the Church in Russia during the nineteenth century and until the Revolution of 1917 has several facets. As regards the government of the Church, the synodal regime, that is administration by the committee known as the 'Holy Synod' with its lay Procurator, continued, and as time went on, it had the effect of binding the Church more closely than before to the Tsarist autocracy. Whereas originally the Procurator had been simply an official who served the Holy Synod, he now became a Minister of State and, as the Tsar's representative, acquired almost dictatorial powers over the Church. This was especially so during the long tenure (1880–1905) of the office by K. P. Pobedonostev (1827–1907), whose whole outlook was ultra-conservative and who strove to make the Orthodox Church the chief bulwark and the unifying bond of the Tsarist regime. He was himself an ardent believer, but he administered the Church as though it were a department of the State and used it to counter all forms of unrest and agitation. The Church, which had a monopoly of religious propaganda and a censorship of religious literature, was a powerful instrument for this purpose. The Procurator controlled appointments to the episcopate, and the bishops were constantly being moved from one diocese to another and so had little opportunity of exercising much influence. Moreover, in each diocese there was a lay bureaucracy that was subject to the Procurator. There was an immense amount of red tape and a good deal of bribery and corruption. Pobedonostev was naturally hated by all the liberal and reformist elements in Russian society, and he made the Church hated too. Its mainstay was the devotion, not unmixed with superstition, of the mass of the uneducated peasants.

The revolutionary upheavals of 1905 brought about the downfall of Pobedonostev. There was at that time a small minority of the clergy who favoured political reform, and a substantially larger section that desired a reform of the whole ecclesiastical system. Many thought that a genuinely representative council or synod of the Church should be constituted which would break the domination of the 'Holy Synod' and restore to the Church power to govern itself under a patriarch. The Tsar vaguely undertook to summon such a council when he thought fit, but he never did so. It should be added that great injury was done to the reputation of the Church as well as to that of the Imperial Household by the sinister influence of the notorious monk Rasputin (1872–1916). This is the darker side of the Church's history, and accounts for its identification in the mind of reformers and revolutionaries with the Tsarist regime and also for its unreadiness for the final crisis when it came.

There was however a brighter side to Russian Orthodoxy in the nineteenth century. There was a revival both of spirituality and of theology. The spiritual revival was inspired to a large extent by the 'startsi' or elders. Western readers are familiar with the portrayal of a 'staretz' in the person of Father Zossima in Dostoyevsky's *The Brothers Karamazov*. They were usually, but not necessarily, monks. They had no formal ecclesiastical office. They lived lives of intense asceticism, were credited with gifts as healers of the body as well as of the soul, and were sought out by multitudes of the faithful. They produced something equivalent to the evangelical awakening in eighteenth-century England. Many of them were steeped in the writings of the Fathers, particularly through the *Philokalia*, a collection of patristic excerpts on the life of the spirit, which won great popularity. This kind of spirituality was not activist but quietist. A young Orthodox priest was once talking to a Western fellow-student about the nature of religion. 'I cannot understand what you Westerners mean by religion,' he said; 'you seem to be always wanting to *do* something for God. Our idea of religion is just the opposite. It is to be still before God, and let him do for us.' It was a kind of spirituality that could enable Christians to endure terrible ordeals with heroic patience, but that would not and did not give them any sense of obligation to work for social justice or political reform.

A theological academy had been founded at Moscow at the end of the seventeenth century, and during the first half of the nineteenth century three more were founded – at St Petersburg (1809), Kiev (1819), and Kazan (1842). The students were recruited from the seminaries which were now established in most dioceses and which trained lay religious teachers as well as priests. A change came over the kind of theology that was taught in the academies. Instead of the Latin scholasticism that had been introduced into Russia by Peter Mogila (1596–1647), there was now a return to the native sources of Orthodox theology in the patristic tradition. More patristic texts were translated into Russian at this time than into any other European language. There was also an extension of the Church's missionary work in the Far East which followed Russia's colonial expansion. Both the Bible and the Liturgy were translated into a large number of popular dialects.

The Russian intelligentsia throughout the nineteenth century were exposed to currents of liberal thought and philosophical speculation from the West, which were favoured by some of the Tsars though opposed by others. Many intellectuals were entirely alienated from Christianity. There developed a deep-seated conflict between the 'Westernizers' and the 'Slavophils'. The Westernizers wanted Russia to identify itself unrestrictedly with Western culture and to take part in the advance of science and secularism. The Slavophils, on the other hand, wanted Russia to stand by her own traditions and would have modernized the old idea of the mission of 'Holy Russia' to the world. But these groups were not sharply defined, and many changes were rung on both the main themes. The Slavophils were naturally in sympathy with the spirit of the Orthodox Church though they were generally critical of the existing ecclesiastical system. There were some profound Christian thinkers, such as A. S. Khomiakov (1804–60), Fyodor Dostoyevsky (1821–81), and V. S. Soloviev (1853–1900), who drew their inspiration from the long tradition of Russian spirituality, and on the eve of the Revolution there were a number of intellectuals, like Nicholas Berdyaev (1874–1948) and Sergius Bulgakov (1871–1944), who had reacted from secularism or marxism to a rediscovery of Christian faith and who in exile were to be pioneers of a renovated Orthodox theology and make a considerable impact on the West.

When at length the Revolution came, the movement towards Church reform which had been at work since 1905 bore fruit. Kerensky's provisional government allowed the Church to assemble a council, to which 265 clergy and 299 laity were elected by the dioceses. In August 1917 it approved a new constitution for the Church under which the patriarchate would be re-established, bishops would be elected by the dioceses, and the laity would participate in the administration of the Church at all levels. On 31 October, six days after the overthrow of the provisional government by the communists, Basil Tikhon (1865–1925), Metropolitan of Moscow, was elected Patriarch. So far from clinging to the *ancien régime*, the Church had thus taken the opportunity to reform itself in a democratic spirit. But the leaders of the Church had not foreseen, any more than anyone else, the triumph of the Bolsheviks in the October Revolution. The new ecclesiastical constitution was scarcely born when the Church was plunged into the necessity of determining its attitude to a revolutionary situation. It is not strange that the line followed by the Patriarch, who was now the Church's spokesman, wavered.

The Bolsheviks were not well-qualified to understand the Russian Church. They were dogmatic marxists, for whom religion was 'the opium of the people', to be eliminated by hook or by crook. Engels had said that Christianity had become the perquisite of the ruling classes which they used to bridle the lower classes. Whatever justification for this view there may have been in Western Europe, it was far from being realistic in Russia where the Orthodox Church was essentially a Church of the people and the ruling classes were for the most part alienated from it. Whatever measures the communists adopted to extirpate religion would hit not the ruling classes but the peasants. This disjunction between marxist dogma and the character of the Russian Church partly explains the fluctuating tactics that the communists have adopted towards the Church since 1917. But their final aim throughout has been to extirpate religion.

So in January 1918 the separation of Church and State and the secularization of education were decreed. The property of the Church was to be confiscated without compensation, and the Church itself to be deprived of juridical existence. Only where the local authorities allowed would the Church continue to be able to make use of its places of worship. These decrees and the Church's protests against them set off widespread anti-religious riots and excesses. Nevertheless, in October 1918 Tikhon addressed a message to Lenin in which he said that the Church blessed every form of earthly government that was permitted by God, and he urged him to celebrate the anniversary of his seizure of power by releasing the prisoners and by stopping the flow of blood. Let the government abandon destruction and organize order and justice. In the following year, Tikhon called upon the faithful to abstain from provocative actions and to obey the government except when its requirements were contrary to the faith.

Graver trouble occurred when during the famine of 1921–2 Tikhon addressed an appeal to foreign churches for relief funds. The money received was appropriated by the government which did not want the Church to have the credit of bringing help to the hungry. The government also now decreed the confiscation of all church property for purposes of famine relief. Tikhon issued a statement allowing the surrender of unconsecrated objects but forbidding the surrender of consecrated objects, for example vessels used in the liturgy. Instead, the faithful should contribute funds of equivalent value. This statement started another violent wave of persecution. The Church was represented as refusing to help the victims of the famine. There were public trials of prominent ecclesiastics; among others, the Metropolitan of St Petersburg was shot. Tikhon himself was imprisoned. It was at this juncture that a group of priests declared their opposition to the patriarch's instructions and organized themselves as the so-called 'Living Church', and to add to the Church's distress other schismatic bodies were formed as well.

After a year's imprisonment, Tikhon was released on his making an official acknowledgement of his past 'faults' and a declaration that he was not an enemy of the Soviet government. He died in 1925, and in his testament reiterated his appeal to the faithful to be loyal to the government. He had foreseen that the regular election of a successor would not be possible, and had designated three Metropolitans as locum-tenentes. Those designated were not able to act since they were put under arrest. But from 1927 to 1943 the Metropolitan Sergius (1867–1944) was able to supervise what was left of the Orthodox Church, basing his policy on Tikhon's testament. It was not until the Second World War that the

Soviet government changed its tactics towards the Church and permitted the election of a new Patriarch. Sergius himself was elected and was succeeded in 1944 by Alexis (1877–1970) and in 1971 by Pimen (b. 1910), both of whom have continued the same policy. A reconstruction of the Church was taken in hand. The church buildings that had been handed over to the 'Living Church', which was by now discredited, were restored. The government had not abandoned its hostility to religion or its anti-religious propaganda and education, but it found that it was expedient to tolerate the Church, provided its political loyalty was maintained and it confined itself to purely religious activities.

In these circumstances, there appears to have been a considerable revival of church life, and contacts with Christians of the West have been renewed. But the Church continues to be severely handicapped by the prohibition of all missionary work and its exclusion from the field of education.

21

Christianity in America

WHAT is known to historians as 'The American Revolution' took place before our period. As a result of the War of Independence (1775–83) the thirteen English colonies in North America had won their freedom and become an independent nation. But for a long time afterwards American history could fitly be described as revolutionary and, if revolution spells the opposite of stability, America's *religious* history was conspicuously so. A number of factors contributed to the surging vitality of religion in the U.S.A. during the nineteenth century. Whereas in Europe it was an autumnal revolution that beset the Churches, in America it was spring.

At first sight, it might be thought that, since Christianity in America came from Europe, it would be a reproduction of European Christianity. American Christianity was indeed a transplantation, but the soil and the circumstances in which it was transplanted, and the characteristics of those who did the transplanting, caused it to develop in a manner all its own. The effects of transplantation were much more marked in North America than in Southern and Central America. The colonists and immigrants in Southern and Central America not only were of one stock but they took with them a single form of Christianity, Roman Catholicism. But in North America – and particularly that part of it that was to become the United States – the case was different. (We must restrict our attention to this part of the continent which itself is continental in its dimensions.) Here the colonists and immigrants from Europe brought with them, sooner or later, all the heterogeneous types of European Christianity. In the U.S. the whole Christian macrocosm, dispersed in Europe among many nations, was to be transplanted into one country.

This circumstance in itself might have produced no more than a religious mosaic, each portion of which was set so that its shape and colour were preserved, or a static juxtaposition of caves of Adullam. But just as the early colonists had been political and religious radicals who had wanted not to transplant European traditions and institutions but to escape from them, so the subsequent waves of immigrants were mostly dissatisfied seekers after a better kind of life and a better kind of religion than Europe had afforded them. Thus the American States were constantly receiving new injections of radical idealism, if not of divine discontent. The immigrants had escaped from the restraints that in Europe were put upon radicalism in religion. They were free to experiment and to do whatever they wanted. It is true that in the colonial period there had been church establishments of one kind or another, but the Revolution had been their death warrant, though in some States they lingered on till early in the nineteenth century. The separation of Church and State became an axiom of the American way of life. The Constitution provided that 'no religious test shall ever be required as a qualification to any office or public trust under the United States', and the First Amendment to the Constitution (1791) declared that 'Congress shall make no law respecting an establishment of religion, or prohibiting the free exercise thereof'. Thus there were no restrictions on private or group enterprise in religion. The U.S. became a paradise of *laissez faire*.

The independent, pioneering spirit, which impelled people to leave Europe in search of a new world, was also favoured and stimulated by the drive to the West and the extensions of the frontier. The frontier situation encouraged a robust, even a riotous, individualism in religion as in everything else, and it largely accounts for the exuberant fissiparity of American Christianity as well as for its extraordinary activism.

These characteristics were not, however, evident directly after the Revolution. The Great Awakening[1] – the counterpart of the Evangelical Revival in England – had by then spent its force. The generation that followed the Declaration of Independence was absorbed in other interests, and the guides of thought reflected the rationalistic and deistic outlook of the Enlightenment in Europe. Vital religion was at a low ebb. Towards the end of the eighteenth century it is reckoned that less than ten per cent of the population were church members. In 1798 the General Assembly of the Presbyterian Church described conditions as follows:

We perceive with pain and fearful apprehension a general dereliction of religious principles and practice among our fellow-citizens, a visible and prevailing impiety and contempt for the laws and institutions of religion, and an abounding infidelity, which in many instances tends to atheism itself. The profligacy and corruption of the public morals have advanced with a progress proportionate to our declension in religion.

If this was anything like a just description of conditions along the Eastern seaboard, they were even worse in the new West.

But there was already on the way what is known as the Second Great Awakening, the starting-point of a recurring series of revivals. This Awakening began in New England among the Congregationalists, Presbyterians, and Methodists. It was especially noticeable among students in the colleges, e.g. at Yale during the presidency of Timothy Dwight (1752–1817). Many new colleges were founded under Christian auspices. A profusion of missionary and philanthropic societies came into being on an interdenominational as well as on a denominational basis: e.g. the American Education Society (1815), the American Bible Society (1816), and the American Sunday School Union (1824). There was a crusading spirit abroad and a mood of apocalyptic expectation. In the East, where church

1. See G. R. Cragg. *The Church and the Age of Reason*. Penguin Books 1960, Chapter 12.

institutions were relatively settled and learning and theology were highly esteemed, the revival was steady and sober in its manifestations. In the South and West and on the frontier it was another matter.

While the Presbyterians were first in the field following the westward-moving population, it was the Methodists and Baptists who won the greatest harvest of souls. Their freer methods of evangelism and more flexible attitude to Church order were better adapted to frontier conditions. They were quite willing to relinquish the need for a learned ministry and to concentrate on a simple, emotional preaching of the Gospel with a view to securing sudden conversions. Camp meetings, often held at night, played an important part in the revival and were sometimes attended by hysterical phenomena.

The glare of blazing camp-fires falling on a dense assemblage . . . and reflected back from long ranges of tents upon every side; hundreds of candles and lamps suspended among the trees, together with numerous torches flashing to and fro, throwing an uncertain light upon the tremulous foliage, and giving an appearance of dim and indefinite extent to the depth of the forest; the solemn chanting of hymns swelling and falling on the night wind; the impassioned exhortations; the earnest prayers; the sobs, the shrieks, or shouts, bursting from persons under intense agitation of mind; the sudden spasms which seized upon scores, and unexpectedly dashed them to the ground; all conspired to invest the scene with terrific interest, and to work up the feelings to the highest pitch of excitement.

Here was revivalism in its original purity, before it was corrupted by professionalism. Even so, two visitors from England, who witnessed such scenes, not inaptly reported: 'They have revived all the irregularities of the Corinthian Church, as though they had been placed on record to be copied, and not avoided.'

These developments in the West not only gave rise to a large proliferation of separatist sects, such as the Mormons, the Shakers, and the Second Adventists, but also had divisive repercussions on the old church systems. In 1801 a Plan of Union had been accepted by the Presbyterians and Congregationalists so that they might combine forces in an attempt to evangelize the West, but it led to so much friction that it had to be abandoned in 1837. In fact revivalism begot not unity but schism. There were many in the older churches who still had a mind for theological precision and who wanted an educated and a disciplined ministry: they looked askance at the libertarianism, the emotionalism, and the extravagances of the revivalists. There were schisms on this account among the Presbyterians, the Lutherans, and the Quakers. But revivalism was not the only cause of schism.

In New England there was a revulsion from Calvinistic orthodoxy that took two forms, Universalism and Unitarianism. It has been said that 'the Universalists believed that God was too good to damn them, while the Unitarians held that men were too good to be damned'. The difference between them appears to have been more social than theological. The Universalists were mostly country folk of mediocre education, whereas the Unitarians were the Brahmans of New England society with their headquarters at Boston. William Ellery Channing (1780–1842) was their prophet. The Unitarians were liberal in their theology, but in all other respects they were extremely conservative, and there were limits to their theological liberality. Ralph Waldo Emerson (1803–82) started life as a Unitarian minister, but soon broke away and became an independent sage. 'The old is for slaves,' he said. 'Go alone. Refuse the good models, even those sacred in the imagination of men. Cast conformity behind you, and acquaint men at first hand with deity.' T. Parker (1810–60), a fervent social reformer and theological radical, found Unitarian orthodoxy too narrow a bed: he ministered to a congregation of his own in Boston.

Slavery was another and much more extensive source of schism in American Christianity. In the eighteenth century New England had been the centre of the slave trade, though a vigorous protest against it had been maintained by the

Quakers. About the time of the Revolution, the spread of liberal and humanitarian ideas, and the belief that 'all men are by nature free and independent', led to a general condemnation of the institution and to the formation of numerous anti-slavery societies. By the turn of the century the obligation to abolish slavery had become almost axiomatic. But then unfortunately the invention of spinning and weaving machinery created a new market for cotton, and the invention of the cotton gin made cotton growing the most profitable and important product of the Southern States. In consequence, slavery came to be regarded in the South as indispensable on economic grounds, and the Churches in the South were not long in finding grounds of both precept and example in the Scriptures which justified the right to hold slaves. In the North, on the other hand, the movement for abolition was all the time growing in strength and determination. This conflict of interest and belief, which issued eventually in the Civil War, also brought about schism in most of the Churches that were spread over both sides of the Mason-Dixon line. The Methodist Episcopal Church and the Baptists split in the 1840s, and the Presbyterians and others as the Civil War approached. The exceptions were the Protestant Episcopal (i.e. Anglican) Church and the Roman Catholics.

The schisms that then took place have not yet been altogether healed, and they were complicated by other sources of division. After the Civil War the American Churches began to be agitated by the scientific theory of evolution and by the higher criticism of the Bible. The first reactions were negative as in England and Scotland, and there were various heresy trials. Although liberalism in theology was winning its way by the close of the nineteenth century, biblical and dogmatic conservatism was more persistent and had a larger following than in the Protestant Churches of Europe. This was notably the case in what is known as the 'Bible Belt' and wherever revivalist movements were influential. A number of further church cleavages

resulted from this so-called modernist–fundamentalist controversy.

The term 'fundamentalism' derives from a Bible Conference of conservative evangelicals at Niagara in 1895.
They took their stand upon 'five fundamentals': the inerrancy of the Scriptures, the deity of Jesus Christ, the Virgin
Birth, the substitutionary theory of the Atonement, and
the bodily Resurrection and imminent bodily Second
Coming of the Lord. From 1909 to 1915 twelve volumes on
The Fundamentals were published in this cause and were very
widely distributed. It has been said that 'the fundamentalist
ministers, with important exceptions, were less well trained
than the liberals and usually had to content themselves with
the less sophisticated and, on the whole, less wealthy congregations. But they remained close to the people and
reigned unchallenged over vast rural areas.'

By this time however progressive Protestant theologians
and preachers had become apostles of the 'social gospel'.
Negatively, this was a reaction against the individualism
and pietism of the conservative evangelicals. Positively, it
focused attention on the social implications of the Christian
faith and the duty of churchmen to promote social justice
in every area of the common life. The mission of the Church
was to build the Kingdom of God on earth. The social
gospel canalized in new directions the inveterate activism
and philanthropy of American Christianity. No doubt it
tended to be too moralistic and utopian, and it was later
severely and penetratingly criticized by Dr Reinhold
Niebuhr[1] and others in the name of a realism that claimed
to be at once more politically radical and more authentically
biblical, but it continues to be a pervasive feature of the
Christian ethos in America.

It remains to be said that in the twentieth century, while
the principal Protestant denominations have preserved their
distinction and social stratification, they have come to
cooperate in many fields of activity along the lines of

1. See pp. 220f.

the ecumenical movement. In 1908 a Federal Council
of Churches was formed, and in 1950 a National Council of
Churches of Christ, which coordinates all interdenominational work.

*

For Roman Catholicism in the U.S.A., the nineteenth century was in some ways even more of a revolutionary epoch
than it was for Protestantism. In the first place, as a result of
immigration from Ireland and Europe, there was a vast
increase not only in the Catholic population but in the
proportion of Catholics in the population as a whole. In
1830 they numbered only three per cent of the population;
by the time of the Civil War they were the largest denomination, and since then their numbers have steadily
continued to increase. The stream of immigration was continuous: the largest wave – which was more like an avalanche – was caused by the Irish potato famine of 1845–6
and the failure of the European revolutions of 1848. This
prodigious growth in numbers was accompanied not only
by remarkable feats in church construction but by many
growing pains. Dioceses had to be multiplied, priests somehow or other recruited, and the life of the Church organized
as best it might be amid the rapid social developments that
were in progress.

The American Catholics had had no bishop of their own
till 1790. Then, when the need to extend the episcopate was
realized, it happened that most of the priests best qualified
for the office were Frenchmen who had emigrated in consequence of the French Revolution, and who naturally were
not in love with democratic institutions. While they were
marked out by their piety and culture, they had little or no
mastery of the English language. They were thus debarred
from preaching, and to their flocks they seemed like alien
intruders. As the number of Irish immigrants increased, the
demand for English-speaking and familiar bishops rose.
There was inevitable friction so long as the French bishops
survived. Moreover, among the Irish priests who came to

America were some colourful adventurers who had been in trouble with their ecclesiastical superiors at home. They were liable to be even more troublesome in freer conditions that were favourable to the formation of factions. The bishops had to cope with a good deal of turbulence, and for a time there was a threat of schisms.

Another source of trouble for the bishops, which also threatened schisms, was the system of 'lay trusteeship'. Under the civil law church property was held by bodies of lay trustees. This arrangement was entirely congenial to the Protestant denominations, and the Catholics had hitherto accepted it in spite of its incongruity with canon law. In fact, when there had been no bishops, there had been no alternative. But now that there were bishops, many of the bodies of trustees were disposed to adhere to their democratic rights. Not only did they claim to control church property, buildings, etc., but to elect their own pastors. The latter claim was objectionable to the bishops anyhow, and all the more so because in some cases the lay trustees were very lax Catholics who were quite happy to be served by unworthy priests. There were several protracted *causes célèbres*, and the bishops were not able finally to make their authority effective until about the middle of the century.

By this time, troubles from within were being succeeded by troubles from without. It is important to remember that the Irish Catholic immigrants, although they came from a rural background, settled in the cities when they reached America. Whereas the German Catholic immigrants moved West and became farmers, the Irish became entirely urbanized. The Church encouraged them to stay in the cities, because so it was much easier to provide religious ministrations for them and to prevent them from lapsing. But these concentrations of a Catholic proletariat in the cities soon began to arouse resentment in the older Americans. They saw a flood of cheap labour lowering their standard of living. The Irish were often shifty, unruly, and improvident. And they were papists and priest-ridden. On all counts this foreign invasion seemed to menace the American way of life with its roots in Puritanism. In the Eastern cities, those who regarded themselves as 'Native Americans' launched a movement to restrict further immigration, to arrest the spread of Catholicism, and to subject Catholics to political proscription. During the decade 1850–60 there were 'no popery' riots, and a secret organization was started by the Nativists called the 'Know-Nothings' (if a member was interrogated, he said 'he knew nothing about it'). Disreputable propaganda was made use of, such as Maria Monk's fraudulent revelations about convent life. While 'Know-Nothingism' was eclipsed by the Civil War, the movement continued afterwards through what was known as the 'American Protective Association' and the Ku-Klux Klan.

One reason for the hostility to the Irish Catholics was the practice of their priests in organizing them in self-contained communities and in preventing them so far as possible from associating with their Protestant fellow-citizens. The Catholics thus appeared to be an alien element in the American democracy, and they were inhibited from participating in the political and cultural life of the nation. In the latter part of the century some influential Catholic leaders arose – notably Cardinal James Gibbons (1834–1921) – who determined to break down this isolation and whose policy was to americanize Catholicism. Another member of this group was John Ireland (1838–1918), Archbishop of St Paul: some remarks of his in a sermon to a Catholic Congress in 1889 may be taken as representative:

We should live in our age, know it, be in touch with it. . . . It will not do to understand the thirteenth better than the nineteenth century. . . . We should speak to our age – of things it feels and in language it understands. We should be in it, and of it, if we would have its ear. For the same reasons, there is needed a thorough sympathy with our country. The Church of America must be, of course, as Catholic as even in Jerusalem or Rome; but as far as her garments assume color from the local atmosphere, she must be

American. Let no one dare paint her brow with a foreign tint or pin to her mantle foreign linings.

There were however other ecclesiastics who looked upon this policy as bound to lead to a dilution and compromise of Catholic principles, and who were not willing to idealize such American dogmas as the separation of Church and State. Controversy on the whole subject rumbled for a long time, and is not yet dead. Towards the close of the last century the controversy was complicated by the fact that some Liberal Catholics in France, who sympathized with the americanizing policy, extolled its enlightened, democratic spirit and fêted its representatives when they visited Europe. This caused alarm in the Vatican, and in 1899 Leo XIII issued an encyclical, entitled *Testem Benevolentiae*, in which he condemned a number of opinions 'which some comprise under the head of Americanism', for example the extolling of the natural virtues above the supernatural on the strange pretext that they were more modern and manly; emphasis on the active virtues to the exclusion of humility, charity, and obedience; the need to adopt new methods in leading non-Catholics to the faith. But all the supposed Americanists, both in the U.S. and in France, hastened to declare that they held none of the condemned opinions, and so Americanism has commonly been described as 'the phantom heresy'.[1]

The truth is that there was little understanding in the Vatican at that time of the situation of the Church in America. The policy of the Americanists has increasingly prevailed and has undoubtedly strengthened the position and prospects of the Church. On the other hand, it continued to be a weakness of American Catholicism that it was so preoccupied with organization and the practical aspects of church life that it neglected theology and made no substantial contributions to American culture. Recently, however, this weakness has begun to be redressed.

1. For the whole story see T. T. McAvoy. *The Great Crisis in American Catholic History 1895–1900*. 1957.

22

The Missionary Movement

IT is a sociological, rather than a theological, paradox that for the Churches of the West the nineteenth century was a period both of formidable reverses and of prodigious expansion. This was equally the case with the Roman Catholic and the non-Roman or Protestant Churches. For, while in Europe the Churches lost for the most part the support of civil governments on which they had hitherto depended and were often harassed by political repression, and also there was a steady alienation both of the intelligentsia and of the proletariat from Christian allegiance, yet at the same time Western Christianity was spreading all over the world as it had never done before, so that Professor Latourette in his *History of the Expansion of Christianity* is able to say that this was the greatest century since the first.

Of the revolutionary changes that took place in the structures of society, in the extension of knowledge and the mastery of physical power, and in the ability to conquer man's chronic enemies – hunger, poverty, disease, ignorance, and war – some were as unfavourable as others were favourable to the Christian mission in the world. We have had occasion to observe the losses that the Churches of Europe sustained on their home ground, so to speak. Now we are to see to what extent these were balanced by gains abroad. It is not within our scope to catalogue, country by country, the expansion of the Church in other continents; we can consider only in the rough the external and internal causes of this expansion and try to assess its strengths and weaknesses. We are concerned with the expansion of Christianity from the view-point of the home Churches rather than with the history of missions in itself. Let us take note first of some of the external or sociological factors that were favourable to missionary enterprise.

Manifestly, the new mechanical inventions, the means of transport, travel, and communication, were as favourable to missionary as they were to commercial enterprise. In the first Christian century the apostolic mission of the Church was greatly favoured by the *pax romana* and the many advantages that it afforded; so in the nineteenth century the Christian mission was even more extensively favoured by the *pax britannica* and all that it symbolized. Moreover, this was the age of colonial expansion, especially by the British, and of the opening up to Western commerce and culture of virgin territories that had never before been explored, as well as of ancient lands and civilizations that had hitherto been closed to the West. Missionaries were beckoned as they had never been before.

That the Industrial Revolution was also favourable to the Christian mission abroad is perhaps borne out by the consideration that it was the countries most involved in that, which were also most active in the propagation of Christianity abroad: Great Britain and the U.S.A., France, Belgium, Germany, and Northern Italy. Missionaries who followed the flag could depend on their home government's protection, even where the administrators and merchants were otherwise unhelpful, and personally detached from the Church. Governments did not directly support Christian missions, but they supported Christian schools, not because they were Christian, but because they were schools. Even the anti-clerical French governments, who were attacking the Church at home, supported it abroad as an agent in the dissemination of French culture. Christians, we know, were pioneers in popular education. Wherever they went, they founded schools which provided what people in Africa and the Orient wanted more than almost anything else.

It should also be remembered that the effect of commercial and imperial expansion was to break up and disintegrate both ancient and primitive cultures, or at least to introduce into them a disturbing ferment, which rendered them more open to the acceptance of Christianity. For societies, like nature, abhor a vacuum. And driving on the whole movement for secular expansion was not only greed for gain and a reckless spirit of adventure, but an infectious optimism about the future of the world. Christians naturally were not immune from this infection, though they had a perspective of their own.

These were extrinsic or sociological factors that were favourable to the spread of Christianity abroad. But the nineteenth would not have been a great century in mission-ary expansion, if there had not been as well a large upsurge of new zeal and devotion within Western Christendom to take advantage of the favouring conditions. That is just what there was. Although in Europe the Churches, both Catholic and Protestant, may have failed by and large to meet the new challenges to Christian belief and to adapt their outlook and their structures to the social, political, and economic revolution that was taking place, yet there was at the same time a genuine revival of spiritual vitality in the Churches, an outcrop of new movements and institutions, and above all an unprecedented sense of obligation to carry the Gospel to all nations.

The eighteenth-century Churches had had no such sense of obligation. Its novelty may be appreciated when it is recalled that as late as 1796 a speaker in the General Assembly of the Church of Scotland dissuaded the Fathers and Brethren from approving a proposal to start missionary work overseas. 'I cannot otherwise consider the enthusiasm on this subject', he said, 'than as the effect of sanguine and illusive views, the more dangerous because the object is plausible.' Another speaker considered that 'to spread abroad the knowledge of the Gospel among barbarous and heathen nations seems highly preposterous, in so far as it anticipates, it even reverses, the order of nature'. It is true that resistance to foreign missions was more prolonged in

Scotland than in England, where the evangelical awakening inspired its converts to want to see the Gospel preached in areas of the world where it had never been preached before. A whole range of missionary societies was founded under this impulse: the Baptist Missionary Society (1792), the London Missionary Society (1795), the Church Missionary Society (1799), the British and Foreign Bible Society (1804), and the Methodist Missionary Society (1813).

No less was there a revival of missionary zeal in the Roman Catholic Church. The Spanish and Portuguese governments, in the day of their imperial power, had been notable patrons of missions, especially of the Society of Jesus. But their day of power was past, and in 1773 the Jesuits had been suppressed by the pope. There was however an astonishing recovery after the *débâcle* of the French Revolution and the Napoleonic wars, especially in France itself.[1] In the hundred years after 1815, more religious orders and congregations came into existence in the Roman Church than in any previous period of the same length. Men and women consecrated themselves to the service of the Church in teeming numbers – to educational and missionary enterprises, to the care of the poor and the sick, as well as to the contemplative life. The traditional Catholic esteem for celibacy assisted the growth of the orders. Celibates were able to do things, both at home and abroad, that could be less easily undertaken by the married. Early in the nineteenth century the Jesuit order was reconstituted and was soon at work again as the spearhead of missionary advance. The revival of piety among the laity was not merely pietistic – absorbed in apparitions, pilgrimages, sentimental religious exercises, and the cult of the miraculous: it provided a good recruiting ground for zealous missionaries.

The loosening hold of Gallican and Febronian ideas about the relations of Church and State, and the rise of the new ultramontanism, helped the Catholic missionary enterprise.

1. See S. Delacroix. *Les Missions contemporaines, 1800–1957.* 1958.

The Church was no longer under the control of civil governments, which had always been suspicious of spontaneous
ecclesiastical activity. Although the popes opposed liberal
constitutions as long as they could and the freedoms which
Lamennais had espoused, they were not slow to take advantage of them. The papacy was able to organize and dispose
its forces, and to set in motion new instruments of evangelism, without a frustrating reference to the civil power.
Liberated from dependence on the State, the Church had a
new power of autonomous action. The transformation of the
Roman Church into a closely-knit and centrally organized
and strictly disciplined army – while from other points of
view it had grave disadvantages – undoubtedly facilitated
a world-wide missionary strategy, and its policy of safe-
guarding its members from dangerous thoughts and unsett-
ling questions, on the basis of its own infallibility, was
calculated to produce effective missionaries – at any rate
to simple-minded peoples.

Most of the Protestant missionaries also went out with a
similar confidence. At least in the early stages, they had a
sharply defined Calvinistic or conservative theology, which
was unaffected by the acids of modernity. Protestantism had
an even greater asset than the central organization of
Roman Catholicism in its congruence with the individualism of the age. It could more easily allow scope for
individual initiative and the enterprise of groups that were
subject to no control but their own inner dynamic. There is
the remarkable case of the China Inland Mission, founded
by James Hudson Taylor in 1865, which, although it had
no denomination behind it, became larger than any other
missionary body in China. Protestantism allowed for this
free-lance type of expansion in a way that Roman Catholicism could not. The Salvation Army had its origins in the
same year, and rapidly spread through the English-speaking world and beyond. Autonomous, interdenominational
movements like the Y.M.C.A. and the Y.W.C.A. were
swiftly organized on an almost world-wide scale. They

received generous financial support, made possible by the increase of wealth in the countries where Christianity was strongest.

*

There is however another side to this whole picture, to which we must now attend. It goes to explain why this great wave of missionary expansion has, since about 1914, been arrested or slowed down. After all, what happened in the nineteenth century? In most areas of the world Christian missions got only quite a small footing proportionately to total populations. Between the wars, for example, the Christians in India numbered only two per cent of the population, in China one per cent, and in Japan half per cent. Admittedly, in many countries the Christians were able to exercise more influence through their schools and other institutions and the quality of their converts than their actual numbers would suggest. But the nineteenth-century missionary movement had serious imperfections and weaknesses, apart from those that mark all human enterprises.

First, while it would be grossly unfair to say that in the age of European imperialism the missionaries just represented European domination like the traders and the administrators, still they did appear to the peoples of Africa and the East far too much in that light. They came as agents of the same culture, though of a different aspect of it. They were there as exporters of European religion, as the administrators were of European methods of government. Most missionaries still regarded Europe as their home, though Roman Catholics, especially monks and nuns, did often settle for good in the countries to which they went on mission. But a foreign, an imperial or colonial, aroma hung about most mission stations. With notable exceptions, missionaries were politically quietist or conservative. They would hardly have been tolerated if they had been inclined to radicalism.

Secondly, in a country like India very few members of the

ruling classes or higher castes were converted. Missions were much more successful among the poor and outcast. This may have been natural and creditable, but missionary statesmen with a longer view would have seen that the best way to christianize a people is to christianize its natural leaders. Here the narrow intellectual outlook of most missionaries was a liability.

For, thirdly, the main motive of missions in the nineteenth century was the evangelical one, common to Protestants and Roman Catholics, of rescuing as many of the heathen as possible from the everlasting damnation which otherwise awaited them. The grand object was to save as many souls as possible for eternal life in the next world. This was a very powerful motive – more powerful, it seems, than any that derives from a more liberal theology about God's dealings with non-Christians or from a more discriminating assessment of the value of other religions. The simple view that everything in non-Christian religions and cultures was evil dominated the missionary outlook for a long time, though individuals were of course often more humane than their creeds. The heathen in his blindness bowed down to wood and stone, and that was that. Only in the latter part of the century did a more sympathetic study of non-Christian religions begin to be fostered, and distinctions were drawn between higher and primitive faiths.

Fourthly, the missionaries had no doubt about the complete superiority of their own Western culture, and therefore their method was to transplant all they could of Christianity in its Western forms. Hence churches and chapels were built in Africa and the East and on South Sea islands in the neo-Gothic architectural styles that were then fashionable in Europe. Native priests were dressed up like European clergymen, and even native bishops, when there came to be such, adorned themselves in the riding attire of eighteenth-century English prelates, which has sometimes been mistaken for that of a Highlander going to a funeral! European music, art, and ways of living were blandly exported. The missionaries would all have echoed Tennyson's refrain: 'Better fifty years of Europe than a cycle of Cathay.' Quite a different attitude has become common now, but it was very late in coming.

For the same reason, missions for the most part were slow to realize the need to train indigenous ministries and an indigenous church leadership. Roman Catholics were more enlightened and far-sighted in this respect, perhaps because theirs is anyhow a manifestly international Church. British missionaries seem to have supposed that British imperial power would last for ever. At any rate, they did not foresee the rapidity with which the older civilizations of the East and the younger peoples of Africa would come to resent European domination and tutelage, and succeed in achieving their independence. As this process gathered pace, Christian missions found themselves at a grave disadvantage. The failure to produce indigenous churches with indigenous leadership has had to be repaired as best it might be. Nowadays the Christian communities founded by the missions are acknowledged to be Churches in their own right, not foreign missions of European or American Churches. They are spoken of as 'the Younger Churches'. Missionaries from the West now gladly work under native church leaders, wherever these are available. They see themselves as colleagues invited to assist the Younger Churches, not as the natural bosses who have come out to run them, and it is a tribute to the spirit of the Younger Churches that they still welcome help from outside, and have not been carried away by the excesses of nationalism and the reaction against colonialism.

There are of course many qualifications that would have to be made if we were surveying the situation in different parts of the world. For instance, the Churches in West Africa are much more advanced as indigenous Churches than those in East and Central Africa.

It remains to be said that one of the most weakening features of the missionary movement was that it transplanted

not only Western Christianity, but Western denomina-
tionalism. A faith, which was supposed to reconcile all men
and all peoples to one another as well as to the one God and
Father of all, often had the effect of splitting them up even
more than they were split up already. Christianity came in
the form of religious sects and parties. Instead of giving the
converts the experience of being brought into a universal
Church which was being built up in forms appropriate to
their own history and traditions, it divided them denomi-
nationally by differences of belief and practice which might
be explicable in Europe or America but were quite unsuitable for export. 'What', it has been asked, 'can it possibly
mean but confusion and distress of mind, when a Northern
Chinese joins the American Southern Baptists, thus adding
the divisive heritage of the American Civil War to a country
already cursed with its own civil wars?' It is not surprising
that it has been left to other agents to unify the people of
China. When one considers how in country after country the
Christian missionary movement thus belied its own creden-
tials, it is amazing that it made as much progress as it did.
It has been the belated realization of this blatant self-
contradiction in the missionary enterprise that has made the
movement towards the union of the Churches so much more
compulsive abroad than it is at home. It is also evidence of
the sacrificial service by which the missions were animated
that they were able to do as much salutary work as they did
in spite of this devastating handicap.

In the present century there has been a steady growth in
interchurch and international cooperation. In addition to
the advances that have been made towards the complete
unification of Churches in some parts of the world, and the
new spirit that has been engendered by the ecumenical
movement, there has been increasing collaboration across
denominational and national boundaries among those who
are responsible for the missionary enterprise. The most
valuable organ of this collaboration has been the *International Review of Missions*, founded in 1912, and its indis-

pensable agency has been the International Missionary Council, founded in 1921.

It stands to reason that in the mission field many matters have arisen, quite apart from the interrelations of Churches and missionary societies, which could best be tackled on an international and interdenominational basis. For example, the relation of the Younger Churches to civil governments became more and more important and more and more difficult, when nineteenth-century liberal democracy as an ideal began to give way to authoritarian and nationalist governments which were liable to be committed to a definite and aggressive ideology and were intolerant of movements and organizations that would not fall in behind the national policies. In such circumstances it was obviously common sense for minority Christian communities to take counsel with one another and, if possible, to act together. The traditional debates and doctrines in Europe about Church and State might still contain useful instruction, but they provided no direct guidance for Churches placed in environments which they had never envisaged.

Again, many thorny problems arose in the mission field which Christians of different Churches could profitably study together with a view to arriving at a common mind and avoiding a conflicting witness; for example, what should be done about the matrimonial relationships of converts in polygamous societies? Also, with the growth of a more positive and sympathetic attitude to non-Christian religions and culture, the Younger Churches, whatever their denominational origin, were equally confronted by such questions as how far non-Christian religions should be regarded as a *praeparatio evangelica*, and their sacred books as counterparts to, and even a substitute for, the Old Testament, and again just how far the Christian mission could rightly go in becoming genuinely indigenous. For instance, should an attempt be made to purify and, as it were, to baptize the initiation rites of pagan tribes or must they be altogether eschewed?

Profound theological issues lay at the back of all these

questions, as was shown when Hendrik Kraemer (1889–1965), a Dutch theologian who had been greatly influenced by Karl Barth and the theology of crisis, published his book, *The Christian Message in a Non-Christian World* (1938),[1] in which he challenged many of the assumptions of liberal theology about the mission of the Church, e.g. the idea that alongside the special revelation of God to Israel and in Christ there is a general revelation through other religions. Two years previously an English translation had appeared of a no less remarkable book by a German Catholic, Otto Karrer, *Religions of Mankind* (1936), which took a much more liberal view of non-Christian religions. 'It is unreasonable', he wrote, 'to believe in a *special* revelation in Christ if we refuse to believe in a *universal* revelation of God to the human race, a revelation, that is to say, accessible, though in diverse degrees, to all men.' This theological debate is still continuing. There is now a new department of theological study called 'Missiology', to which Catholics and Protestants are both contributing.

1. In 1956 he published a sequel, *Religion and the Christian Faith*. 1956.

23

The Ecumenical Movement

THE word 'ecumenical' means world-wide. It has a traditional as well as a modern application. Traditionally, it was
applied to those creeds and councils of the Church that were
universally accepted, in distinction from local creeds and
synods. In this sense it is convenient to spell it 'oecumenical',
as in the expression 'the oecumenical documents of the
faith'. In its modern application, which began in the
nineteenth century, 'ecumenical' no doubt denotes an *ideal*
of universality. It points to what the separated Churches of
Christendom have in common despite their divisions and to
their will to attain to the unity that they ought to display.
The ecumenical movement could not at first be described
as 'oecumenical' in the traditional sense since it was not
formally recognized by the Roman Catholic Church which
stood aloof from it. That limitation has now happily been
removed, and there is a very lively 'Catholic ecumenism'.

It is possible to trace the antecedents of the ecumenical
movement from the sixteenth century onwards, and to discover many interesting but abortive attempts that have
been made since then to bridge the divisions between the
Churches. But it is generally agreed that the movement, as
it is now known, dates from the International Missionary
Conference that was held at Edinburgh in 1910. It had been
prepared for by the formation of various trans-denomi-
national bodies during the nineteenth century, notably the
Evangelical Alliance (1846). Of particular importance was
the World's Student Christian Federation (1895), which
drew together the Student Christian Movements in various
countries. It was under these auspices that those who were

to become the initiators and leaders of the ecumenical movement first met and got to know one another. Whatever their own denominational background, they realized that they had much more in common with other Christians than they had been led to suppose, and it seemed intolerable to them that they should set out to serve Christ and his cause in the world without being able to conduct themselves as friends and fellow-workers.

The ecumenical movement, as it developed had what may be called three prongs. The first prong was the missionary movement, which was the *raison d'être* of the Edinburgh Conference. It was the continuation committee appointed by that Conference which launched the *International Review of Missions* and was the seed-bed of the International Missionary Council, of which we have already spoken.

The second prong came to be known as 'Life and Work'. It sought to find out how Christians could assist one another in bringing their faith to bear on the general life of society – in politics, industry, education, international relations, etc. There had of course been various antecedents preparing the way for this – for instance, the nineteenth-century Christian Socialist movements and the American 'social gospel'. But 'Life and Work' had one supreme architect and inspirer, Nathan Söderblom (1866–1931).

Söderblom was the son of a Swedish Lutheran pastor, and his early years were spent not far from the Arctic Circle in conditions of great simplicity. As a young man he served as pastor of the Swedish Church in Paris, and devoted the time he could spare from his not very exacting duties to the study of ancient, particularly Persian, religions – studies that eventually bore fruit in his Gifford Lectures on *The Living God*, which were published posthumously in 1933. Söderblom next became a professor of the history of religions, first at Uppsala and then at Leipzig.

In 1914 the archbishopric of Uppsala fell vacant, and the King of Sweden appointed the comparatively unknown professor in preference to two eminent bishops who were recommended for the office. Conservative heads were shaken, but the king had made a wise choice. Söderblom's experience in other countries had given him an unusual acquaintance with the currents of theological thought. He spoke five languages with equal fluency. He was a ready-made ecumenical leader, passionately concerned about Christian unity and the witness of the Church to social justice.

He had hoped that, even during the First World War, it might be possible to hold a conference that would show there was a deeper Christian unity than could be shaken by the disasters of the war. This proved to be impossible, but his desire was fulfilled in the Universal Christian Conference on Life and Work which was held at Stockholm in 1925. There was a deep-rooted and long-standing division among Christians between those who held that the task of the Church was to save souls out of the present evil world and prepare them for an eternal destiny, and those who held that the task of the Church included the transformation of this world. These attitudes have sometimes been called 'world-renouncing' and 'world-affirming': there have naturally been many varieties of each.[1] It was inevitable that this divergence should come out in the Life and Work movement from the first.

It cannot be said that Stockholm 1925 produced very tangible results, but it helped Christians of different traditions to understand one another, and it brought together into personal relations church leaders who had been in hostile camps during the war and were still suspicious of one another. The Conference laid down certain general principles, such as the free and full development of human personality as a supreme value above property or profit, and it declared for a 'Christian internationalism', But the question was: how were such general principles to

1. See Ernst Troeltsch. *The Social Teaching of the Christian Churches.* Eng. trans., 1931; H. Richard Niebuhr. *Christ and Culture.* 1952.

be carried out in practical politics, and who was going to be responsible for carrying them out? We shall come back to this point.

For the British record, it should be said that a similar conference had been held at Birmingham in 1924, in the preparations for which representatives of all the Churches in England took part, including the Roman Catholics, though they had to withdraw before the conference actually took place. It was known as 'Copec': 'Conference on Politics, Economics, and Citizenship'. The twelve volumes of commission reports that were published in preparation for it are a good index of the extent to which Christian social thinking was by this time permeating the Churches in England. The conference was presided over by William Temple, who played a leading part not only in 'Life and Work', but in all aspects of the ecumenical movement.

Its third prong was known as 'Faith and Order'. The initiator in this case was an American episcopalian, Charles Harold Brent (1862–1929), who was Bishop of the Philippines and later of Western New York. As early as 1910 he had been instrumental in persuading the Protestant Episcopal Church in the U.S.A. to launch a proposal for a conference on Faith and Order to which should be invited representatives of 'all Christian communions throughout the world which confess our Lord Jesus Christ as God and Saviour'. But Churches are not institutions that rush recklessly into action when they get a big idea. Seventeen years were to elapse before the first World Conference on Faith and Order was held at Lausanne in 1927. This conference, which was attended by 400 delegates, had several significant features.

Although the Roman Catholic Church stood aloof, the Orthodox Churches of the East were represented. A liaison was thus effected between the Eastern and Western Churches, and a way was opened for a better understanding of Eastern Orthodoxy by Western Christians, already begun by Western contact with the Russian theologians who settled in the West after the Bolshevik Revolution. Another striking feature of the Lausanne Conference was the quality of the delegates. The Churches sent some of their most eminent divines. For example, the Church of England was represented by Bishop Gore and Bishop Headlam, two of its most weighty spokesmen. Further, there was a remarkable combination of outspoken frankness about the differences between the Churches with a sense of underlying unity. Everyone felt that an enterprise had been started which must be carried further.

There were thus three clearly distinguished prongs of the ecumenical movement. The next notable event was the Missionary Conference held at Jerusalem in 1928. It was now that the terms 'Older' and 'Younger' Churches came into use. Indians and Chinese and Africans were no longer to be looked upon as objects for missionary work from the West: they were partners in a common undertaking – the World Mission of the Church. It was also coming to be seen that the Church in the West was itself in a missionary situation: before long the epithet 'post-Christian' would be invented to describe it. There seemed to be an alarming penetration of a godless secularism into all lands, including those that were nominally Christian. The point was later made in the phrase, *France, pays de mission*.

Another series of ecumenical conferences was held just before the Second World War, but in between the conferences a great deal of further work was done through commissions and publications. There had also by now been many parallel developments in various localities. In England, in addition to Copec, there had been, as an outcome of an 'Appeal to all Christian People' by the Lambeth Conference of 1920, conversations between representatives of the Church of England and the Free Churches with a view to a possible reunion, and also between Anglicans and Roman Catholics at Malines in Belgium under the leadership of Cardinal Mercier (1851–1926) and Viscount Halifax (1839–1934). Nothing very definite came of either, but they were signs that the theologians of separated Churches were at least getting on to speaking terms.

Elsewhere, church unions were actually coming into existence. This was the time when the union of the Church of Scotland and the United Free Church was consummated. The three branches of Methodism in England were united in 1932. In 1925 four groups of Canadian Churches had formed the United Church of Canada. Not least, the scheme of Church Union for South India was steadily taking shape; it had the important characteristic that it was to be a union of episcopal and non-episcopal churches.

Various motives were at work in all this. There was a growing conviction that it was the nature of the Church of Christ to be one, and that schism was intrinsically scandalous. There were also strong economic arguments for union, e.g. the absurd wastage of Christian effort through overlapping and competing organizations at a time when the pinch was beginning to be felt of a shortage of ministers. It was also being perceived that united churches are in a stronger position than divided churches to collaborate with friendly governments and to withstand hostile ones. The last consideration weighed more and more as totalitarianism gathered strength. When the next series of ecumenical conferences met in 1937–8, it was in a world that already lay under this heavy menace and the threat of a global war.

Two of these conferences were held in Britain: Life and Work at Oxford in July 1937, and Faith and Order at Edinburgh shortly afterwards. Life and Work had as its title this time 'Church, Community, and State', which reflected the concerns that were pressing upon all Churches. This conference, of which J. H. Oldham (1874–1969) – a veteran from Edinburgh 1910 who had been at the centre of the ecumenical movement ever since – was chief organizer, was prepared for by a series of volumes of exceptionally high quality. Oldham had realized, and was bringing others to realize, that, if the Christian faith was to bear creatively upon the life of the world, it was not enough for clerics and theologians and ecclesiastical assemblies to pass resolutions about what ought to be done. Theologians were not qualified by their training, nor were ecclesiastics by their interests, to say how politics or industry or international relations should be conducted. All these secular spheres had in modern times become exceedingly technical and complicated, and only men who had an expert, inside knowledge of them, gained from experience, could say what it was possible to do and what ought to be done. Beneficial changes in society must be brought about by lay people, who were in responsible positions of power and whose words could be made flesh.

The Oxford Conference therefore set its face against vague generalizations and abstract resolutions, and it was followed up, during and, still more, after the Second World War, by the promotion of what in some countries were called 'lay institutes' and in others the 'frontier' movement. In either case, means were sought of enabling Christian laymen to help one another to understand, and reach right decisions about, the questions that arose in their own fields of social responsibility, whether in government or administration, education or industry, the legal or other professions. Among the most impressive examples of this development were the Evangelical Academies founded in Germany after the war. Groups of lay people – for example journalists or technicians or doctors – would attend the Academies for advanced courses concerning the bearing of their faith as Christians upon their jobs. The whole movement was provided with a centre at the Ecumenical Institute at Bossey in Switzerland, where international courses of the same kind were organized.

This whole development revealed the need for a new kind of theology for the laity, which would illuminate the problems that actually press upon men and women who have to cope with the life of the contemporary world. Traditional and conventional theology seemed now to have been far too much dominated by purely ecclesiastical and clerical interests, and to have been fabricated by men who had only a remote acquaintance with what was actually going on at the centres and growing points of power. Nowhere was this range of questions opened up more fruitfully than in *The Christian News-Letter*, which Oldham started and edited during the war.

The Edinburgh Conference on Faith and Order in 1937 was attended by representatives of 123 Churches. There was no delegation from the German Evangelical Church, because the Nazi government had refused them passports. This was a serious loss to the Conference – apart from the gravity of what it portended – because the Germans always have much of substance to contribute. Nevertheless, both this and the Oxford Conference did much to cement the bonds between the leaders of the Churches that were so soon to be engulfed in the war and to be cut off from communication with one another. Relations between Christians on opposite sides of the conflict were never embittered in the Second World War as they had been in the first, when preachers and theological professors had presented arms with shocking slickness.

But the 1937 Conferences had a more positive outcome. A committee had been appointed to work out a constitution for a World Council of Churches, which would draw the participants in the ecumenical movement more closely and permanently together, and also coordinate the various prongs in the movement. Work on this constitution, which had made progress before the outbreak of the war, was inevitably hampered by its incidence. But contact was maintained between the church leaders in the allied countries and in the Nazi-occupied territories, largely through the courageous ingenuity of G. K. A. Bell (1883–1958), Bishop of Chichester. When the war ended, preparations for the inauguration of the World Council of Churches went rapidly ahead.

The third ecumenical conference that had been held

before the war was another Missionary Conference – at Tambaram near Madras. About half of the 470 delegates came from the Younger Churches, and it is said that never had so polyglot an assembly gathered in the name of Christ. Those who were present testified to the sense of equality that prevailed among the delegates: this may have been helped by the circumstance that there were fewer delegates with great official prestige. One of the things emphasized at Tambaram was the need to raise the standard of training for Christian leadership everywhere, and especially in the Younger Churches. It was the considered conviction of the Conference that 'the present condition of theological education is one of the greatest weaknesses in the whole Christian enterprise', and if the war had not supervened something imaginative might have been done about that.

The World Council of Churches was inaugurated at Amsterdam in 1948. Representatives were present of 147 different Churches from 44 different countries. The principal non-participants were the Roman Catholics, whose exclusive claim to be the one true Church still kept them apart, some groups of ultra-conservative Protestants who instead founded rival international organizations, and the Russian Church. The Moscow Synod condemned the World Council of Churches as a non-ecclesiastical body with political aims of an anti-democratic character. Later on, however, more cordial relations were established between Moscow and Geneva where the World Council of Churches set up its headquarters.

The World Council of Churches does not claim to be a super-Church or a substitute for a united Church. It is a council of Churches which aims at forwarding cooperation and understanding between those that belong to it and at fostering the movement towards Christian unity everywhere. It incorporates the previously separate activities of the three previously distinct prongs, and also another prong of the ecumenical movement that had come into existence by this time, namely the Christian Youth movements which had already held international conferences at Amsterdam in 1939 and at Oslo in 1947.

It is not to be supposed that in the World Council peace and harmony have reigned supreme. Strong tensions have always been at work. There is, first of all, the tension between the Catholic and Protestant constituents in the movement. Then, the Eastern Orthodox Churches have always been inclined to take a line of their own, and to be uneasy with the outlook of the West. Not least, there has been the tension between the activism of the Anglo-Saxons and what seemed to them the eschatological quietism of many continental theologians. After listening to Karl Barth at Amsterdam in 1948, an American delegate from the Far West said: 'If I were Barth, I'd quit this assembly and go fishing. And when I fished, I wouldn't bait my hook nor wet the line: I'd expect the Lord to make the fish flop out of the water right into my frying pan.' The Americans had got the same impression at Oxford in 1937, when they had summed up the continental attitude as 'Sit, brothers of the Son of Man, and leave it all to God.'

As we have seen, this was certainly to misunderstand Barth's own teaching, but it may be that his would-be disciples had given a good deal of pretext for it. The same tension was no less conspicuous at the second Assembly of the World Council at Evanston, Illinois, in 1954, when the main subject for consideration was Christian Hope. But, whatever the tensions, all who have taken part in these gatherings seem to have been driven to the conclusion that they must stay together and patiently work away at their differences. There is a large organization at Geneva which gives the member churches of the World Council plenty to do by reason of the industry of its many departments and officers. Fears have sometimes been expressed that the ecumenical movement would get bogged down in a vast centralized bureaucracy.

There have been corresponding developments in each country where there are a number of Churches that belong to the World Council. In Britain, all the non-Roman Churches are represented on the British Council of Churches which was constituted in 1942 under the leadership of William Temple. It has taken under its wing and coordinated a variety of interdenominational activities – in the fields of education, interchurch aid, youth work, etc. From time to time it has sponsored commissions that have produced reports on particular subjects, such as *The Era of Atomic Power* (1946). In some cities and areas, local councils of churches were affiliated to the British Council of Churches.

By common consent, the most serious limitation of the ecumenical movement was for a long time its top-heaviness. It tended to be a head without a body. The actual participants in the movement were mostly church leaders, whether lay or clerical, and theologians. The ordinary church members in all denominations lagged far behind, and in most cases were not even aware that their representatives were drawing closer together. During the 1960s there was much improvement in this respect. Not only during the annual Week of Prayer for Christian Unity each January, but at other times as well, Christians of all denominations are now accustomed to coming together for common prayer and worship as well as for many other kinds of activity. There are, however, still many obstacles in the way of church union, as was shown by the set-back received in 1969 by the long prepared scheme for Anglican–Methodist union in England. On the other hand, the English Presbyterians and Congregationalists joined forces in 1972 in the United Reformed Church, and the widespread entry of the Roman Catholic Church into the ecumenical movement has had an encouraging and enriching effect at all levels. Kinds of collaboration now take place as a matter of course that would have been unthinkable a generation ago.

The obstacles to closer unity are by no means only theological. What have been called 'non-theological factors' may be even more important. That is to say, what really keeps churches apart may not be their advertised differences in regard to the faith and ordering of the Church but dogged local attachments to traditional buildings and customs and sociological groupings which ordinary church members do not want to see disturbed. Even when a union had been agreed upon by church delegates, the most recalcitrant obstacles to its realization have been found to lie in non-theological factors of that kind. Whether the church leaders could have done more than they succeeded in doing to carry their Churches along with them, who shall say? In oft-quoted words William Temple called the ecumenical movement 'the great new fact of our era': it is too early yet to say whether this was a piece of prophetic insight or of wishful thinking.

24

A Decade of Fermentation

God made yeast, as well as dough, and loves fermentation just as dearly as he loves vegetation – *Emerson*

FERMENTATION: the features of the process are an effervescence, with evolution of heat, in the substance operated on, and a result- ing alteration of its properties – *Oxford English Dictionary*

DURING the 1960s the world at large was beset by some- thing more than fermentation and effervescence. In addition to wars and threats of wars, and revolutionary political changes and transfers of power, specially in Africa, there were many unprecedented occurrences ranging from men landing on the moon to breakdowns of law and order in universities all over the world. For a lively and generously documented characterization of the fantastic turmoil of the period, see Christopher Booker's *The Neophiliacs* (1969).

Hitherto, churches had been looked upon as havens of stability and conservation in comparison with the flux and fever to which secular life and instutions are always more or less subject. But during this decade the Churches, above all the Church of Rome, the most conservative of them all, were infected with the universal restlessness and passion for change and innovation. But we must avoid exaggeration. In many respects the Churches have gone on functioning as they did before, though with straitened resources, di- minished congregations, and serious leakages in their ministries, with the warning of graver shortages and ad- versities to come. And anyhow the unwonted restlessness in the Churches has been neither universal nor uniform in its manifestations. Probably no stronger words than 'fer- mentation' and 'effervescence' are needed to describe what has been happening.

To illustrate this general statement, we may take a two-fold dip into the decade and glance first at the disturbances in the Roman Catholic Church, and then at new fashions of Christian thinking and speaking in the non-Roman Churches of the West – fashions that are sometimes denominated 'the new theology' and 'the new morality'.

*

When Cardinal Roncalli (1881–1963) was elected pope in 1958, there may have been general relief that he did not take the name 'Pius', but no one could have guessed what were to be the effects of his five years' pontificate. It has been said of the College of Cardinals who elected him that 'no one had the slightest suspicion of the real personality of the man they had chosen, or of what his coming was to mean for Catholicism and the world as a whole'.[1] Whatever may have been thought about John XXIII in the Curia at Rome, he quickly charmed the outside world with his informal and unconventional style and his warmhearted accessibility. It soon became evident that there was a new atmosphere in the Vatican and that fresh air was being let into its corridors of power. *Aggiornamento* (bringing up to date) became the watchword of the day. But John XXIII might have left behind him little more than the image of a lovable and transparently good old man who for a brief period had lent an unfamiliar complexion to the papal office, if he had not taken the decisive step of summoning the Second Vatican Council.

His sensational announcement on 25 January 1959 that he was going to do that has been described as a *coup d'état*.

With it, in fact, Pope John put an end to his predecessors' authoritarian monologue and gave the word to the whole Church, bishops, priests, and laymen included; he dealt a blow at Roman centralization and at the privileges of the Curia, opening the way to recognition of the pluralism and federalism of the national and continental Churches; he reconstructed the primacy of the Church's spiritual mission, subordinating to its pastoral ends the

1. Carlo Falconi. *The Popes in the Twentieth Century.* 1967, p. 313.

legalism of its lawyers and the temporalism of its diplomatists; he gave an impulse to the progressive secularization of the ecclesiastical community by extending greater responsibilities to laymen; and, finally, he brought the Catholic Church in a certain sense into the vanguard of ecumenism, thrusting it towards an embrace not only with other Christian communities but even with other faiths.[1]

But when Pope John made his startling announcement, these consequences were only latent and could not have been foreseen. Between January 1959 and the opening of the first session of the Council in October 1962 a determined effort was made by the conservative forces in the Curia, which were primarily responsible for all the preparatory arrangements, to make sure that the Council would be conducted on safely traditional lines. Only when the proceedings actually began did it become clear that a large majority of the bishops was no longer willing to be dictated to by the Curia. They successfully insisted on plotting their own course, and in doing so they had the pope's support.

Though John XXIII did not live to see the end of the Council, it was apparent before he died that the effects of his bold initiative would be epoch-making. It was not only that the documents finally adopted by the Council represented definite changes of teaching and policy with regard to such matters as the bases of dogma, the nature of the Church and its government, religious liberty, and ecumenical relations. What John XXIII had done was to reveal to an astonished world and, in the first instance, to the Church itself that there were innumerable Roman Catholics of every rank and provenance who had been waiting, consciously or unconsciously, for release from the centralized authoritarian straitjacket which for too long had been imposed upon them.

The result was that in the space of a few years there was no less than a general change of climate in the Church. There were many manifestations of it of which only a few can be noted here. Roman Catholic theologians[1] can now with impunity publish work on doctrinal and other subjects, and indeed on the foundations of belief, that would make Pius XII, let alone Pius X and Pius XI, turn in their tombs. The writings of Père Teilhard de Chardin (1881–1955), the Jesuit theologian and scientist, which were not allowed to be published in his lifetime, became bestsellers and stimulated an exceedingly open religious dialogue in many countries. Vatican II had balanced the one-sided emphasis of Vatican I on the authority of the papacy with stress on the complementary authority of the bishops ('collegiality' suddenly became a vogue word). More than that, the public docility and uncritical submissiveness of the hierarchy towards the pope and of other ranks in the Church towards the hierarchy began to disappear, and cardinals and bishops were seen to be standing up to the papacy, and priests to their bishops, with an independence that had been unheard of in modern times. Roman Catholicism had all at once become Critical Catholicism. Controversial attitudes to Luther and the Reformation and to non-Roman traditions were also being revised. We have already spoken of the new openness and freedom in ecumenical relations.[2] Along with all this, remarkable changes in liturgy and in the style of worship were being introduced, including the substitution of the vernacular for Latin. Has a great Church ever acquired a new look so swiftly?

It must of course be added that these changes were not set in motion without contention and opposition. It was only to be expected that there would be resistance to innovation and *aggiornamento* both in the Curia at Rome, which would find it hard to relinquish its power even if it wanted to, and elsewhere as well. Moreover, the attitude of John XXIII's successor has been ambivalent. When Pope Paul VI (b. 1897) was elected in 1963, it was known that he was

1. e.g. Hans Küng, Karl Rahner, S.J., Edward Schillebeeckx, O.P., etc.
2. See p. 267 supra.

a man of very different temperament and talents from Pope John, but he was supposed to be a progressive who would tactfully but firmly consolidate the reforms that had been begun and carry forward the policy of *aggiornamento*. In many respects he has done that, but in others he has appeared to be swayed by reactionary influences and to have been reluctant to accept the full implications of collegiality, dialogue, and decentralization.

This was strikingly the case when the pope reserved for his own decision the question of the Church's attitude to population control and contraception, and disregarded the findings of a commission that had been appointed to advise him. His encyclical *Humanae vitae* (1968) was widely criticized inside as well as outside the Church, and its non-infallible character was emphasized and taken advantage of by those who disagreed with it. Likewise, Paul VI's rigid attitude to priestly celibacy in the Latin Church[1] and his will to prevent an open reconsideration of this disciplinary rule, while applauded in some quarters, have been resented and defied in others, notably in Holland. It must be allowed that in present circumstances the pope's position is not an enviable one. It is much too early yet to say how far the fermentation in the Church of Rome is likely to proceed. What does seem certain is that it will be impossible to put the clock right back as was done by Pius X in his ruthless suppression of the modernist movement or to restore the *status quo ante* Pope John XXIII.

*

Our other dip into the Christian ferment of the sixties will have less coherent or tangible results and admit of even less confidence about its likely outcome. After the Second World War theology in Britain, and in other countries too, seemed to be in a fairly quiescent state. No new heresies or orthodoxies had been striking the headlines. English

1. Married priests are accepted in the Uniate Churches of the East that are in communion with Rome.

divines, as their manner is, had more or less assimilated the neo-orthodox theology, of which Barth and Brunner were the continental apostles, and in doing so had toned it down and drawn its sting. It is true that in Germany Rudolf Bultmann was reported to be causing a lively controversy with his claim that the gospel must be 'demythologized', but Bultmann was too radical a critic of the New Testament and philosophically too much of an existentialist to attract many followers in England. If there was a fashion in England, it was the cultivation of what was called a 'biblical theology', which was sometimes advertised as being 'post-liberal' or 'post-critical'. It was supposed that the storms of the age of Liberalism and Modernism had been safely weathered and that theologians could concentrate again on the positive exposition of their faith and its corollaries. The editor of a British theological journal remarked that the topics which really seemed to excite his readers and bring in correspondence were such matters as baptism and episcopacy, and not any fundamental issues of belief. The biblical theologians were happy talking among themselves and were neither keen nor successful in drawing others into the conversation. It was a period when theology was doughy rather than yeasty.

The 1960s changed all this, at any rate for the time being. The most famous – or notorious – episode that contributed to a new fermentation was the publication in 1963 of *Honest to God* by John Robinson (b. 1919), then Bishop of Woolwich. Dr Robinson had previously been known as an effective dean of chapel in Cambridge, as a good New Testament scholar, and as an exponent of the current biblical theology. He wrote *Honest to God* in a respite from his new experiences in South London, not as a manifesto, but as an attempt to clear his own mind and give expression to his dissatisfaction with accepted ideas about God, Christ, the Church, prayer, etc. In 1612 an earlier John Robinson had made the celebrated remark that 'the Lord hath more truth to break forth out of his holy word'. The Bishop of Woolwich seemed to be saying instead that nowadays there was more truth to break forth out of the writings of Rudolf Bultmann, Paul Tillich and Dietrich Bonhoeffer. The theological pundits were soon observing that those authorities differed much from one another, but what the pundits observed was of little consequence, for *Honest to God* quickly became a bestseller on a world scale and a universal talking-point. How far this was due to the facts that its author was a bishop and that it was launched with a sensationally entitled article in a Sunday newspaper, no one can be sure. Certainly, no bishop had sparked off such a commotion since Dr Barnes, the former Bishop of Birmingham, who in his time had crossed swords with more than one Archbishop of Canterbury. While some of the devout were shocked by *Honest to God*, multitudes of readers welcomed it both as a frank and patently honest acknowledgement of the need for a new deal in theology and as an attempt to express the gist of the Christian faith in a fresh frame of reference.

Although Dr Robinson's *cri de cœur* reached farthest afield, his was not a solitary voice, for just about the same time – in addition to the dramatic developments in Roman Catholicism – a number of other books appeared which had originated quite independently but had also a fermenting character. It may suffice to mention a volume of essays by a group of Cambridge theologians which was significantly entitled *Soundings* (1962). Their aim was to call attention to a number of basic questions which were being complacently ignored or soft-pedalled in the Church. At the same time, they said that it was premature to expect any speedy answers to them. It was a time for making soundings, not for charting solutions or constructing a new theological system.

Before long, there was quite an avalanche of publications of one kind and another for or against what was misleadingly called 'the new theology'. This expression was misleading because it implied that a positive and constructive reinterpretation of the Christian faith was being launched by a consortium of divines, whereas all that had happened in fact was the appearance of a variety of independent and inchoate essays that were designed to voice, rather than to satisfy, a need.

It is true that in the U.S.A. a group or school of young theologians was apparently coming out if not with a new theology, at least with a new anthropology. But the so-called 'death of God' theologians[1] or 'Christian atheists' did not really form a coherent group with a common mind, nor was what they said as new in reality as it was to most people in appearance. In the nineteenth century Feuerbach had transmuted theology into anthropology and Nietzsche had proclaimed that God was dead. Still, these American theologians were not simply repeating what Feuerbach or Nietzsche had said. What led to their being classed together was their common determination to take seriously the complete secularization of contemporary culture. In sharp contrast to the sacral culture of the middle ages which was pervaded at every point by reference to God, our culture had dispensed with the concept of God. Bonhoeffer had clearly stated their presupposition, though he was not himself a Christian atheist.

Man has learned to cope with all questions of importance without recourse to God as a working hypothesis. In questions concerning science, art, and even ethics, this has become an understood thing. . . . It is becoming evident that everything gets along without 'God', and just as well as before.

While the American 'death of God' theologians started from this acknowledgement of the secularization of contemporary culture, they proceeded along independent lines of thought or had different objectives. Some took the view that the only possible way to be a Christian in the twentieth century was to accept the axioms of secularization and to

1. The most prominent of them were Thomas Altizer, Paul van Buren, William Hamilton, and Gabriel Vahanian.

construct a faith in which the concept of God was dispensed with. Others were more affected by the alleged meaninglessness of the term 'God' according to certain forms of linguistic analysis. Others again accepted the secularization of culture as a fact but did not accept it as normative for Christian faith. They looked upon it as a challenge to discover ways of experiencing and point to the transcendence and ineffable mystery of God within a culture that seemed to exclude him. Or, as Bonhoeffer had put it, it was a call to the 'abandonment of a false conception of God, and a clearing of the decks for the God of the Bible'.

The death of God movement could indeed move in two contrasted directions. On the one hand, it might sell out completely to the presuppositions of contemporary secular atheism. Or, on the other hand, it might welcome the demolition of all the facile and conventional ways of speaking about God, to which theologians as well as preachers and propagandists have all too readily been habituated, so that God might once again be heard speaking for himself in a world from which he was reputed to be absent. In other words, Christian atheism might lead to a rediscovery of the truth that

> The sunne holds down his head for shame,
> Dead with eclipses, when we speak of thee.

Much the same could be said of 'secular Christianity'[1] which was another name that was adopted for what purported to be a radically new Christian theology. This also naturally presupposed the secularization of modern culture. Instead of deploring it, it accepted it as providential, i.e. as providing conditions in which men might be free to attain to a maturity and 'coming of age' that was not possible in a civilization dominated by the Church and controlled by religious sanctions. Some would-be 'secular Christians'

1. The late Professor Ronald Gregor Smith (1913–68) of Glasgow University was one of the most sensitive and sophisticated exponents of this theme: see his book *Secular Christianity* (1966).

went further and affirmed that the Christian gospel, rightly understood, was exclusively about secular existence and personal relations in this world, and that all thought of a Beyond, of an eternal order in which human destiny would be fulfilled, must be henceforth eliminated.

It was ironic that, at a time in history when the secular survival (let alone, fulfilment) of man was more imperilled than it had ever been before, professing Christians should have been proposing to jettison the most persuasive article in their creed, namely the proclamation of the reality of a kingdom which is *not* of this world. But history, and not least church history, is full of ironies like this, that is of creeds and causes turning into their opposites. In the memorable words of P. T. Forsyth:

> This is the irony of history – when the very success of an idea creates the conditions that belie it, smother it, and replace it. Catholicism becomes the Papacy. The care for truth turns to the Inquisition. The religious orders, vowed to poverty, die and rot of wealth. A revivalist movement becomes a too, too prosperous and egoistic Church. Freedom as soon as it is secured becomes tyranny.

No voices were heard in the 1960s declaring that 'the world is sweet to the lips, but bitter to the taste. It pleases at first, but not at last. It looks gay on the outside, but evil and misery lie concealed within' (J. H. Newman).

There was irony too in the advocacy by Christian clerics of a 'new morality' such as on the face of it would be as acceptable as possible to a 'permissive' society. There was of course more to it than that, and much that was worthy and well said. Moral codes and patterns of behaviour do need to be kept under constant review in the light of changing social conditions. In this sense they are relative and not absolute. Moreover, Christianity, which in the New Testament is presented as a deliverance from the rigours of legalism, has ever been liable to revert to new forms of that from which it should be a liberation. Traditional Christian morality has inclined to be a text-book morality and to keep people in leading strings, laying insufficient stress on the value and importance of personal freedom and responsibility and on the rights and duties of the individual conscience. So-called 'situation-ethics' directed attention to these facts and so to the truth that making a moral decision means not asking what general rule is relevant and acting upon it, but reckoning with the circumstances and potentialities of each case or situation and having the insight to judge what is the best course of action in this particular instance. Insofar as the proponents of what was loosely named 'the new morality' were saying these things there was good reason to welcome what they said, and it was unreasonable to charge them with surrendering to the popular demand for permissiveness or licentiousness.

But often those who were publicized as the spokesmen of the new morality, especially when their utterances were reported in the press, seemed to be justifying, if not encouraging, all kinds of laxity and to be contrasting an ethic of law with an ethic of love in a grossly simplified and misleading manner. The impression was given that Christianity had nothing more to say than 'love and do what you will', and that it now had nothing definite or peremptory to declare about the norms of conduct that make for the good life and the common good; and this at a time when firm guidance about, and witness to, such norms were urgently needed both by individuals who were ceasing to have any wholesome framework of standards and by societies that were tending to drift into moral confusion and anarchy and so preparing for themselves a reaction to a new and harsh authoritarianism ('freedom as soon as it is secured becomes tyranny'). It was certainly ironic that Christianity, which through much of its history and in many of its forms has been too moralistic and officiously censorious,[1] should at this juncture have appeared in its effervescent mani-

1. 'Legalistic moralism has lain like a blight on the history of Christendom' (E. Brunner).

festations to be morally nerveless and palely to reflect the hedonism of the age.

It is too soon to say whether or not the effervescence of the sixties will prove to have been evanescent. Anyhow it has not caused the author of this book to alter the Epilogue with which he concluded it when it was first published in 1961.

25

Epilogue

THIS book has been intended, within its necessary limits, to give a fair and representative impression of what has been going on in the Churches, especially of Britain and Europe, since the end of the eighteenth century. If 'the age of revolution' had by now given way to an era of stability, it would be easier to offer some concluding reflections. But notoriously this is not so. The revolution, in the broad sense in which we have been using the term, continues and shows no signs of slowing down or of coming even to that kind of settled rhythm in which some historical periods have run quietly on. However, it is not our business here to prophesy about the future either of the world or of the Church. Even a few comments on the past must be taken as no more than provisional or an interim report.

How have the Church or the Churches stood up to the age of revolution? When Thomas Fuller in the middle of the seventeenth century was writing his *Church History of Britain*, he said that 'an ingenious gentleman' told him he had better make haste with his history 'lest the Church of England be ended before the History thereof'. Many during our period, who have had no love for the Churches, expected them to collapse or to wither away, and at times it looked as though such expectations might be fulfilled. There have been Christians too who have thought that ecclesiastical institutions were doomed and that the faith which they enshrined could survive only by way of death and resurrection. For example, in 1852 the great Anglican preacher, F. W. Robertson of Brighton, said:

As to our 'incomparable Church', why it does not require a prophetic spirit to see that in ten years more she must be in fragments, out of which fragments God will reconstruct something for which I am content to wait, in accordance with his usual plan, which is to be forever evolving fresh forms of life out of dissolution and decay.

It would not be inconsistent with Christmas faith to hold that the Church as a visible society might be put to death and disappear.

But that is not what has happened, though in some countries it has seemed at one time or another to be a real or impending possibility. If the full measure be taken of the revolutionary changes that have taken place in the worlds of thought and invention, in political and social structures, and in the conditions of living and working, and if the rootedness of the Churches in the pre-revolutionary order or the *ancien régime* be borne in mind, then their survival with so many of their ancient characteristics and appurtenances intact is remarkable, to say the least. They have not survived because they were well-prepared for the turmoil in which they were to be ineluctably involved, nor because, when it came upon them, they showed ready powers of adaptation to new circumstances and of taking time by the forelock. On the contrary, we have seen how recalcitrant they were to change, how blind or short-sighted in the days of visitation, how disposed to stone or silence or jettison the would-be prophets or reformers in their midst, and how lacking in the imaginative compassion and sensitive humanity that might have given them a secure standing in the hearts of peoples when they were deprived of earthly privileges and the active support of governments.

Nevertheless, the Churches would not have been able to survive, except as monuments on the margin of society, unless they had to some extent changed with the times and adjusted their teaching and practice to the new climate of thought and the new structures of society. We have seen various examples of more or less successful essays in adjustment. If they appear to have been inadequate or misguided, it would be foolish to dismiss them as totally ineffective or as without lasting value and instruction. Christians in the twentieth century, who on the whole have been less adventurous than the nineteenth-century 'liberals' whom they affect to have surpassed, have still much to learn from them. Dietrich Bonhoeffer, the courageous German theologian who was put to death by the Nazis, wrote in his *Letters and Papers from Prison*:

> There are so few nowadays who have any real interest or sympathy for the nineteenth century. ... Hardly anyone has the slightest idea what was achieved ... by our own grandfathers. How much of what they knew has already been forgotten! I believe people will one day be utterly amazed at the fertility of that age, now so much despised and so little known.

But even when full justice has been done to the achievements of the reformers of Christian thought and institutions, it may still seem astonishing that the Churches have survived with so little alteration, at any rate in their façades. In the same year that Frederick Robertson foresaw the break-up of the Church of England, James Martineau was contemplating the possible realization of a new unity of the Churches. 'Whatever unity may yet arise in Christendom,' he said, 'will be no less different from any thing we have yet known than the factory from the monastery, the locomotive from the packhorse, or *The Times* newspaper from the illuminated manuscript.' So far the Churches have survived without being united and without any such degree of transformation. The reason that they have been able, with their predominantly archaic outlook, to hold as much ground as they have, many be found less in their own inherent vitality than in the non-emergence of any satisfying alternative to them.

A. N. Whitehead prophesied that 'that religion will conquer which can render clear to popular understanding some eternal greatness incarnate in the passage of temporal fact'. The Churches may not have been much of a hand at doing that, but it has been suspected that, despite the archaism in which they were embedded, they had more to say to the final point than any new faiths that have been adumbrated or propounded. Marxism and fascism, as constructive faiths, have by their fruits repelled free men. 'Scientific humanism', which probably hits off the creed of most intellectuals, and of multitudes of non-intellectuals too, in the West, hardly promises to meet the total needs of the human person and of human communities. It is much stronger in its criticism of the Churches than in revealing a capacity to do better what they have done badly. 'Believe me,' said Napoleon III shrewdly, 'one never really destroys a thing till one has replaced it.' This appears to be true of religious, as well as of other, institutions that aim at satisfying the basic and enduring human needs. Many Christians have assimilated the fruits of science and of humanism, even if the Churches have not yet candidly acknowledged their duty to recast their teaching and their *mores* accordingly, or gone nearly far enough towards incarnating in the contemporary world the traditional faith which they represent. By the middle of the twentieth century, when Christian thinkers were by no means up to date with their homework, it was becoming clear that far-reaching and largely new questions were being put to them by linguistic philosophers and Freudian psychologists.

All in all, while the Churches have survived and their future is still open, it can hardly be said that they have revived in such a way as to offer an assurance to the dispassionate observer that they will not become mere survivals in a world that will have no further use for them. It is too soon to assess the promise of what appear to be the liveliest growing points in the Churches at present, such as the Liturgical Movement[1] which seeks to restore corporate worship as a communal activity that awakens in popular understanding the 'eternal greatness incarnate in the passage of temporal fact', or the rediscovery of the Bible[2]

1. See, e.g., J. D. Benoit. *Liturgical Renewal*. 1958; A. R. Shands. *The Liturgical Movement and the Local Church*. 1959.

2. See, e.g., W. Neil. *The Rediscovery of the Bible*. 1955; J. E. Fison. *The Faith of the Bible*. 1957.

as a revelation of the truth about man's origin and destiny and the relations in which he stands to both the eternal and the temporal. It is possible that such movements may capture the imagination and command the allegiance of many who are at present spiritually unenfranchised; on the other hand, they may, like other movements that have been hopefully launched, only 'pick up a few recruits . . . and remain the preoccupation of small sects'. There are eager young churchmen who seem to want to narrow, instead of extend, the boundaries of the Church. But, as Paul Tillich has said, 'if religion is the special concern of special people and not the ultimate concern of everybody, it is nonsense or blasphemy'.

Christopher Dawson once observed that 'men today are divided between those who have kept their spiritual roots and lost their contact with the existing order of society, and those who have preserved their social contacts and lost their spiritual roots'. To survey the history of the Church since the French Revolution is to be made aware of this schism in the soul of modern man and in the souls of many Christian men. It does not enable one to say with confidence whether or not the schism can be healed.

SUGGESTIONS FOR FURTHER READING

BURGESS, H. J., *Enterprise in Education: The Work of the Established Church in the Education of the People Prior to 1870* (S.P.C.K., London, 1958).

CARPENTER, S. C., *Church and People, 1789–1889: A History of the Church of England from William Wilberforce to 'Lux Mundi'* (S.P.C.K., London, 1933).

CHADWICK, W. O., *The Victorian Church*, 2 vols. (A. & C. Black, London, 1966–70).

CLARKE, B. F. L., *Church Builders of the Nineteenth Century: A Study in the Gothic Revival in England* (S.P.C.K., London, 1938).

DAVIES, HORTON, *The English Free Churches* (O.U.P., London, 1952).

ELLIOTT-BINNS, L. E., *English Thought 1860–1900: The Theological Aspect* (Longmans, Green, London, 1956).

ELLIOTT-BINNS, L. E., *Religion in the Victorian Era* (Lutterworth Press, London, 1936).

HALES, E. E. Y., *The Catholic Church in the Modern World: A Survey from the French Revolution to the Present* (Eyre & Spottiswoode, London, 1958).

LATOURETTE, K. S., *Christianity in a Revolutionary Age*, 5 vols. (Eyre & Spottiswoode, London, 1959–63).

LLOYD, ROGER, *The Church of England in the Twentieth Century*, 2 vols. (Longmans, Green, London, 1946, Vol. I; 1950, Vol. II).

MACKINTOSH, H. R., *Types of Modern Theology: Schleiermacher to Barth* (Nisbet, London, 1937).

MACQUARRIE, J., *Twentieth Century Religious Thought* (S.C.M. Press, London, 1963).

NICHOLLS, D., *Church and State in Britain since 1820* (Routledge & Kegan Paul, London, 1967).

NICHOLLS, J. H., *History of Christianity 1650–1950* (Ronald, New York, 1956).

NORMAN, E. R., *Church and Society in England 1770–1970* (O.U.P., Oxford, 1976).

STORR, V. F., *The Development of English Theology in the Nineteenth Century, 1800–60* (Longmans, Green, London, 1913).

TULLOCH, JOHN, *Movements of Religious Thought in Britain During the Nineteenth Century* (Longmans, Green, London, 1885).

WAND, J. W. C., *A History of the Modern Church from 1500 to the Present Day* (Methuen, London, 1946).

WARRE CORNISH, F., *A History of the English Church in the Nineteenth Century*, 2 vols. (Macmillan, London, 1910).

WEBB, C. C. J., *A Study of Religious Thought in England from 1850* (Clarendon Press, Oxford, 1933).

WILLEY, BASIL, *Nineteenth-Century Studies* (Chatto & Windus, London, 1956; Penguin Books, London, 1964).

WILLEY, BASIL, *More Nineteenth-Century Studies* (Chatto & Windus, London, 1956).

WOOD, H. G., *Belief and Unbelief since 1850* (C.U.P., Cambridge, 1955).

Chapter 1: The Gallican Church: The Revolution and Napoleon

HALES, E. E. Y., *Revolution and Papacy 1769–1846* (Eyre & Spottis-woode, London, 1960).

McMANNERS, J., *The French Revolution and the Church* (S.P.C.K., London, 1969).

PHILLIPS, C. S., *The Church in France 1789–1848* (Mowbray, London, 1929).

Chapter 2: Theological Reconstruction in Germany

BARTH, KARL, *From Rousseau to Ritschl* (S.C.M. Press, London, 1959).

CREED, J. M., *The Divinity of Jesus Christ* (C.U.P., Cambridge, 1938).

HARRIS, HORTON, *David Friedrich Strauss and his Theology* (C.U.P., Cambridge, 1973).

Chapter 3: Christianity in England 1790–1830

COWHERD, R. G., *The Politics of English Dissent* (Epworth Press, London, 1959).

HOWSE, E. M., *Saints in Politics: The 'Clapham Sect' and the Growth of Freedom* (University of Toronto Press, Toronto, 1952).

OVERTON, J. H., *The English Church in the Nineteenth Century 1800–33* (Longmans, Green, London, 1894).

WATKIN, E. I., *Roman Catholicism in England to 1950* (O.U.P., London, 1957).

Chapter 4: The Anglican Revival 1830–45

BRILIOTH YNGVE, *The Anglican Revival* (Longmans, Green, London, 1925).

BROSE, O. J., *Church and Parliament: The Reshaping of the Church of England 1828–60* (O.U.P., London, 1959).

CHURCH, R. W., *The Oxford Movement: Twelve Years 1833–45* (Macmillan, London, 1891).

FABER, GEOFFREY, *Oxford Apostles* (Faber & Faber, London, 1933).

WEBB, C. C. J., *Religious Thought in the Oxford Movement* (S.P.C.K., London, 1928).

Chapter 5: Conflicts in Scotland

HENDERSON, H. F., *Erskine of Linlathen: Selections and Biography* (Oliphant, London and Edinburgh, 1899).

MCLEOD CAMPBELL, J., *The Nature of the Atonement* (James Clarke & Co., London, 1959).

WATT, HUGH, *Thomas Chalmers and the Disruption* (Thomas Nelson, Edinburgh, 1943).

WHITLEY, H. C., *Blinded Eagle: An Introduction to the Life and Teaching of Edward Irving* (S.C.M. Press, London, 1955).

Chapter 6: Liberal Catholicism and Ultramontanism in France

DANSETTE, A., *Religious History of Modern France* (Nelson, Edinburgh, 1961).

PHILLIPS, C. S., *The Church in France 1848–1907* (S.P.C.K., London, 1936).

VIDLER, A. R., *Prophecy and Papacy: A Study of Lamennais, The Church and the Revolution* (S.C.M. Press, London, 1959).

Chapter 7: Coleridge and Maurice

COLERIDGE, S. T., *Confessions of an Inquiring Spirit* (A. & C. Black, London, 1956).

HIGHAM, FLORENCE, *Frederick Denison Maurice* (S.C.M. Press, London, 1947).

VIDLER, A. R., *F. D. Maurice and Company* (S.C.M. Press, London, 1966).

Chapter 8: The Christian Social Movement

BINYON, G. C., *The Christian Socialist Movement in England: An Introduction to the Study of its History* (S.P.C.K., London, 1931).

CHRISTENSEN, T., *Origin and History of Christian Socialism 1848–54* (Universitetsforlaget, Aarhus, 1962).

INGLIS, K. S., *Churches and the Working Classes in Victorian England* (Routledge & Kegan Paul, London, 1963).

JONES, P. D'A., *The Christian Socialist Revival 1877–1914* (Princeton University Press, 1968).

MAYOR, S., *The Churches and the Labour Movement* (Independent Press, London, 1967).

RECKITT, M. B., *Maurice to Temple: A Century of the Social Movement in the Church of England* (Faber & Faber, London, 1947).

VIDLER, A. R., *A Century of Social Catholicism 1820–1920* (S.P.C.K., London, 1964).

WICKHAM, E. R., *Church and People in an Industrial City* (Lutterworth Press, London, 1957).

Chapter 9: From Strauss to Ritschl

EDGHILL, E. A., *Faith and Fact: A Study of Ritschlianism* (Macmillan, London, 1910).

MOZLEY, J. K., *Ritschlianism* (Nisbet, London, 1909).

REARDON, B. M. G., *Liberal Protestantism* (A. & C. Black, London, 1968).

SCHWEITZER, A., *The Quest of the Historical Jesus* (A. & C. Black, London, 1910).

Chapter 10: Science and Christian Belief in England

GILLISPIE, C. C., *Genesis and Geology: A Study in the Relations of Scientific Thought, Natural Theology, and Social Opinion in Great Britain, The Impact of Scientific Discoveries Upon Religious Beliefs in the Decades Before Darwin* (Harper Torchbooks, New York, 1959).

LACK, DAVID, *Evolutionary Theory and Christian Belief* (Methuen, London, 1957).

MILLHAUSER, M., *Just Before Darwin. Robert Chambers and Vestiges* (Wesleyan University Press, Middletown, Conn., 1959).

MOORE, J., *The Post-Darwinian Controversies. A Study of the Protestant Struggle to come to terms with Darwin in Great Britain and America 1870–1900* (C.U.P., Cambridge, 1979).

Chapter 11: The Bible and the Broad Church

DAVIDSON, R. T., and BENHAM, W., *The Life of A. C. Tait* (Macmillan, London and New York, 1891).

FABER, GEOFFREY, *Jowett* (Faber & Faber, London, 1957).

HORT, A. F., *Life and Letters of F. J. A. Hort*, 2 vols. (Macmillan, London, 1896).

PROTHERO, R. E., *Life and Correspondence of Arthur Penryn Stanley* (Murray, London, 1893).

Chapter 12: The English Free Churches

EDWARDS, MALDWYN, *After Wesley* (Epworth Press, London, 1935).

EDWARDS, MALDWYN, *Methodism and England* (Epworth Press, London, 1943).

PEEL, A., *These Hundred Years: A History of the Congregational Union 1831–1931* (Congregational Union, London, 1931).

ROSS, S., *Nonconformity and Modern British Politics* (Batsford, London, 1975).

THOMPSON, D. M. (Ed.), *Nonconformity in the Nineteenth Century* (Routledge & Kegan Paul, London, 1972).

UNDERWOOD, A. C., *A History of the English Baptists* (Kingsgate Press, London, 1947).

Chapter 13: The Pontificate of Pius IX

AUBERT, R., *Le Pontificate de Pie IX* (Bloud et Gay, Paris, 1952).

HALES, E. E. Y., *Pio Nono: A Study in European Politics and Religion in the Nineteenth Century* (Eyre & Spottiswoode, London, 1954).

HOLMES, D. J., *The Triumph of the Holy See; a short history of the papacy in the xixth century* (Burns Oates, London, 1979).

WARD, WILFRID, *William George Ward and the Catholic Revival* (Macmillan, London, 1893).

Chapter 14: Ritualism and Prayer Book Revision

BELL, G. K. A., *Randall Davidson* (O.U.P., London, 1938).

BENTLEY, J., *Ritualism and Politics in Britain* (O.U.P., Oxford, 1978).

JASPER, R. C. D., *Prayer Book Revision in England 1800–1900* (S.P.C.K., London, 1954).

MARSH, P. T., *The Victorian Church in Decline* (Routledge & Kegan Paul, London, 1969).

SPARROW SIMPSON, W. J., *The History of the Anglo-Catholic Revival from 1845* (Allen & Unwin, London, 1932).

Chapter 15: Stands Scotland Where It Did?

BLACK, J. S., and CHRYSTAL, G., *The Life of William Robertson Smith* (A. & C. Black, London, 1912).

FLEMING, J. R., *A History of the Church in Scotland 1843–74* (T. & T. Clark, Edinburgh, 1927).

FLEMING, J. R., *A History of the Church in Scotland 1875–1929* (T. & T. Clark, Edinburgh, 1933).

SIMPSON, P. CARNEGIE, *The Life of Principal Rainy*, 2 vols. (Hodder & Stoughton, London, 1909).

Chapter 16: Catholic Modernism

BARMANN, L. F., *Baron von Hügel and the Modernist Crisis in England* (C.U.P., Cambridge, 1972).

REARDON, B. M. G., *Roman Catholic Modernism* (A. & C. Black, London, 1970).

VIDLER, A. R., *The Modernist Movement in the Roman Church* (C.U.P., Cambridge, 1934).

VIDLER, A. R., *A Variety of Catholic Modernists* (C.U.P., Cambridge, 1970).

Chapter 17: Ebb and Flow in English Theology

CARPENTER, JAMES, *Gore: A Study in Liberal Catholic Thought* (Faith Press, London, 1960).

MOZLEY, J. K., *Some Tendencies in British Theology from the Publication of 'Lux Mundi' to the Present Day* (S.P.C.K., London, 1951).

RAMSEY, A. M., *From Gore to Temple* (Longmans, Green, London, 1960).

VIDLER, A. R., *20th Century Defenders of the Faith* (S.C.M. Press, London, 1965).

Chapter 18: Kierkegaard

HOHLENBERG, JOHANNES, *Søren Kierkegaard* (Routledge & Kegan Paul, London, 1954).

KIERKEGAARD, S., *Journals* (O.U.P., London, 1938).

LOWRIE, WALTER, *A Short Life of Kierkegaard* (O.U.P., London, 1943).

Chapter 19: The Theology of Crisis

BARTH, KARL, *The Epistle to the Romans* (O.U.P., London, 1933).

BETHGE, E., *Dietrich Bonhoeffer* (Collins, London, 1970).

HORTON, W. M., *Contemporary Continental Theology* (Harper Bros., London and New York, 1938).

WILLIAMS, D. D., *Interpreting Theology 1918–52* (S.C.M. Press, London, 1953).

Chapter 20: Eastern Orthodoxy

CURTISS, J. S., *Church and State in Russia: The Last Years of the Empire, 1900–17* (Columbia University Press, New York, 1940).

HAMMOND, PETER, *The Waters of Marah* (Rockliff, London, 1956).

MEYENDORFF, JEAN, *L'Église Orthodoxe, hier et aujourd'hui* (Éditions du Seuil, Paris, 1960).

TIMASHEFF, N. S., *Religion in Soviet Russia 1917–42* (Sheed & Ward, London, 1943).

ZERNOV, N., *Eastern Christendom* (Weidenfeld & Nicolson, London, 1961).

Chapter 21: Christianity in America

DRUMMOND, A. L., *Story of American Protestantism* (Oliver & Boyd, London and Edinburgh, 1949).

MAYNARD, T., *The Story of American Catholicism* (Macmillan, New York, 1941).

SPERRY, W. L., *Religion in America* (C.U.P., Cambridge, 1945).

SWEET, W. W., *The Story of Religions in America* (Harper Bros., London and New York, 1930).

Chapter 22: The Missionary Movement

LATOURETTE, K. S., *A History of the Expansion of Christianity* Vols. IV and V (Eyre & Spottiswoode, London, 1938–46).

NEILL, STEPHEN, *A History of Christian Missions* (Penguin Books, London, 1964).

Chapter 23: The Ecumenical Movement

BLOCH-HOELL, N., *The Pentecostal Movement* (Allen & Unwin, London, 1964).

DUFF, EDWARD, S. J., *The Social Thought of the World Council of Churches* (Longmans, Green, London, 1956).

FEY, H. E., *The Ecumenical Advance 1948–1968* (S.P.C.K., London, 1969).

GOODALL, N., *The Ecumenical Movement* (O.U.P., London, 1961).

GOODALL, N., *Ecumenical Progress: a decade of changes in the Ecumenical Movement 1961–1971* (O.U.P., London, 1972).

ROUSE, RUTH, and NEILL, STEPHEN, *A History of the Ecumenical Movement 1517–1948* (S.P.C.K., London, 1954).

Chapter 24: A Decade of Fermentation

COX, H. E., *The Secular City* (S.C.M. Press, London, 1965).

HALES, E. E. Y., *Pope John and his Revolution* (Eyre & Spottiswoode, London, 1965).

KÜNG, H., *The Living Church: Reflections on the Second Vatican Council* (Sheed & Ward, London, 1963).

OGLETREE, T. W., *The 'Death of God' Controversy* (S.C.M. Press, London, 1966).

ROBINSON, J. A. T., *Honest to God and the Debate* (S.C.M. Press, London, 1963).

ROBINSON, J. A. T., *Christian Freedom in a Permissive Society* (S.C.M. Press, London, 1970).

INDEX

READ MORE IN PENGUIN

In every corner of the world, on every subject under the sun, Penguin represents quality and variety – the very best in publishing today.

For complete information about books available from Penguin – including Puffins, Penguin Classics and Arkana – and how to order them, write to us at the appropriate address below. Please note that for copyright reasons the selection of books varies from country to country.

In the United Kingdom: Please write to *Dept. EP, Penguin Books Ltd, Bath Road, Harmondsworth, West Drayton, Middlesex UB7 0DA*

In the United States: Please write to *Consumer Sales, Penguin Putnam Inc., P.O. Box 12289 Dept. B, Newark, New Jersey 07101-5289.* VISA and MasterCard holders call 1-800-788-6262 to order Penguin titles

In Canada: Please write to *Penguin Books Canada Ltd, 10 Alcorn Avenue, Suite 300, Toronto, Ontario M4V 3B2*

In Australia: Please write to *Penguin Books Australia Ltd, P.O. Box 257, Ringwood, Victoria 3134*

In New Zealand: Please write to *Penguin Books (NZ) Ltd, Private Bag 102902, North Shore Mail Centre, Auckland 10*

In India: Please write to *Penguin Books India Pvt Ltd, 11 Community Centre, Panchsheel Park, New Delhi 110017*

In the Netherlands: Please write to *Penguin Books Netherlands bv, Postbus 3507, NL-1001 AH Amsterdam*

In Germany: Please write to *Penguin Books Deutschland GmbH, Metzlerstrasse 26, 60594 Frankfurt am Main*

In Spain: Please write to *Penguin Books S. A., Bravo Murillo 19, 1° B, 28015 Madrid*

In Italy: Please write to *Penguin Italia s.r.l., Via Benedetto Croce 2, 20094 Corsico, Milano*

In France: Please write to *Penguin France, Le Carré Wilson, 62 rue Benjamin Baillaud, 31500 Toulouse*

In Japan: Please write to *Penguin Books Japan Ltd, Kaneko Building, 2-3-25 Koraku, Bunkyo-Ku, Tokyo 112*

In South Africa: Please write to *Penguin Books South Africa (Pty) Ltd, Private Bag X14, Parkview, 2122 Johannesburg*

READ MORE IN PENGUIN

THE PENGUIN HISTORY OF THE CHURCH

The Early Church   Revised Edition   Henry Chadwick

The story of the early Christian church from the death of Christ to the Papacy of Gregory the Great. Professor Henry Chadwick makes use of the latest research to explain the astonishing expansion of Christianity throughout the Roman Empire.

Western Society and the Church in the Middle Ages   R. W. Southern

In the period between the eighth and the sixteenth centuries the Church and State were more nearly one than ever before or after. Professor Southern discusses how this was achieved and what stresses it caused.

The Reformation   Owen Chadwick

In this volume Professor Owen Chadwick deals with the formative work of Erasmus, Luther, Zwingli, Calvin, with the special circumstances of the English Reformation, and with the Counter-Reformation.

The Church and the Age of Reason   Gerald R. Cragg

This span in the history of the Christian church stretches from the age of religious and civil strife before the middle of the seventeenth century to the age of industrialism and republicanism which followed the French Revolution.

A History of Christian Missions   Stephen Neill

This volume of *The Penguin History of the Church* represented the first attempt in English to provide a readable history of the worldwide expansion of all the Christian denominations – Roman Catholic, Orthodox, Anglican, and Protestant.

The Christian Church in the Cold War   Owen Chadwick

In this concluding volume Owen Chadwick surveys the difficulties encountered by the Eastern and Western churches, from the end of Second World War and the era of a divided Europe, to the fresh global challenges and opportunities facing Christians now.